*Learning English*

**Band 1**

**Teacher's Resource Book**

Herausgegeben von

Stephanie Ashford
Maria Dashöfer
Hermann Fischer
Alexander Hick
Harald Peter
Hannelore Zimmermann

Ernst Klett Verlag
Stuttgart Düsseldorf Leipzig

*Learning English*
# Challenge 21 · Band 1 · Teacher's Resource Book

**Herausgegeben von**

Stephanie Ashford, B.A. Hons., Villingen-Schwenningen; OStR'n Maria Dashöfer, Mannheim; StR Hermann Fischer, Münster; StR Alexander Hick, Weinheim; StD Harald Peter, Kirchzarten; Stud. Ass. Dr. Hannelore Zimmermann, Donaueschingen

*Challenge 21 Band 1 – Werkteile*

| | | |
|---|---|---|
| **Schülerbuch** | Klettnummer 3-12-510510-2 | |
| **Doppel-CD 'Selected Texts'** | Klettnummer 3-12-510515-3 | (mit ausgewählten Texten und Liedern aus dem SB) |
| **Kassette 'Selected Texts'** | Klettnummer 3-12-510514-5 | (mit ausgewählten Texten und Liedern aus dem SB) |
| **CD 'Additional Texts'** | Klettnummer 3-12-510518-8 | (mit Hörverstehenstexten) |
| **Kassette 'Additional Texts'** | Klettnummer 3-12-510516-1 | (mit Hörverstehenstexten) |
| **Workbook** | Klettnummer 3-12-510512-9 | |

**Symbols used**

 Additional/supplementary activity

 Text recorded on double CD/cassette 'Selected Texts', printed in SB

 Text recorded on CD/cassette 'Additional texts', printed in TRB only

 Copymaster in TRB and on CD-ROM

 Copymaster on CD-ROM only

 Copymaster in TRB only

( i ) Additional background information

**Abbreviations**

| | |
|---|---|
| EA | *Einzelarbeit* |
| GA | *Gruppenarbeit* |
| HA | *Hausaufgaben* |
| KA | *Klassenarbeit* |
| KV | *Kopiervorlage* |
| L | *Lehrer/Lehrerinnen* |
| OHP | *Overhead projector* |
| p./pp. | *page/pages* |
| PA | *Partnerarbeit* |
| S | *Schüler/Schülerinnen* |
| S. | *Seite* |
| SB | *Schülerbuch* |
| TA | *Tafelanschrieb* |
| TRB | *Teacher's Resource Book* |

 Gedruckt auf Recyclingpapier, hergestellt aus 100% Altpapier.

1. Auflage  A 1  5 4 3 2 1 | 2005 2004 2003 2002 2001

Alle Drucke dieser Auflage können im Unterricht nebeneinander benutzt werden, sie sind untereinander unverändert.
Die letzte Zahl bezeichnet das Jahr dieses Druckes.
© Ernst Klett Verlag GmbH, Stuttgart 2001. Alle Rechte vorbehalten.
Internetadresse: http://www.klett-verlag.de

Redaktion: Gillian Bathmaker, BA (hons), Virginia Maier, M.A., Noreen O'Donovan

Umschlaggestaltung & Grafik: Hanjo Schmidt, Stuttgart.
Satz: DTP-Verlag.
Repro: Lihs GmbH, Medienhaus, Ludwigsburg.
Druck: Wilhelm Röck, Weinsberg
Printed in Germany.
ISBN 3-12-510511-0

# Contents

## Projektarbeit

Praktische Hinweise . . . . . . . . . . . . . . . . . . . . . . . . . . . . . . . . . .5
Evaluation form . . . . . . . . . . . . . . . . . . . . . . . . . . . . . . . . . . . . .5
KV 1: Project planning . . . . . . . . . . . . . . . . . . . . . . . . . . . . . .6
KV 2: Project evaluation . . . . . . . . . . . . . . . . . . . . . . . . . . . .7

## 1 Who cares what I think?

Didaktisches Inhaltsverzeichnis . . . . . . . . . . . . . . . . . . . . . . . .8
Einleitung . . . . . . . . . . . . . . . . . . . . . . . . . . . . . . . . . . . . . . . . .9
**First impressions** . . . . . . . . . . . . . . . . . . . . . . . . . . . . . . . . . .9
**Rebels** . . . . . . . . . . . . . . . . . . . . . . . . . . . . . . . . . . . . . . . . . .9
The Rebel . . . . . . . . . . . . . . . . . . . . . . . . . . . . . . . . . . . . . . . . .9
**Personal appearance** . . . . . . . . . . . . . . . . . . . . . . . . . . . . .10
Fired from Rolls Royce for Dangerous Hair . . . . . . . . . . . . . .10
Who cares what I think? . . . . . . . . . . . . . . . . . . . . . . . . . . .10
Listening comprehension: Interview with an American Teenager 10
**Time and money** . . . . . . . . . . . . . . . . . . . . . . . . . . . . . . . .12
Music makes the world go round for teenagers . . . . . . . . .12
**Every generation has its day** (N'oubliez jamais) . . . . . . .13
World AIDS Day . . . . . . . . . . . . . . . . . . . . . . . . . . . . . . . . . .13
Young give up condoms as Aids fear fades . . . . . . . . . . . . .13
**Under Pressure** . . . . . . . . . . . . . . . . . . . . . . . . . . . . . . . . .14
The Pressure Cooker (1) . . . . . . . . . . . . . . . . . . . . . . . . . . . .14
The Pressure Cooker (2) . . . . . . . . . . . . . . . . . . . . . . . . . . . .14
**Project: Creating a poster** . . . . . . . . . . . . . . . . . . . . . . . .15
KV 1: 'Who cares' survey . . . . . . . . . . . . . . . . . . . . . . . . . .16
KV 2: Personal fact sheet . . . . . . . . . . . . . . . . . . . . . . . . . .17
KV 3: Listening comprehension:
       Interview with an American teenager . . . . . . . . . .18
KV 4: N'oubliez jamais . . . . . . . . . . . . . . . . . . . . . . . . . . . .19
KV 5: AIDS Awareness . . . . . . . . . . . . . . . . . . . . . . . . . . . .21
KV 6: Collecting information . . . . . . . . . . . . . . . . . . . . . . .22
KV 7: Test: Children of 8 join alcohol casualty list . . . . . .23

## 2 A British jigsaw

Didaktisches Inhaltsverzeichnis . . . . . . . . . . . . . . . . . . . . . . .24
Einleitung . . . . . . . . . . . . . . . . . . . . . . . . . . . . . . . . . . . . . . . .25
**A British Jigsaw** . . . . . . . . . . . . . . . . . . . . . . . . . . . . . . . . .25
**About Britain** . . . . . . . . . . . . . . . . . . . . . . . . . . . . . . . . . .26
Listening comprehension: Wales and the Welsh . . . . . . . . .27
**The British way of life** . . . . . . . . . . . . . . . . . . . . . . . . . . .28
The new Brits: single, stoned and selfish . . . . . . . . . . . . . .29
**Notes from a small island** . . . . . . . . . . . . . . . . . . . . . . . .30
Part 1: Marmite and village fêtes . . . . . . . . . . . . . . . . . . . .30
Part 2: A lonely island . . . . . . . . . . . . . . . . . . . . . . . . . . . .31
Part 3: Two nations . . . . . . . . . . . . . . . . . . . . . . . . . . . . . .31
**The two Ashingtons** . . . . . . . . . . . . . . . . . . . . . . . . . . . .32
**City streets** . . . . . . . . . . . . . . . . . . . . . . . . . . . . . . . . . . . .32
Revealed: Britain's filthiest air . . . . . . . . . . . . . . . . . . . . . . .32
Greening of the Midlands grime . . . . . . . . . . . . . . . . . . . . .32
**Focus on Birmingham** . . . . . . . . . . . . . . . . . . . . . . . . . . .33
Quick & Quirky: Facts about Birmingham . . . . . . . . . . . . .34
**Project: Presenting a town / region** . . . . . . . . . . . . . . . .34
KV 1: Listening comprehension:
       Wales and the Welsh . . . . . . . . . . . . . . . . . . . . . . .35
KV 2: Round Britain game . . . . . . . . . . . . . . . . . . . . . . . . .36
KV 3: Round Britain review questions . . . . . . . . . . . . . . . .37
KV 4: Round Britain crossword . . . . . . . . . . . . . . . . . . . . .39
KV 5: Test: Two towns and two nations . . . . . . . . . . . . . .40

## XtraFile The British political system

Didaktische Hinweise . . . . . . . . . . . . . . . . . . . . . . . . . . . . . . .41
KV 1: Government in Britain quiz . . . . . . . . . . . . . . . . . . .42
KV 2: The British political system . . . . . . . . . . . . . . . . . . .43
KV 3: British politics game . . . . . . . . . . . . . . . . . . . . . . . .44
KV 4: Test: Translation: Australia and the Monarchy . . . .46

## 3 Making the grade

Didaktisches Inhaltsverzeichnis . . . . . . . . . . . . . . . . . . . . . . .47
Einleitung . . . . . . . . . . . . . . . . . . . . . . . . . . . . . . . . . . . . . . . .48
**Education: What's the point?** . . . . . . . . . . . . . . . . . . . . .48
16+ . . . . . . . . . . . . . . . . . . . . . . . . . . . . . . . . . . . . . . . . . . . .49
**School life in Britain** . . . . . . . . . . . . . . . . . . . . . . . . . . . .49
**Records of achievement** . . . . . . . . . . . . . . . . . . . . . . . . .50
Personal statement . . . . . . . . . . . . . . . . . . . . . . . . . . . . . . .50
Listening comprehension: Work experience . . . . . . . . . . . .50
Academic Report . . . . . . . . . . . . . . . . . . . . . . . . . . . . . . . . .51
**Single-sex education** . . . . . . . . . . . . . . . . . . . . . . . . . . . .51
Performance and achievement . . . . . . . . . . . . . . . . . . . . . .52
Regardless of sex, it's cool to do well . . . . . . . . . . . . . . . . .52
**Them & Us** . . . . . . . . . . . . . . . . . . . . . . . . . . . . . . . . . . . .53
**Independent schools:** Fettes College . . . . . . . . . . . . . . .54
**Schools of the future** . . . . . . . . . . . . . . . . . . . . . . . . . . .55
IT revolution in the classroom . . . . . . . . . . . . . . . . . . . . . .55
Laptop to oust books . . . . . . . . . . . . . . . . . . . . . . . . . . . . .55
**Project: A new centre of learning** . . . . . . . . . . . . . . . . .55
KV 1: 16+ Role play: Model answer . . . . . . . . . . . . . . . . .56
KV 2: The school systems in Britain and America . . . . . .57
KV 3: Educational systems . . . . . . . . . . . . . . . . . . . . . . . .59
KV 4: Personal data sheet . . . . . . . . . . . . . . . . . . . . . . . . .60
KV 5: Listening comprehension: Work experience . . . . . .61
KV 6: Making a phone call: Model answer . . . . . . . . . . . .62
KV 7: Test: Real Life U . . . . . . . . . . . . . . . . . . . . . . . . . . . .63

## 4 Meet Britain's Press

Didaktisches Inhaltsverzeichnis . . . . . . . . . . . . . . . . . . . . . . .64
Einleitung . . . . . . . . . . . . . . . . . . . . . . . . . . . . . . . . . . . . . . . .65
**Meet the press** . . . . . . . . . . . . . . . . . . . . . . . . . . . . . . . . .65
Quality & popular press . . . . . . . . . . . . . . . . . . . . . . . . . . .65
Circulation & readership . . . . . . . . . . . . . . . . . . . . . . . . . . .65
**Sales figures** . . . . . . . . . . . . . . . . . . . . . . . . . . . . . . . . . . .66
*Mail on Sunday* climbs into second position . . . . . . . . . . .66
Average sales figures . . . . . . . . . . . . . . . . . . . . . . . . . . . . . .67
**News coverage in quality and popular papers** . . . . . . .67
Mystery of crash pilot's last message . . . . . . . . . . . . . . . . .67
7 Minutes From Safety . . . . . . . . . . . . . . . . . . . . . . . . . . . .67
**What makes the news?** . . . . . . . . . . . . . . . . . . . . . . . . .68
Top Ten Stories . . . . . . . . . . . . . . . . . . . . . . . . . . . . . . . . . .68
**Paparazzi!** . . . . . . . . . . . . . . . . . . . . . . . . . . . . . . . . . . . . .69
**The right to know** . . . . . . . . . . . . . . . . . . . . . . . . . . . . . .69
Headline News . . . . . . . . . . . . . . . . . . . . . . . . . . . . . . . . . . .69
The right to know . . . . . . . . . . . . . . . . . . . . . . . . . . . . . . . .69
**A journalist's day** . . . . . . . . . . . . . . . . . . . . . . . . . . . . . .70
Listening comprehension: Working on a regional newspaper .71
**Further assignments** . . . . . . . . . . . . . . . . . . . . . . . . . . . .72
**Project: A comparative study of British newspapers** . . . .72
Glossary: The Press . . . . . . . . . . . . . . . . . . . . . . . . . . . . . . .72
KV 1: Using statistics . . . . . . . . . . . . . . . . . . . . . . . . . . . . .73
KV 2: Writing an article . . . . . . . . . . . . . . . . . . . . . . . . . . .74

# Contents

(4 Meet Britain's Press)

KV 3: **Role play cards** .................................75
KV 4: **Listening comprehension:**
           Working on a regional newspaper ...........77
KV 5: **Test: talking in Whispers** ....................78

## 5 Welcome to America

Didaktisches Inhaltsverzeichnis .......................79
Einleitung ...........................................80
**Photos of America** ..................................80
**Physical features and time zones** ...................80
Listening comprehension: A conference call ...........81
Hunting Mr Heartbreak .................................81
**Climate and weather in the USA** .....................83
Temperature, rainfall and snowfall ...................83
Extreme weather conditions ...........................83
Hurricane wreaks havoc on battered Gulf states .......84
**Population** .........................................84
Population trends by region from 1990 to 1997 ........84
West, South are building more population muscle ......84
**Focus on the South** .................................85
The southernisation of America .......................85
**Southern rock** ......................................86
Sweet Home Alabama ...................................86
**Project: Planning a trip to the US** .................87
KV 1: **Listening comprehension: A conference call** ...88
KV 2: **Conference call** (Transcript) .................89
KV 3: **Tricky situations** (Role cards) ...............90
KV 4: **Tandem crossword** .............................92
KV 5: **Test: Notes from a big country** ...............94

## XtraFile  The American political system

Didaktische Hinweise .................................95
Checks and balances ..................................95
Listening comprehension: Radio address to the nation ..95
The US political system ..............................96
Klassenarbeit ........................................96
KV 1: **Checks and balances quiz** .....................97
KV 2: **Listening comprehension:**
           Radio address to the nation ................98
KV 3: **The US political system: 'Checks and balances'** ..99
KV 4: **Test: Translation: Government and politics** ..100

## 6 Life in the city: Atlanta

Didaktisches Inhaltsverzeichnis ......................101
Einleitung ...........................................102
**Facts and figures** ..................................102
Atlanta Timeline .....................................102
**Introducing Atlanta** ................................103
Listening comprehension: Talking about Atlanta .......104

**World's busiest airport** ............................106
Atlanta flying high, via world's No. 1 airport .......106
**What's on the minds of Atlantans** ...................107
**Congestion, urban sprawl and quality of life** .......108
**The best place to live?** ............................109
A sense of community .................................109
**Changing communities – multi-cultural communities** .109
Atlanta's new main street: Buford Highway ............110
**From Terminus to Atlanta** ...........................110
**Project: Improving your town** .......................111
KV 1: **Listening comprehension:**
           Talking about Atlanta ......................112
KV 2: **Questionnaire: Talking about Atlanta** ........113
KV 3: **Role play cards** .............................114
KV 4: **Survey sheet** ................................115
KV 5: **Test: America's cities:**
           They can yet be resurrected ................116

## 7 Glued to the tube – TV in the USA

Didaktisches Inhaltsverzeichnis ......................117
Einleitung ...........................................118
**The influence of television** ........................118
Are you glued to the tube? ...........................118
Growing up on television .............................118
Did you know? American viewing habits ................118
**What's on?** .........................................118
TV Guide .............................................118
**Typical TV: Game shows and soap operas** ............120
The longest running daytime game show in the USA:
The Price is Right! ..................................120
All My Children: One of the longest running soaps in history .120
**Ratings and guidelines** ............................121
**TV stations and networks in the USA** ...............123
Media Research .......................................123
**Talking TV!** .......................................124
Listening comprehension: 'The Shock of Recognition' ..124
**Blame the couch potatoes** ..........................125
**Project: A panel discussion** .......................126
KV 1: **The Truman Show** .............................127
KV 2: **Discussing TV** ...............................128
KV 3: **Media research** ..............................129
KV 4: **Listening comprehension:**
           The Shock of Recognition ..................130
KV 5: **TV board game** ...............................131
KV 6: **Test: TV and me** .............................133

Lösungen zu den Kopiervorlagen .......................134

Worterklärungen zu den Tests .........................142

Zusätzliche Materialien ..............................143

Hinweise zur Benutzung der CD-ROM ....................144

# Projektarbeit

## Einleitung

*Handlungsorientierte Arbeit bzw. Projektarbeit, bei der Studenten und Studentinnen selbstständig in Gruppen (oder alleine) zu bestimmten Themen Recherchen anstellen, Material zusammenstellen und auf verschiedene Arten präsentieren, ist ein zunehmend wichtiger Bestandteil des heutigen Unterrichts.*

*Im Voraus von L klar erarbeitete Kriterien und Parameter sind Voraussetzung für gelungene Projektarbeit. In den in 'Challenge 21' vorgeschlagenen Projekten am Ende eines jeden Kapitels werden jeweils klare Anweisungen zur Erarbeitung des Behandlungsfeldes für S gegeben. Folgende Tipps mögen dem L zusätzlich bei der Vorbereitung von Projektarbeit behilflich sein.*

### Project time

Decide in advance:
- how much time students will need to do research for a project.
- how much class time you want to spend on a project.
- how much time you will expect students to spend on project work at home.
- how much time students will need to complete the project.

*Examples:*
- Research: 1 homework assignment;
  Project work: 1 week's lessons and homework; Completion/presentation: 1 week/10 days later.
- Complete project: 2–3 'project days' at school in which students work only on the project and do not attend other lessons.
- Individual student assignment in which student has a given period (1–3 months) to complete project on his/her own.

### Preparation & planning

- Study and discuss aspects of the project to be done at the end of each chapter in the SB with students when starting work on a new chapter. This will enable the students and the teacher to start gathering material whilst the chapter is being covered.
- Copymaster 1 (Project planning) on p. 6 can be handed out to students when they start work on the project in order to help them organize and record work planned and in progress.

### Effective group work

- Groups should have between three and five members and should be composed of members with mixed English abilities.
- Check that group members have individual responsibilities (e.g. group secretary, group speaker, source/material researcher, group progress monitor) to ensure that everyone participates.
- Insist on group members alternating responsibilities in the course of the project.
- Devise project-related 'mini-assignments' to be completed by students in English at every meeting (e.g. reading articles and responding, reporting to the class about experiences, completing worksheets) to make sure that groups speak English amongst themselves.
- Refer students to the 'Skills files' in the Student's Book, especially p. 129 (Giving a talk or presentation), p. 139 (Projects & groupwork) and pp. 140/141 (Questionnaires and surveys).

### Evaluation

- Copymaster 2 (Project evaluation) on p. 7 can be handed out to students so that they can evaluate their work as individuals and as part of a team.
- The evaluation form below can be copied and used by the teacher to evaluate a group and/or an individual on completion of a project.

---

## Evaluation form

Project title: _____

Student's name/Group members: _____

| Criteria | 1 | 2 | 3 | 4 | 5 | 6 | Comments/suggestions |
|---|---|---|---|---|---|---|---|
| Contributions/ideas | | | | | | | |
| Co-operation (in group) | | | | | | | |
| Content | | | | | | | |
| Quality of written work | | | | | | | |
| Oral fluency | | | | | | | |
| Oral accuracy | | | | | | | |
| Style of delivery | | | | | | | |
| Coherence | | | | | | | |
| Use of different media | | | | | | | |
| General impression | | | | | | | |

**Final grade:** ☐    Signed: _____ (teacher)   Date: _____

# Project planning

Name: _____    Class: _____

Project title: _____

Aspects to be dealt with:

- _____    • _____
- _____    • _____
- _____    • _____
- _____    • _____

Information needed:                  Sources of information / help:

- _____    • _____
- _____    • _____
- _____    • _____
- _____    • _____

Progress report:

| Name | Task | Deadline | Material used | Task complete |
|------|------|----------|---------------|---------------|
|      |      |          |               |               |
|      |      |          |               |               |
|      |      |          |               |               |
|      |      |          |               |               |
|      |      |          |               |               |
|      |      |          |               |               |
|      |      |          |               |               |
|      |      |          |               |               |
|      |      |          |               |               |
|      |      |          |               |               |
|      |      |          |               |               |
|      |      |          |               |               |
|      |      |          |               |               |
|      |      |          |               |               |
|      |      |          |               |               |

# Project evaluation

Name: _____   Class: _____

1. **What have you learned from the project?**

   _____
   _____
   _____

2. **What aspect(s) did you find the most interesting / useful? Why?**

   _____
   _____
   _____

3. **What aspect(s) did you find the least interesting / useful, and why?**

   _____
   _____
   _____

4. **Future reference: When doing a project in future ...**

   … I will _____

   … I won't _____

   … I would like my teacher to _____

5. **Self-evaluation**

| Personal progress | none | some | a lot |
|---|---|---|---|
| I have improved my knowledge of the topic. | | | |
| I have made a point of speaking English with my classmates and teacher. | | | |
| I am more confident in speaking English (less worried about making mistakes). | | | |
| I can speak English more fluently. | | | |
| I can speak English more accurately. | | | |
| I can write English more accurately. | | | |
| I have improved my English vocabulary. | | | |
| I can take notes and summarise the content of authentic texts. | | | |
| I can use grammar books and dictionaries to solve my language problems. | | | |

| Teamwork | none | some | a lot |
|---|---|---|---|
| I have taken an active part in discussions. | | | |
| I have taken an active part in decisions. | | | |
| I have taken an active part in looking for material. | | | |
| I have contributed ideas to the group. | | | |
| I have helped other people in my group when they needed it. | | | |
| I have completed my tasks on time. | | | |

# 1 Who cares what I think?

## Didaktisches Inhaltsverzeichnis

|  | Title | Text type / Topic | Skills & Tasks |  |
|---|---|---|---|---|
|  | **First impressions** (SB S. 6) | • photos | • Speaking: describing pictures and discussing opinions<br>• Vocabulary: terms for describing one's appearance |  |
| 🎙 | **The Rebel** (SB S. 7) | • poem (194 words)<br>• being a rebel | • Reading: for gist<br>• Speaking/writing: presenting an original poem in rap form<br>• Grammar: asking and answering questions/the present tense |  |
|  | **Fired from Rolls Royce for Dangerous Hair** (SB S. 8) | • newspaper article (230 words)<br>• appearance and its consequences | • Reading: for detail<br>• Speaking: role play<br>• Translation<br>• Grammar: the present perfect |  |
|  | **Who cares what I think?** (SB S. 9) | • survey | • Speaking: talking about values and goals | **1** TRB, S. 16<br>**2** TRB, S. 17 |
| 🎙 | **Interview with an American Teenager** (SB S. 9) | • interview<br>• how young people see themselves | • Listening comprehension | **3** TRB, S. 18 |
|  | **Time and money** (SB p. 10) | • bar charts<br>• young people's pocket money and leisure time | • Speaking: talking about and comparing statistical information<br>• Writing: statistical information<br>• Vocabulary: terms for comparing statistics |  |
|  | **Music makes the world go round for teenagers** (SB S. 11) | • newspaper article (260 words) | • Reading: for detail<br>• Speaking: presenting and comparing opinions about the world of pop music |  |
|  | **Every generation has its day** (SB S. 12) | • mind map<br>• lifestyles then and now | • Speaking/writing: talking about and documenting opinions about lifestyles<br>• organizing ideas in thematic groups |  |
| 🎙 | **N'oubliez jamais** (SB S. 12) | • song (290 words) | • Listening comprehension | **4** TRB, S. 19/20 |
|  | **Young give up condoms as Aids fear fades** (SB S. 12) | • newspaper article (665 words)<br>• young people and AIDS | • Reading: for gist<br>• Speaking: expressing and discussing opinions and ideas<br>• Writing: organizing ideas in table form<br>• Grammar: phrases with prepositions/tenses | **5** TRB, S. 21<br>**6** TRB, S. 22 |
| 🎙<br>🎙 | **The Pressure Cooker (1)** (SB S. 15)<br>**The Pressure Cooker (2)** (SB S. 18) | • radio play (1000 words)<br>• radio play (545 words)<br>• youth-related problems | • Reading: for detail<br>• Speaking: talking about stressful situations<br>• Writing: letters/original scene endings<br>• Grammar: question tags |  |
|  | **Project: Creating a poster** (SB S. 19) |  |  |  |
|  | **Test: Children of 8 join alcohol casualty list** | • newspaper article (343 words) |  | **7** TRB, S. 23 |

# Who cares what I think? 1

## Einleitung

Unter der Kapitelüberschrift 'Who cares what I think?' wird ein direkter Bezug zur Erlebniswelt der Zielgruppe des Buches hergestellt. Die Redeanlässe beziehen sich dabei zunächst auf Dritte, bevor das „Ich" der Redeanlass ist. Die S werden immer wieder dazu aufgefordert, sich zu den Dingen zu äußern, die in ihrem Leben einen großen Platz einnehmen.

## First impressions  SB S. 6

→ *Ausgangsfrage:* When you see people for the first time, what do you pay attention to especially?
Die Nennungen werden als TA festgehalten und dann – unter Berücksichtigung der weiteren Fragestellungen Describing people unter den Bildern – auf die Fotos angewendet.
Zu erwartende Nennungen: *hair, eyes, age, clothes, hands, legs, voice, way of expressing oneself, interest, gestures, ...*

### Describing people

● (S. 'Grammar file', SB S. 149.) Die Aufgaben unter den Fotos sollen hauptsächlich mündlich in GA oder PA erarbeitet werden. Mögliche Angaben (*adjectives & opposites*):
friendly ≠ unfriendly • relaxed ≠ nervous; uptight • angry ≠ conciliatory; calm • reserved ≠ open; extrovert • trendy ≠ conservative, traditional; nervous ≠ relaxed; calm • in a good mood ≠ in a bad mood; angry • stylish ≠ old-fashioned • open-minded ≠ narrow-minded • charming ≠ boorish

→ How would you describe the ideal teacher? The ideal friend?

## Rebels  SB S. 7

### Creating a poem

Die Zeilen des Gedichtes werden von den S in Stillarbeit/PA zusammengesetzt und das Ergebnis mit dem Originalgedicht verglichen.

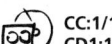
CC:1/1
CD1:1  **The Rebel** (Originalgedicht von D.J. Enright)

When everybody has short hair,
The rebel lets his hair grow long.
When everybody has long hair,
The rebel cuts his hair short.
When everybody talks during the lesson,
The rebel doesn't say a word.
When nobody talks during the lesssons,
The rebel creates a disturbance.
When everybody wears a uniform,
The rebel dresses in fantastic clothes.
When everybody wears fantastic clothes,
The rebel dresses soberly.
In the company of dog lovers,
The rebel expresses a preference for cats.
In the company of cat lovers,
The rebel puts in a good word for dogs.
When everybody is praising the sun,
The rebel remarks on the need of rain.
When everybody is greeting the rain,
The rebel regrets the absence of sun.
When everybody goes to the meeting,
The rebel stays at home and reads a book.
When everybody stays at home and reads a book,
The rebel goes to the meeting.
When everybody says, Yes please,
The rebel says, No thank you.
When everybody says, No thank you,
The rebel says, Yes please.
It is very good that we have the rebels,
You may not find it very good to be one.
*From* Rhyme Times Rhyme, London: Chatto & Windus, 1974, p. 9.

### Comprehension

Die Fragen 1. und 2. werden mündlich in der Klasse behandelt. Danach lässt sich eine Diskussionsphase anschließen; die Ergebnisse werden schriftlich festgehalten. Mögliche Lösungen:
1. *The rebel is a person who just wants to be different because he likes to be different. • The rebel decides to go against what is expected of him/her because he/she doesn't agree with others' expectations. • The rebel "rebels" only because he/she wants to attract attention. • The rebel acts the way he/she does in order to protest against the rest of society.*
2. *In a society we need rebels. If there were no rebels, people would all be the same. • Democracy allows people to have their own opinions, tastes, style. However, it will be difficult and lonely for you to choose to be a rebel because others do not understand you. • You might not at all agree with how a rebel acts.*

### Grammar

Das *present tense* und die Fragebildung werden hier wiederholt und in PA eingeübt. Mögliche Fragen/Antworten:
a)/b) When does the rebel dress in fanstastic clothes? • When everybody wears a uniform. • When does the rebel dress soberly? • When everybody dresses in fantastic clothes. • When does the rebel create a disturbance? • When nobody talks during the lessons.

### Over to you

● Das Gedicht in Rap-Stil von mehreren (möglichst freiwilligen!) S vorlesen lassen zur Übung von Aussprache und Intonation. Die Struktur des Gedichts wird dann als Vorlage verwendet, um ein eigenes Gedicht zu schreiben. Präsentation: vor der Klasse als Rap (oder, wenn es den S lieber ist, als freier Vortrag.)
HA: in GA oder Einzelarbeit eigenes Gedicht (oder 'The Rebel') mit musikalisch-rhythmischer Begleitung auf Kassette aufnehmen und der Klasse präsentieren.

→ "It's getting more and more difficult to be different." In groups, discuss whether you agree or disagree with this statement, and come up with a statement for your group giving reasons for your opinion.

→ PA (Rollenspiel): Einige Situationen vorgeben, z. B. Two guests in restaurant; two passengers on a train; etc. S eine der Situationen aussuchen und zweimal spielen lassen: einmal mit und einmal ohne 'Rebel'. Anschließend kurze Diskussion als Klasse: "Is it possible to be a 'rebel' and a 'conformist'?"

# 1 Who cares what I think?

## Personal appearance
SB S. 8–9

### Talk about it

● *Die 'Pre-reading'-Aufgaben sollen mündlich erarbeitet werden. Die Ergebnisse können als TA oder OHP festgehalten werden.*
Groups which have uniforms/rules: *police, armed forces, nurses, football/sports clubs (on and off the pitch), clubs and bands.*
Why rules/uniforms are sometimes necessary or advantageous: *to avoid danger to self and others, e.g. wearing jewellery when you do sport; to be easily recognisable as a group; to make differences in wealth less noticeable, etc.*

### Fired from Rolls Royce ...
SB S. 8

### Comprehension

1. Mortiboy lost his job because he refused to have his hair cut, even though his training manager had told him to do so. The training manager thought that the spikes might be a hazard to people working with Peter.
2. Mortiboy didn't believe that his hair was dangerous and he therefore refused to have it cut. He thinks that he should be allowed to look the way he wants.
3. (Offene Meinungsangabe)

### Translation

*Bristol, England.*
*Der gerichtliche Einspruch eines 18 Jahre alten Punk-Rockers, der von Rolls Royce auf Grund der Tatsache gefeuert wurde, dass die 4 Inch langen Spikes seiner Frisur die Augen seiner Kollegen gefährden würden, wurde am Dienstag abgelehnt.*
*Ein Arbeitsgericht in dieser Stadt an der Westküste erfuhr, dass Peter Mortiboy, dessen ungewöhnliche Bekleidung 18 Ohrringe, ein mit Zacken versehenes Hundehalsband, Stahlarmbänder und ein Piercing durch die Nase aufweist, von Rolls Royce wiederholt gewarnt wurde, dass seine äußere Erscheinung nicht den Anforderungen der Firma entspräche.*
*Nach Aussagen von Ausbildungsleiter Howard Perry kündigte der Luxuskarossenhersteller ihm seinen Ausbildungsplatz im Technical College von Rolls Royce und seinen Job, in dem er 120 £ pro Woche als auszubildender Techniker erhielt, als er im letzen Juni begann Spikes zu tragen.*

### Grammar

(S. 'Grammar file', SB, S. 142 & 144.) Mögliche Antworten:
1. *I go to school every day and I have never been late.* • *I always learn my English vocabulary but I have never passed an exam.* • *I have a shower every morning but I have never really enjoyed it.* • *We travel to Italy every year but we have not yet learned Italian.*
2./3. *I practice the violin for an hour a day but I haven't been able to learn this concerto.* • *She practices the violin for an hour a day but she hasn't been able to learn the concerto.* • *I eat a low-fat diet but I still haven't lost any weight.* • *He eats a low-fat diet but he still hasn't lost any weight.*

### Role play

*S bereiten Rollenspiel in PA vor. Einige Paare vorspielen lassen. Wenn möglich, vorgespielte Versionen auf Video oder Kassette aufnehmen. Anschließend in KA sprachliche Aspekte bzw. Schwierigkeiten und Verhalten (positiv und negativ!) besprechen.*

## Who cares what I think?
SB S. 9

### Over to you

 *Kopiervorlagen 1 & 2: TRB, S. 16 & 17/CD-ROM*

● *Diese Ausgangsfrage stellt einen Redeanlass dar, der als Hinführung zu der Erstellung des 'Personal fact sheet' dient. Die Fragen können entweder in Einzelarbeit oder in Form von Interviews von S beantwortet werden. S auffordern, eigene Mittel (PCs, Bilder, etc.) zur Erstellung eines eigenen 'Personal Fact Sheet' zu benutzen.*
*Die möglichst weitgehend selbst gestalteten 'Personal Fact Sheets' sollen dann im Klassenzimmer ausgehängt werden.*

→ *'Survey' (Kopiervorlage 1) anonym ausfüllen lassen, einsammeln und neu verteilen. S sollen zu fünf Angaben Stellung nehmen (agree/disagree/reason).*

### Listening comprehension
SB S. 9

 *Kopiervorlage 3: TRB, S. 18/CD-ROM*
*Lösungen: TRB, S. 134*

 CC:1/1
CD:1 **Interview with an American teenager**

*Keith Wong tells of the time when his grandfather had to sneak into the United States from China because immigration laws prevented him from coming here. His grandfather was then detained for six months in a cold, lonely cell at Angel Island. Keith also knows that with dedication, persistence, and hard work, his family has firmly and successfully established itself in San Francisco, California, after three generations. Those experiences have influenced Keith in fundamental ways: he works diligently to be successful in school, treasures his parents, brother and sister (and dog, Riki), and hopes to have an impact on the world – maybe even to be the person who discovers the cure for AIDS. Although his country didn't warmly welcome his ancestors, sixteen-year-old Keith loves the United States and feels he has the responsibility to help others and be informed about issues. Now, Keith, who can rarely keep a smile from his face, hopes to become an Eagle Scout and attend the college of his choice.*

**How would you describe yourself?**
I'm just an average kid with pretty high expectations though I'm not sure if I'll reach all of my expectations! I'm going to try. I think I care a lot about other people too, like the homeless. I think I have some sort of intelligence. I have some basic skills. That's how I describe myself, just your everyday person.

**Who are your heroes?**
My heroes? I don't think I like one person for everything they are. I think that everybody has like sports heroes or something. They might be good in sports, but maybe their personal life may not be that good. Like Michael Jordan, he's one of the best basketball players, but he owed a lot of money to bettors. Other people might think of him as a hero, but I don't. Just because he's a good basketball player and he can say he's sorry for it, people say, "Oh, okay, let's forgive him." But I think people should stick to people close to home and look at what they've done to help other people. I think people that volunteer at these homeless shelters are the people that give so much and make a difference in the world.

**Have you heard the term "American dream?" What's yours?**
I think back a long time ago the American dream was when you came over to America and made a name for yourself and did better

than you would have before. I think right now the American dream is just getting your education and finding a job, and not living in poverty and supporting yourself and your family. And just living happily. I think that's the American dream right now.

I just want a good job that I can support my family with. Work with people that are easy to work with. Belong to organizations like Boy Scouts and help the younger kids shape their views so that they can grow up to be successful, too. That's what I want to do, to help other people.

**In what way would you like to make a difference in society?**
Maybe if I worked for the Environmental Protection Agency (…) – if I could go out there and bust some of the bad guys or bring in somebody that was real bad. Or if I go into chemistry or something, maybe I could discover a cure for AIDS! Well, maybe not that big, but anything that would make a little bit of difference in the world would be good.

**How would you describe a good citizen?**
Hanging out your flag would be one of the things a citizen should do. I think during the holidays you have to show (patriotism). I also think (reciting) the Pledge of Allegiance is a big thing. And believing in your country also. You know how some people are saying, "Oh, Americans are all so bad"? They should just do something about it instead of complaining. I think that's what they should do.

**If you had the opportunity to live anywhere in the world, including the United States, where would you choose?**
I like San Francisco the most, just because it's so culturally diverse. It's a beautiful city, I think. We take everything for granted, but we have everything we ever need here – we can plant our own food and all that, too. I also think America is still the best country in the world. There's a lot of problems in America, but not as bad as the other countries. Like there's no wars being fought; there's no terrorism within America, except I guess you could call the Waco, Texas, thing or the bomb in New York a form of it. But like in England, they have the IRA and stuff like that.

**Do you think politicians are trustworthy?**
I think we expect them to be, but then there are a lot of politicians that are concerned only with themselves. I don't think they're really doing that much for the community of the citizens. They should stop arguing and try to reach a compromise.

And then, there are just a lot of negative attitudes about the government, with all these groups like ACT-UP or those hippie-type groups, the pro-choice people, and all rap songs, too. (…)

**What do you think the country is going to be like in fifty years?**
I hope that America would be the model for all the nations in the world and that maybe all the other nations would be like America in fifty years. Maybe everybody would have a democracy and everybody would have an equal say and there wouldn't be any racism. I think racism by then will probably be gone, because everybody grows out of everything. I don't think there will be any more wars.

I hope that America has a good president that everybody likes and that there wouldn't be any different views between Republicans and Democrats and others. I wish the parties would all work together. I hope that in fifty years everybody will work for the common good. I think it's possible, if everybody tries hard enough to work with each other and just tries to meet halfway. That's what I want America to be in fifty years.

**Do you think teenagers care about the country and are informed about issues?**
At (my school), everybody knows a lot about the subjects right now in the world, but in the other schools, I find that people don't really care because their schools don't focus on the subjects and current events right now. I think that a majority of the kids probably don't really care about what's happening now, but as you get older, I guess it becomes more apparent to you.

**Do you think Americans care about their country?**
No. I think they care most about themselves and they just expect to receive everything all the time. They expect the government to do everything for them, when they don't do anything for themselves to help their situation.

**What it is like to attend a magnet-school like Lowell?**
It's a pretty tough transitional time, because junior high was so much smaller and a lot easier. I was spoiled in that I didn't really have to work hard for As in junior high. Then when I got to Lowell, I had to work hard just to get Bs. I work three and a half, sometimes four hours a night on homework. My mom's also making me prep for the SAT. Lowell's stereotype is as a nerd school. *(Laughter)* It's a college preparatory school. Lowell has a lot of courses that most other schools in San Francisco don't have, like advanced placement and honors classes. You can select your own classes and your own time schedule. The majority of teachers at Lowell are very old, and I think these older teachers are a lot harder than the younger teachers that are coming out now.

**Tell me about the Chinese education that you've had.**
My parents encouraged me to go to Chinese school when I was in first grade. I went to Chinese schools in Chinatown, Saturday from nine to twelve. I memorized old poems, stories, and learned new vocabulary words. We had a test every week too. I haven't been going though since I graduated from eighth grade.

The best thing that I learned was the old poems, because they usually told about how life was back in China, like farming or feudal wars a long time ago. There is one lesson I liked about this guy who tells a sort of ten commandments of life, saying how to respect your parents and respect everybody else around you. And he told about life and if there are bad times, what to do. Probably the hardest thing he said to do was respecting what your parents say all the time, because your views are a lot different than your parents' views. But I get along well with my parents.

I speak Chinese pretty well. I used to speak it better before, but over the years I haven't spoken it that much. I used to speak a lot of Chinese with my parents when I was little, and with grandparents every time I saw them because they don't know any English.

**I was wondering what you thought of the stereotype of Asian students as extremely smart. I'm sure you've heard of that.**
Yes! *(Laughing)* I think that stereotype is true because most of the Asians around me are really smart. And I think it's because our ancestors had to work harder in China for everything they had. They had to work in the field every day. I think the view back in China was that America was this great land that you can find success in if you try hard enough, so they all try harder – and a lot of them succeed.

But there are problems with that. My school has a majority of Chinese students. So they're setting up new rules to limit the number of Chinese people going. You've got to get perfect scores to get in. But I heard of some people that did get everything perfectly and still didn't get in – just because they're Chinese. They're lowering the standards for other races and making the standards a lot tougher for Asians mostly. I guess they want to racially mix it. I think they should just let whoever's qualified come in.

**What's the difference between the Asians who are doing really well in school and business and the ones who are dropping out of school and getting into trouble?**

# 1 Who cares what I think?

I think the main difference is the parents. Of the kids that work hard, maybe their parents really encourage them to do better. I know a lot of dropouts that still live at home and their parents don't really care what they do – maybe because their parents just came over from China and have two jobs or something and they're never at home. So they can't even offer their kid any guidance. The only people kids could hang around with was gangs and other kids that had no support from anybody at home either. So they just roam around together causing trouble.

Basically, my mom guided me, my brother, and my sister along on what to do. I'm going to the same high school that my brother and sister went to. My mom wants me to go to college. She's instilled our attitudes and our values. She only worked until about one o'clock when I was younger, so she was always there for me (after school). And my dad always came home around dinner time, so I could talk to him too.

**What kind of Chinese customs does your family follow?**
Well, there's the Moon Festival. We usually eat moon cake to signify that. Moon cake is kind of a Chinese version of fruit cake. I don't really like it. It's hard and sweet, with some kind of beans in it.

And then we have the Chinese New Year. My dad makes those red signs with little sayings like "good luck bringing in the New Year." My mom makes lanterns out of the money they give out during Chinese New Year. There's customary food that you eat, like moo shu pork and stuff called dzai – a vegetarian dish. We usually go to visit the family on New Year's. The Chinese New Year's parade is also a big thing – lots of tourists go there. I think I went to one or two before; my dad was in it one time. But I think once you see it, there's not much reason to go again because they just have the same line dances and a dragon and those big guys on stilts.

There's a lot of other holidays, but we don't really observe some of them. My parents aren't that traditional because we're a Christian family and we celebrate all the Christian holidays. We just celebrate the major Chinese holidays because it's good to keep in touch with your own ancestry and your own customs, and at the same time, have the American ones, like the Fourth of July.

Church is very big in my life right now. We go to church every Sunday. I think Christian values are what I live with every day – how I deal with hardships and the suffering that goes on. I think Christianity has taught me how to get out there and give a lot. I do day camp in the summertime to help kids learn and try to be better people.

Adapted with permission from Who Cares What I think?
© 1994 Close Up Foundation, Alexandria, Virginia, U.S.A.

## Time and Money                                     SB S. 10–11

### Collecting information

1. S sollen kurz ihre eigenen Antworten zu den Fragen a)–d) ausdenken (evtl. als HA) und dann diese mündlich in Form eines ‚Minivortrages' der Klasse mitteilen.
Mögliche Antwort:
"I get 100 Euros a month pocket money and I spend most of it on magazines and going out with friends. I usually spend about 25 Euros a month on CDs and about twice as much on clothes. I don't spend much time talking on the phone but I spend about 3 hours a day sending SMS messages! I only watch television for about an hour a day."
2. S befragen einander und halten Antworten in Kurzform fest (note taking). Diese notes dienen als Vorlage für die nächste Übung.

### Making comparisons

Mögliche Antworten: *Kurt spends more money on CDs than I do.*
• *Inge gets as much pocket money from her parents as Thomas (does).* • *Sabine spends the most money on clothes.* • *Florian spends the least amount of time talking on the telephone.*

### Talking about statistics

(S. ‚Skills file', SB, S. 131.)
1. a) Around 15% of …
b) Around 12% of …
c) Almost a quarter of …
d) … roughly the same amount …
2. a) more – less – than
b) Between – dropped by almost
c) In the same period – from over – to just over

### Over to you

● Dieser Teil wird schriftlich vorbereitet: die S schreiben ihre Lösungen auf eine OH-Folie, so dass eine Präsentation der Ergebnisse und deren Kontrolle/Verbesserung leichter umzusetzen ist. Mögliche Ergebnisse:
*In 1986, more boys than girls spent no time doing homework. In 1996, more boys than girls spent no time doing homework. Between 10 and 15 per cent of 10- to 13-year-olds get no pocket money at all.*

→ Find similar statistical information (on the Internet/in youth magazines) and present it to your class.

→ Write three multiple-choice survey questions concerning how pupils spend their time and money. Ask 5 of your classmates to respond to your questions. Present your results as a bar chart. (Skills files, SB, pp. 140 &131)

## Music makes the world go round …          SB S. 11

### Comprehension

Diese Fragen werden mündlich bearbeitet.
1. The Oasis tour is a good example of how important music is to teenagers. Within hours, no more tickets for the concert were available, because fans had done everything from blocking hotlines to sleeping outside the box offices in order to get a ticket.
2. The survey shows that teenagers spend lots of money on music because it seems to be all that matters for almost 25% of them. Apart from music, teenagers are also interested in clothes, the style of which is strongly influenced by pop stars.
3. The survey found out that music matters, but the text doesn't. Even if a song text is not clear to teenagers, they still listen to the song as long as they like the music.
4. Almost 50% of teenagers don't care about what pop stars do, as long as they like their music. Consequently, they do not necessarily think badly of a pop star's music even though the star is known to be involved in drugs.

### Over to you

(S. ‚Skills files', SB, S. 129 & 132.) Diese Aufgabe bietet einen direkten Bezug zum Alltag der S. Aufgabe 1. mündlich als Klasse besprechen.
Aufgabe 2. sollte von S in Einzelarbeit zu Hause vorbereitet und dann als ‚Referat' mit Diskussion vorgetragen werden.

# Who cares what I think? 1

*Aufgabe 3. sollte zuerst mündlich mit TA bearbeitet werden. S können dann ggf. eine eigene schriftliche Version anfertigen.*

## A step further

*Diese Aufgaben sind im Schwierigkeitsgrad etwas höher und sollten daher im gelenkten L/S-Gespräch und als TA erarbeitet werden. Mögliche Antworten:*
1. a) *You hear new words and expressions and start using them yourself. You start using English words that you know from songs when you are speaking German.* • *Sometimes slang and bad language is used in songs but when you have heard the song and the words often this language begins to sound OK to you and you start using it in a normal context. (e.g. „verpiss dich" from the song by Tic Tac Toe)* • *You hear and adopt new grammatical and sentence structures.*
b) *(Individuelle Angaben)*
2. *clothes, hairstyles, fashion in general, commitment to humanitarian institutions (Live3, AID, supporting child war victims, etc.)*
3. *Who: sports figures; politicians; teachers; parents; friends; TV personalities; etc.*
*What: Television; radio; magazines; newspapers; Internet; advertisements; etc.*

## Every generation has its day    SB S. 12–14

● *Die Fragen im SB werden als Einstieg mündlich erarbeitet, bevor der Song 'N'oubliez jamais' vorgespielt wird.*
*'Lifestyles: then & now'-Diagramm: S könnten entweder ein Diagramm für sämtliche Generationen oder ein Diagramm pro Generation zeichnen.*

→ *Design a diagram showing teenagers' relationships to their parents or to other figures in authority.*

 CC:1/2
CD:17    **Listening: N'oubliez jamais**    SB S. 12

 *Kopiervorlage 4: TRB, 19/CD-ROM*
*Songtext: SB, S. 120*
*Lösung zu 4 2/2: TRB, S. 134*

## World AIDS Day    SB S. 12

*Das World AIDS Day Plakat soll einen Gesprächsanlass als Einstieg in die Thematik und zum anschließenden Text bieten. Für diese Gesprächsphase kann auf einen Aufschrieb verzichtet werden, da der sich anschließende Text noch ausreichend Gelegenheit für schriftliche Arbeiten bietet. Sinnvoll ist auch ein 'brainstorming' zum Thema „AIDS", das als Stichwort sicherlich bei dem 'Lifestyles: then and now' Diagramm auftaucht.*

→ *Folgende Einstiegsfragen wären denkbar:*
• Does this poster get your attention? Why/Why not? What do you think should be included? What do think is too much?
• Which of the suggested activities would you most/least like to organize? Why?
• Think of other special days, e.g. Mother's/Father's Day, World Children's Day, German Reunification Day. What is the difference between World AIDS Day and these other days? Do you think these special days make sense/are necessary?
*Mögliche Antworten:* Some of these days get more attention, some less. The AIDS problem has been around for some time now, so people may not want to hear much about it and thus don't pay as much attention to it as they should. Advantage of having an AIDS day: to cope with AIDS, much money is needed, and the World AIDS Day is a major contribution to raising money.)
• Check the media: how is people's attention in your country drawn to World AIDS day?
*Mögliche Antworten:* Similar posters • Radio spots • TV documentaries • TV shows • …

 *Kopiervorlage 5: TRB, S. 21/CD-ROM*

## Young give up condoms …    SB S. 12–14

### Collecting information

*Beim Textverständnis, diesmal in Tabellenform, werden S angehalten, sich auf zentrale Punkte des Textes zu konzentrieren. Bei der Bearbeitung von Aufgaben 1. und 2. kommt es darauf an eine klare und übersichtliche Tabelle zu entwerfen. Aufgabe 3. (das Ausfüllen der Tabelle) entspricht praktisch dem Unterstreichen zentraler Textstellen als Alternative zu 'Questions on the text'.*
*Mögliche Antworten:*
1./2. *Kopiervorlage 6: TRB, S. 22/CD-ROM*
*Lösungen: TRB, 134*
3. *New research: Findings (ll. 3–8): compared to five years earlier more young people are having regular sex, with more partners, without using condoms.* • *Reasons (ll. 12–25): People don't settle down until they are older so they have more partners. Women have become more relaxed about casual relationships.*
*Charlotte (ll. 29–40): 24, estate agent, used to be terrified of becoming infected and always insisted on using a condom, now not worried about getting AIDS anymore because she's had lots of partners and hasn't caught AIDS yet!*
*Insurance salesman (ll. 45–50): 23, insurance salesman, used to be afraid of getting AIDS and used condoms, but doesn't use condoms anymore because he thinks a cure for AIDS will be found soon, thinks today's generation doesn't care anymore.*

### Your opinion

*(Individuelle Meinungsangabe. S. auch 'Skills file', SB, S. 132.)*
*Mögliche Antwort:*
In my opinion Charlotte and the insurance salesman behave very irresponsibly. I think that it is very important to use a condom when you have sex because you can never know whether your partner has AIDS or not.

### Working with words

*Zwingt noch einmal zur Textlektüre: die Ausdrücke sind in die eigene Vokabelliste zu schreiben.*
1. a) *according to (l. 5)*
b) *to be more likely to (l. 42)*
c) *to be terrified of (l. 32)*
d) *to be worried about (l. 30)*
e) *the change in (l. 13)*
f) *to decline to (l. 45)*
g) *an increase in (l. 9)*
h) *to insist on (l. 34)*
i) *at risk of (l. 2)*
j) *a survey on (l.51)*
2. *Soll als Transferübung schriftlich bearbeitet und als „Themenliste" festgehalten werden. Weitere Beispiele:*

# 1 Who cares what I think?

AIDS partly accounts for a change in young people's sexual behaviour. • In many parts of the world, young people are worried about a potential war. • Young people who smoke are more likely to die of lung cancer.
(S. auch 'Skills file', SB. S. 133.)

### Grammar

Übung: schriftlich ins Heft (HA mit Besprechung in der Folgestunde)
1. has revealed (l. 3) • have had (l. 7) • has risen (l. 11) • has been eroded (l. 20) • hasn't been hammered (l. 23) • hasn't happened (ll. 34/35) • have changed (l. 36)
2. a) (has) sent off • has not been asked
b) ask • have ... been learning
c) was • went • hasn't done • hasn't got/doesn't have
d) haven't seen • left
3. –

### Over to you

• (S. auch 'Skills file', SB, S. 131 & 132.) Als Einleitung zur Diskussion um AIDS und Schwangerschaft bietet sich eine 'brainstorming session' mit Erstellen einer 'mind map' an. Folgende Fragen könnten als Ausgangspunkt gestellt werden:
What can you do to protect yourself against AIDS/pregnancy? What would you do if you found out that you/your partner had AIDS/was pregnant?
Die zweite Aufgabe sollte als Projekt in selbstständiger GA oder PA erarbeitet werden, mit anschließender Präsentation des Materials im Klassenzimmer.
Weitere Informationen zum Thema „AIDS" gibt es bei:
http://www.AIDS.com

## Under pressure    SB S. 15–19

Das Hörspiel 'The Pressure Cooker' thematisiert viele Probleme, die eine zentrale Bedeutung für die Zielgruppe haben: Schulnoten, Erwartungen der Eltern, Liebe und Freundschaft, Problembewältigung, Familienverhältnisse. Im SB werden 2 von den insgesamt 5 Szenen des Hörspiels abgedruckt (2 und 5). (Gesamttext: s. Quellenangabe, SB, S. 17)

### Before you read

• Diese Punkte lenken auf die Thematik des Hörspiels hin. Freie Meinungsangaben der S sind beabsichtigt. Beim vierten Punkt sollen S den 'Pressure cooker' symbolisch betrachten.
Mögliche Antworten:
Under pressure: At school: when there are tests, when reports and grades are given out, when speaking in class or giving a talk • At home: going out late, smoking, boyfriend/girlfriend who parents don't like, losing or breaking s.th. important, etc.
Who to turn to: parents, brother/sister, other relatives (grandparents, aunts, uncles) or 'near' relatives (neighbours, godparents), best friends at school, partner, etc.
Things young people might do when under extreme pressure: cry, shout, go out cycling/running, listen to very loud music, write poems, write a letter to an agony aunt, visit a friend, ring a friend up, run away from home, try to hurt s.o., commit suicide.
A pressure cooker is a special pan which cooks food very quickly under pressure. The play could be about someone who feels under such pressure that he or she could explode.

 CC:1/2  CD1:2  **The Pressure Cooker (1)**    SB S. 15–17

### Comprehension    SB S. 17

1. Schriftliche Erarbeitung in PA im Unterricht (oder als Vorbereitung zu Hause). Liste:
coming home late • not helping enough at home, e.g. dusting, hoovering, cooking a meal/cooking potatoes in the pressure cooker • not working hard enough for exams • going to university: Andrea wants to go to drama college • Andrea's brother Ian who always does everything right • seeing her boyfriend Graham and going out too often • staying in and not seeing Graham anymore before the exams are over.
2. She is jealous. She thinks her mother loves him more because he had no problems at school and is now at university.
3. Andrea's mother has prepared the potatoes and carrots in the pressure cooker. Andrea says that she hates potatoes cooked in the pressure cooker, and claims her mother knows this. Her mother says that she had to cook them in the pressure cooker because she was in a hurry. She had asked Andrea to prepare dinner.
The pressure cooker is symbolic of the tension between Andrea and her mother. Her mother is always in a rush and doesn't pay attention to her needs. Andrea feels that her mother doesn't like her or respect her wishes.

### Grammar

1. Pass my lipstick, will you? (l. 32) • Oh, Andrea, you've not let me down, have you? (l. 37) • I bet she did well, didn't she? (l. 46) • But I'm sure she got good marks, didn't she? (l. 49) • It's always Ian, isn't it? (l. 59)
2. a) ..., couldn't you?;
b) ..., did you?
c) ... didn't he?
3. Mögliche Antworten:
a) You are not really listening to me, are you?
b) That was a really good film we saw last night, wasn't it?
c) You haven't put my pen in your pencil case, have you??
4. (s. Kästchen, SB, S.17)

### Over to you

• Diese Punkte schließen die Arbeit mit Teil 1 des Hörspiels ab und dienen gleichzeitig als Einleitung zum zweiten Teil.
Die Dialoge in PA/GA entwerfen und vorspielen lassen. S ihrer Fantasie freien Lauf lassen, was die Fortsetzung des Hörspiels angeht. (Möglichst nichts verraten!)
Der letzte Punkt kann schriftlich in Einzelarbeit (eventuell als HA) erarbeitet werden.

 CC:1/3  CD1:3  **The Pressure Cooker (2)**    SB S. 18–19

### Comprehension    SB S. 19

1. Mögliche Antworten:
I think it will be the hospital to say that Andrea has woken up/to say that Andrea has died. • It could be Andrea's mother saying that she is going to go to the hospital after all. • It could be Andrea's boyfriend ringing to see what is wrong with her.
2. The safety valve's letting off a bit of steam. I'll turn the heat down: it'll stop in a minute. (ll. 15/16)
You've got to have a safety valve on a pressure cooker. Could blow up if you didn't. (ll. 18/19)

# Who cares what I think? 1

*That means the pressure's back to normal. Unless the safety valve's got blocked ... I've heard of that happening. (ll. 67–69)*
*Very stressful situation: Problems in relationships with parents/ partners; conflicts with parents and /or siblings; fights with friends; problems at school.*
*Your life can be compared to a pressure cooker in these situations because you need to "let off steam" very carefully. Having someone who listens to you about your problems can be the "safety valve" that helps you to to do this. Sometimes someone can help you to calm down, which is like turning the heat down on a pressure cooker. However, if you find no way of letting off steam or reducing the pressure you are under it could cause you to become very ill or be very dangerous to you.*
*3. Bad results at school • rows with her mother, especially about Andrea wanting to go to drama college and not university • Andrea's boyfriend has started going out with her best friend • her best friend and her (ex)boyfriend laugh about the letter she wrote to an advice column.*

### Letter writing

*Bei dieser Aufgabe soll sowohl auf den Inhalt als auch auf formelle Aspekte eines englischen Briefes geachtet werden.*

→ What happens next? Write a follow-on scene.

## Project: Creating a poster    SB S. 19

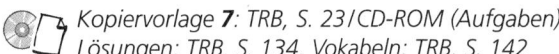 *(S. 'mind map' zu diesem Kapitel auf der CD-ROM.)*
HA: S suchen (möglichst englischsprachige) Materialien aus Zeitungen, Zeitschriften, Internet, etc. Eine Unterrichtsstunde für das Erstellen des Posters einplanen. S arbeiten in PA. HA: Fertigstellen des Posters und vorbereiten der Präsentation. Eine Stunde für die Präsentation des Materials einplanen. Möglich wäre hier auch eine fächerübergreifende Einheit mit den Fächern: BK (Gestaltung des Posters), Deutsch (ähnliche Problematik/deutsche Jugendliteratur), Informatik (Beschaffung von Informationen im Internet, Gestaltung am Computer).
*Zusätzliche Hinweise zur Projektarbeit: TRB, S. 5–7 und 'Skills files', SB, S. 121 & 139.*

## Test: Children of 8 join alcohol casualty list

*Kopiervorlage 7: TRB, S. 23/CD-ROM (Aufgaben)*
*Lösungen: TRB, S. 134, Vokabeln: TRB, S. 142*

# 'Who cares?' survey

**Who cares what I think?** 1

1. How would you describe yourself?

2. Who are your heroes?

3. What's your idea of a "best friend"?

4. What do you hope to achieve in your life?

5. In what way would you like to "make a difference" in society?

6. What's your idea of a good citizen?

7. If you could live in any country in the world (including your own), which one would you pick and why?

8. It is often said that politicians cannot be trusted. Is this true or false in your opinion? Why?

9. What role do you think Germany will play in Europe and the world in 50 years?

10. What can you think of that might help your country to be a better place?

# Personal fact sheet

Who cares what I think? 1

Illustration

**About me:**
..................................................
..................................................
..................................................

**What I hope to achieve:**
..................................................
..................................................
..................................................

**My heroes:**
..................................................
..................................................
..................................................
..................................................

**My description of a best friend:**
..................................................
..................................................
..................................................
..................................................

**My idea of a good citizen:**
..................................................
..................................................
..................................................

**Which country I would live in and why:**
..................................................
..................................................
..................................................

**How I can make a difference in society:**
..................................................
..................................................
..................................................

**How I can help my country:**
..................................................
..................................................
..................................................

Illustration

**Listening comprehension**      **Who cares what I think?  1**

# Interview with an American teenager

**dedication** [ˈdedɪˌkeɪʃn] *Hingabe*
**to have an impact** to make a difference
**to volunteer** to offer to help people for no payment
**Boy Scout** *Pfadfinder*: an Eagle Scout is the highest rank of Boy Scout
**Pledge of Allegiance** [ˌpledʒəvəˈliːdʒns] a spoken promise of o.'s loyalty to the USA
**ACT-UP** AIDS activist group
**pro-choice people** those who are in favour of women's right to choose to have an abortion

**to become apparent** [-ˈ--] to become clear
**magnet school** school at which there is a focus on a particular area of study (e.g. the Arts)
**to prep** short for 'to prepare'
**SAT** (Scholastic Aptitude Test) examination that pupils take in the US as part of the entrance requirements for many universities and colleges
**nerd** *Streber*
**college preparatory school** [prɪˈpærətrɪ] school that prepares pupils for college or university

**advanced placement and honors classes** higher level classes that advanced pupils take in high school and for which they sometimes receive units of credit that help them fulfill requirements for their university or college degrees
**scores** *Ergebnisse*
**attitude** how one feels and thinks about s.th.
**to observe** *here:* to celebrate
**hardship** difficult or unpleasant situation

A. As you listen to the text, tick true (T) or false (F).

|   | T | F |
|---|---|---|
| 1. Keith does not see himself as an average person. | | |
| 2. Keith's hero is Michael Jordan. | | |
| 3. He believes that it is important for people to help each other. | | |
| 4. The American dream has not changed over the years, according to Keith. | | |
| 5. Keith would like to make a difference in the world, but he has no ideas as to how he can. | | |
| 6. Good citizens hang out their flags, he says. | | |
| 7. New York is his favorite city and the United States is his favorite country in the world. | | |
| 8. Too many politicians are only concerned with themselves. | | |
| 9. Keith hopes that not all nations in the world will be like America in 50 years. | | |
| 10. The political parties should work together for the common good of all people. | | |
| 11. Even if schools focused more on current events, teenagers still wouldn't care about them. | | |
| 12. Americans care about their country because their government does everything for them. | | |
| 13. Keith works very hard to be a good pupil. | | |
| 14. Keith speaks Chinese very often. | | |
| 15. The stereotype that Asian pupils are very smart is false, according to Keith. | | |
| 16. The Asian kids who don't do well have problems because they listen to rap music. | | |
| 17. Keith's family observe all Chinese holidays. | | |

B. Listen to the interview again and find out the correct answers.

C. Correct the false statements. Work with a partner if you wish. Write your solutions on the back of this task sheet.

# N'oubliez jamais (1/2)           Who cares what I think?  1

## N'oubliez jamais

Fill in the missing words to the song.

Papa, why do you _____ all the same old songs?
Why do you _____ with the melody?
'Cause down on the street _____ going on,
There's a brand new _____ and a brand new song.

5  He said:
In my life there was so much _____ ,
Still I have no _____ ,
Just like you I was such a _____ ,
So dance your _____ dance and never forget …

10 REFRAIN
N'oubliez jamais,
I heard my father say,
Every generation has its way,
A need to disobey.

15 N'oubliez jamais,
It's in your _____ ,
A need to _____ ,
When _____ get in the way,
N'oubliez jamais.

20 Mama, why do you _____ to the same old songs?

Why do you _____ only harmony?
'Cause down on the street _____ going on.
There's a brand new _____ and a brand new song.
She said:
25 In my _____ there's a young girl's passion
For a lifelong duet,
And someday soon someone's _____ will haunt you,
So sing your _____ song and never forget …

REFRAIN

30 What's this game?
_____ for love or fame,
It's all the same.
One of these days you'll say
That love will be the _____ ,
35 I'm not so _____ …

REFRAIN

Don't you ever forget …
Our love …
Every generation … has its way to go …
40 Ain't it so … ?
N'oubliez jamais … N'oubliez …

*Music & Text: Cregan, Jim / Kunkel, Russ © Universal / MCA Music Publ., A.D.O. Universal Studio /Cregan Music /Olas Music*

# N'oubliez jamais (2/2)     Who cares what I think? 1

**Comprehension**

1. This song is a kind of conversation – who is taking part in it?
2. How would you describe the tone of this song? Is it happy, sad, reflective? Write down lines that support your opinion.
3. In this context phrases like *"the same old songs"* (l. 1) and *"brand new songs"* (l. 4) have more than one meaning. What do you think they mean?
4. What is meant by the phrase *"'cause down on the street something's goin' on"* (l. 3)?
5. What advice did the singer get from his parents?
6. What themes and issues are presented in this song?
7. a) Fill in the table below, comparing the values and interests of your generation with those of your parents' generation.

| My interests/values | My parents' interests/values |
| --- | --- |
| 1. | 1. |
| 2. | 2. |
| 3. | 3. |
| 4. | 4. |
| 5. | 5. |
| 6. | 6. |
| 7. | 7. |

b) In your own words, explain the phrase *"every generation has its way"* (l. 13).

c) Is it true that *"every generation has its way"*? Give reasons for your answer.

# AIDS awareness — Who cares what I think? 1

## Slogans

*People use slogans to put across ideas quickly and effectively. All slogans are short. Some slogans use humour to make their point, whereas others are serious. Others use rhyming phrases or a few vivid, descriptive words. Above all, the key to an effective slogan is that it is easy to remember. Slogans can also be used together with an illustration. Here's an idea for a postcard promoting AIDS awareness.*

Now come up with your own idea for an AIDS awareness postcard in the space below. Be sure to include an original slogan. As you plan, think about the type of audience you are trying to reach. What age group are they? What are their interests? What type of illustration would best catch the attention of this group?

# Collecting information

**Who cares what I think?** 1

## Young give up condoms as Aids fear fades (SB, pp. 12–13)

Fill in the table with information from the text on pp. 12–13.

| Research results | Charlotte Davis (24, estate agent) | Anonymous person (23, insurance salesman) |
|---|---|---|
| Findings: | Previous attitude / reasons: | Previous attitude / reasons: |
| Reasons for findings: | Current attitude / reasons: | Current attitude / reasons: |

# Test — Who cares what I think? 1

## Children of 8 join alcohol casualty list

A record number of underage drinkers, including some as young as eight, are being admitted to hospital suffering from alcohol-related illnesses. A study by casualty staff at Alder Hey children's hospital in Liverpool reveals that the number of children attending the hospital with alcohol-related problems has grown tenfold in the past decade. In 1985 just 20 children were treated for alcohol-related problems. Last year, the figure was 200.

Similar rises were reported by 20 large hospitals across the country, with figures from 250 accident and emergency units suggesting an estimated 50,000 teenagers are now being admitted drunk to casualty departments each year. [...]

Experts blame the rise on children maturing earlier and a lack of parental control. Children identify the glamorisation of drink by pop stars and advertisers as a contributing factor. Simon, 13, came close to dying after drinking 15 measures of vodka. He had begun an evening of illicit drinking, in Hastings, East Sussex, at a friend's house. He received superficial injuries in a drunken brawl, but the amount of alcohol consumed left him with serious alcoholic poisoning. His mother, Gail, 37, said: "Another drink could have killed him. I've explained the dangers – I just pray this will teach him a lesson." [...]

Phillip, 12, had his stomach pumped at a Bristol hospital after collapsing drunk at a youth club disco. He had drunk six alcopops and a large bottle of cider, smuggled in by older boys. [...]

Buying drink is not a problem for Tony, 14, and his friends waiting outside an off-licence in Birmingham's city centre: "First you see if they will sell it to you. If they don't, you pay off a tramp – they'll always buy you a drink."

In the village of Congresbury, near Bristol, young teenagers buy homemade cider through older friends. Martin, 13, said: "We do it at weekends. You can't go home when you're out of your head, so we get a tent and camp out somewhere. We tell our parents we're staying at each others' houses."

(343 words)

© Times Newspapers Limited, *24th August 1997*.
*Photocopying allowed for classroom use only.*

## Content

1. Why are the conclusions of these hospital reports so surprising according to the text?
2. Why are increasing numbers of children consuming alcohol according to the text?
3. What do youngsters do in order to get alcohol?

*(Your teacher will tell you which of the following tasks you should complete.)*

## Comment

1. What measures do you think should be taken to prevent young people from consuming alcohol?
2. Do you think that it is justified to say today's youth is much better off than the young people of 20 or 30 years ago?

## Form

1. The writer includes several direct quotations and statistics in this text. What function do these elements have and what effect do they have on the reader?
2. Would you consider this to be a persuasive text? Why or why not?

## Language

1. Provide the noun form of the following words.
    a) suffering (l. 2)
    b) suggesting (l. 11)
    c) estimated (l. 11)
    d) contributing (l. 15)
2. Explain the following in a complete sentence.
    a) "... *teach him a lesson.*" (ll. 22–23)
    b) "... *staff at Alder Hey children's hospital ... .*" (ll. 3–4)
3. Change the following sentences from the active to the passive, or vice versa.
    a) The distressing conclusions have been reported by several researchers.
    b) Children convince older youths to buy them alcohol.
4. Provide the opposites and synonyms of the words as indicated.
    a) grown (opposite) (l. 6)
    b) received (synonym) (l. 18)
5. Provide the correct verb forms by using the past or the present perfect (simple or progressive).
    a) Yesterday, a 37-year-old mother (to have to) take her son to hospital because he had drunk too much alcohol. Fortunately, he (survive).
    b) Susan (13) (consume) alcohol regularly for two years now. Her brother Brian (14) (never/touch) a glass of alcohol.

# 2 A British jigsaw

## Didaktisches Inhaltsverzeichnis

| Title | Text type / Topic | Skills & Tasks | |
|---|---|---|---|
| **A British jigsaw** (SB S. 20/21) | • collage of photos<br>• typical view of Britain | • Speaking: describing pictures and discussing clichés<br>• Vocabulary: terms for describing one's appearance<br>• Writing: collecting information in table form | |
| **About Britain** (SB S. 22) | • fact file (530 words) | • Reading: for detail<br>• Speaking/writing: defining and understanding definitions<br>• Vocabulary: mind maps, geographical and statistical terms<br>• Grammar: questions | |
| **Wales and the Welsh** (SB S. 23) | • personal account (1270 words) | • Listening comprehension | 1 TRB, S. 35 |
| **The New Brits: single, stoned and selfish** (SB S. 24) | • newspaper article (656 words)<br>• cartoon | • Reading: for detail<br>• Speaking/writing: short survey and summary; talking about cartoons<br>• Vocabulary: compound nouns<br>• Grammar: tenses; gerund | |
| **Marmite and village fêtes** (SB S. 26) | • travelogue (362 words)<br>• national stereotypes | • Reading: for detail<br>• Language: adjectives<br>• Style: identifying rhetorical devices<br>• Speaking: preparing an illustrated talk | |
| **A lonely island** (SB p. 27) | • travelogue (478 words)<br>• insularity | • Reading: for detail<br>• Language: defining terms and paraphrasing<br>• Writing: translation | |
| **Two nations** (SB S. 28) | • travelogue (353 words)<br>• regional differences | • Reading: for detail<br>• Writing: short story or news report; giving an opinion<br>• Style: comparing writing styles | |
| **The two Ashingtons** (SB S. 28) | • statistics | • Writing: comparing statistics<br>• Speaking: role play (small talk) | |
| **Revealed: Britain's filthiest air** (SB S. 30) | • newspaper article (290 words)<br>• environmental problems | • Reading: for gist and detail<br>• Writing: sketch map of Britain<br>• Vocabulary: semantic field 'pollution' | |
| **Greening of the Midlands grime** (SB S. 31) | • newspaper article (216 words)<br>• environmental consciousness | • Reading: for detail<br>• Grammar: adverbs<br>• Language: sentence structure<br>• Writing: news report | |
| **Focus on Birmingham** (SB S. 32) | • statistics<br>• socio-economic factors | • Language: expressing figures<br>• Writing: analysing and interpreting statistics<br>• Speaking: giving a talk | 2, 3, 4 TRB, S. 36 – 39 |
| **Quick & Quirky: Facts about Birmingham** (SB S. 34) | • interesting facts (345 words) | • Reading: for detail<br>• Speaking/writing: Presenting information<br>• Grammar: passive voice | |
| **Project: Presenting a town/region** (SB S. 35) | | | |
| **Test: Two towns and two nations** | • newspaper article (343 words) | | 5 TRB, S. 40 |

# A British jigsaw 2

## Einleitung

*In diesem Kapitel wird die Vielfalt von Land und Menschen dargestellt. Dabei erhalten die S Gelegenheit, landeskundliche Kenntnisse aufzufrischen und zu vertiefen. Der Titel des Kapitels soll dabei als Metapher dienen: Einem Puzzle ähnlich werden regionale Besonderheiten erst dann stimmig und sinnstiftend, wenn sie als Gesamtbild betrachtet werden.*

*Das Puzzle setzt sich aus Einzelbildern Großbritanniens zusammen. Darunter finden sich Reiseeindrücke eines Amerikaners, Momentaufnahmen aus der Region Midlands mit Schwerpunkt Birmingham und ein Vergleich der Lebensstandards zwischen Nord- und Südengland.*

*In den politischen und wirtschaftlichen Übersichten wird Nordirland mit einbezogen, obwohl es nicht zur geografischen Einheit Britain gehört, wohl aber zur politischen Einheit United Kingdom.*

## A British jigsaw        SB S. 20–21

*Die Puzzlebilder sollen in erster Linie als Sprechanlässe dienen. Sie geben einen Einblick in die Vielfalt Großbritanniens und weisen gleichzeitig auf Klischees über Großbritannien hin.*

→ *Mögliche Einstiegsfragen:*
- Have you ever been to Britain?
- Do you recognize any of the photos?
- Where do you think the photos were taken?
- Divide the photos into groups and explain your categories. (e.g. London, rural scenes, free-time, city life, traditions.)
- Choose one of the pictures and describe it in as much detail as possible to your partner.
- Comment on similarities and differences with similar phenomenon in your country.

→ *Um einen generellen geografischen Überblick zu vermitteln, kann das Würfelspiel auf Kopiervorlage 2 (TRB S. 36/CD-ROM) ohne Fragekärtchen eingesetzt werden.*

### Looking at the jigsaw puzzle        SB S.21

1. *Abgebildet sind (von oben, l. nach r.):*
Welsh flag • English breakfast/egg and bacon • Houses of Parliament and Big Ben • London rain/rainy day scene • London transport/London buses and taxis • Bed & Breakfast/B&B • map of Glastonbury area • English/British bobby/policeman • working-class houses/street • English countryside • country road/lane with hedges • (red) telephone box • Scottish soccer/football fans • milk bottle on doorstep/milk delivered to doorstep • cricket on the village green/game of cricket • terraced housing/houses with Asian children • seaside resort/beach scene with pier

2. *S begründen ihre Wahl mit Hinweisen auf Film und Fernsehen, Bücher und Zeitschriften. Die bekanntesten Bilder sind vermutlich:* London buses, Big Ben, telephone box. *Die weniger bekannten Bilder sind vermutlich:* Welsh flag, milk bottle on doorstep, Ordnance Survey map.

*Diese Aufgabe soll als Anreiz dienen, mehr über Land und Leute zu erfahren.*

### Talking about clichés

1. Products: *British beer, tea, biscuits, marmalade (NB marmalade is always made with oranges otherwise it is called 'jam'), cars (Rolls Royce, Jaguar, mini)*
Places: *London, Liverpool, Manchester, Cornwall, Buckingham Palace, Houses of Parliament, Wimbledon, Wembley*
People: *the Royal Family (Queen Elizabeth, Prince Charles, Prince William, Princess Diana), Tony Blair, David Beckham (soccer player), Kevin Keegan (Ex-England football manager and ex-player for HSV), David Coulthard (Formula I racing driver), The Spice Girls.*
Food: *fish and chips, roast beef*
Bands: *The Beatles, Take That, Oasis, The Spice Girls*
Sports: *Manchester United, Glasgow Rangers, All England Tennis Tournament (Wimbledon); Isle of Man Motorbike Race, horse-racing*

2. a) Clichés: *It's always raining. • It's always foggy in London • It's always cold. • The food is bad. • British people have a good sense of humour. • All English businessmen wear bowler hats. • All British houses have a lawn. • Britain is poor and dirty. • The British can't speak any foreign languages. • English football fans are all hooligans. • English holidaymakers spend all their time getting drunk. • The British understate.*

b) *S unterscheiden zwischen eigener Erfahrung (soweit vorhanden) und Klischees.*
Advantages of clichés: *simplified view of reality, easy to understand, make quick judgements possible.*
Disadvantages: *often oversimplified or outdated; judgements made on such a basis may be wrong.*

3. *S diskutieren Übereinstimmung ihres eigenen Deutschlandbildes mit den folgenden Klischees. Sie beschreiben Unterschiede, Nachteile und Vorzüge eines schnellen Urteils.*
Mögliche Klischees: *Bavaria • Black Forest • Berlin • Brandenburger Gate • beer • wine • men in leather trousers • Munich • fast, expensive, reliable cars • Porsche • Mercedes • Volkswagen • soccer (Bayern Munich) • Formula 1 racing (Michael and Ralf Schuhmacher) • tennis: Boris Becker and Steffi Graf • Hitler, WW II • sauerkraut, dumplings; sausages • loud, rude, overweight people • well-organized • no sense of humour • hard-working • great respect for authority • arrogant • prompt*

### Fact finding

1. *The Internet, books, newspapers and magazines, movies, an atlas, maps, etc.*
2. a)/b)/c) *s. 'Information about Britain' auf nächster Seite*

### Abbreviations and acronyms

| | | | |
|---|---|---|---|
| a.k.a | also known as | No. | number |
| a.s.a.p. | as soon as possible | p.a. | per annum |
| c/o | care of | p.t.o. | please turn over |
| CV | curriculum vitae | s.a.e. | stamped addressed envelope |
| e.g. | for example | | |
| i.c. | I see | VIP | very important person |
| i.e. | that means/that is | w/o | without |
| IOU | I owe you | | |

### Over to you

● *S erfinden Abkürzungen in Gruppen (z. B. so = show off) und tauschen sie dann mit anderen Gruppen. Aus dem Zusammenhang sollen die Bedeutungen zu erraten sein.*

# 2 A British jigsaw

## Information about Britain

### England
**Capital city:** London
**Main industries:** manufacturing industry declining but still very important in some regions • 10% of workforce employed in agriculture • 74% of workforce in service industries • one of the world's leading financial centres
**Languages spoken:** English (but also: Hindu, Urdhu, etc.)
**Natural resources:** coal
**Other features:** most densely populated country in UK
**Famous people:** Elizabeth I, Isaac Newton, Charles Darwin, Charles Dickens, Alred Hitchcock, Michael Caine, Joan Collins, William Shakespeare, Hugh Grant, Naomi Campbell, George Michael, Stephen Hawking, Gary Oldman
**Sports:** football, tennis, cricket, polo
**Food:** chocolate, beer

### Scotland
**Capital city:** Edinburgh
**Main industries:** traditional industries (coals, steel, ship building) declining • high-tech industries growing • most important area in Britain for fishing and forestry
**Languages spoken:** English, Gaelic, Scots dialect
**Natural resources:** offshore oil and gas
**Other features:** Highlands, mountainous
**Famous people:** Robert Burns, Alexander, Graham Bell, Adam Smith, William Wallace, Sir Alexander Fleming, Kenny Dalglish, Sean Connery
**Sports:** football, tennis, cricket, polo, highland games, e.g. tossing the caber
**Food:** haggis
**Other:** collies • whisky • tartans/kilts • bagpipes

### Wales
**Capital city:** Cardiff
**Main industries:** steelmaking remains important • new computer industries
**Languages spoken:** English, Welsh
**Natural resources:** coal
**Other features:** smallest country in the UK
**Famous people:** Richard Burton, Shirley Bassey, Shakin' Stevens, Tom Jones
**Sports:** rugby
**Food:** laverbread
**Other:** strong musical (singing) tradition • Welsh corgies

### N. Ireland
**Capital city:** Belfast
**Main industries:** 75% of employees now in service industries • textiles • ship building in decline • sheep and cattle farming
**Languages spoken:** English, Gaelic (Irish)
**Other features:** 50% Protestant and 38% Catholic population • part of UK, but not of Great Britain
**Famous people:** Van Morrison, Kenneth Branagh, Gerry Adams, Ian Paisley, Liam Neeson, James Galway, Seamus Heaney
**Sports:** golf, hurling
**Other:** whiskey, Irish setters, fine ale

## About Britain
SB S. 22–23

[i] The term 'Britain' is used loosely here to refer to the United Kingdom as a whole. This is common (colloquial) usage, though not correct in a strict sense. (Great) Britain and Ireland are two separate geographical units in the British Isles. Hence the full name of the political unit: the United Kingdom of Great Britain and Northern Ireland.

The flags in the background represent England (red cross on white background), Scotland (white X on blue background), Wales (red lion on green and white background) and Northern Ireland (red X on white background. The Union Jack (often mistakenly thought of as the English flag but actually the flag of Great Britain) is a combination of the Scottish, English and N. Irish flags.

*Nachdem S im ersten Teil des Kapitels in erster Linie über Klischees und ihr eigenes (subjektives) Bild von Großbritannien gesprochen haben, geht es hier um einen faktischen/geografischen Überblick.*

### Comprehension
SB S. 23

1. (top left) Countries of Britain/the UK • (centre) Different landscapes • (bottom left) Size and distance
2. climate, resources, landscape, past history, industrial development, recent economic trends.

### Working with words

1. a country which belongs to a larger group of countries: member state • the countries of Europe other than Britain (Iceland & Ireland): continental Europe • information about mountains, rivers, etc.: geographical facts
2. If a country has 'a rural population' it means that most people in that country live in the country. • If a country has 'an urban population' it means that most people who live in that country live in towns or cities • 'densely populated' means that many people live together in a small area • 'population density' refers to the number of people living in a defined area.
3. Population: (number of) people, rural population, urban population, densely populated, unemployed, to move, approximate population, to be spread (evenly), to grow (slowly)
Geography: England, Scotland, Wales, N. Ireland, (highest) mountain/Ben Nevis, the Highlands, (longest) river/Severn, the Bristol Channel, (largest) lake/Lough Neagh, (highest) waterfall/Eas a chual, (deepest) cave/Ogof Ffynnon Ddu, mainland, Europe, the Channel, 242,000 square metres, south coast, extreme north, the coastline, islands, landscapes, mountain ranges, flat, open spaces
Climate: mild, temperate, weather changes, (extremes of) temperature, daily weather, depressions, (south-westerly) winds, rainfall

### Over to you

*S vermeiden geschlossene Fragen. Stattdessen benutzen sie Fragen mit Fragewörtern wie who, what, when, where, why usw. Beispiele:*
How far is it from the most southerly point to the most northerly point of Great Britain? • Which is the biggest country in Great Britain? • How many inhabitants does Britain (England, Scotland, Wales, etc.) have? • What is the shortest distance between Britain and France? • Where is it? • Where is the highest mountain in Great Britain? • What is its name?

# A British jigsaw 2

## Listening comprehension SB S. 23

*Kopiervorlage 1: TRB, S. 35/CD-ROM*
*Lösungen: TRB, S. 135*

CC:1/3
CD:18  **Wales and the Welsh** (Transcript)

Welsh? What's the difference between the Welsh and the English? They are both governed by the same parliament, they both speak the same language, they both can be found on the same island without any distinctive borders, so aren't the Welsh and the English the same?

If you agree with that, you couldn't be further from the truth, but it is an easy mistake to make. For too long now, the Welsh nation has been mistaken for an area of England or even Ireland, the language is thought to be Gaelic (if known at all), and the people are assumed to have the same characteristics as the English. I suppose other small countries around the world suffer the same fate – and if I'm honest even I only have a basic knowledge of other small countries even in the EU. But it does prove frustrating when I get asked where I'm from and have to draw the imaginary map of Britain on the palm of my hand and explain to yet another Joe Bloggs what and where exactly Wales is.

So what makes us Welsh different from the rest of the people in the UK? The first thing for me that springs to mind is language. The Welsh language is one of the oldest surviving (as in not yet dead) languages in Europe, but only around a fifth of the nation speak it fluently. For many years, Welsh was regarded as a useless language and at the turn of this century it was banned in schools as the teaching language and also amongst the children in their playtime. If you were caught speaking Welsh, you were severely punished. So to avoid this, children were discouraged by their parents from speaking Welsh at home too. Welsh was seen as a working class language and if you wanted to succeed in life, you had to speak English. This, for the most part was especially true in the south. Wealthy English businessmen would set up in South Wales and the Welsh provided a cheap work force. Generally, only the middle class 'educated' would seem to 'succeed' (as it were) by leaving the green pastures of home and seeking their fortune elsewhere. Having said that, Welsh is witnessing a comeback through its reappearance in secondary school curriculums because it is now compulsory as a subject up to the age of 14. Also, there seems to be a general interest in wanting to learn Welsh and more and more adults are making use of evening classes to learn or to improve their Welsh. Many seem to want to find their roots and identity once more, and the language would seem the sensible place to start.

As for the Welsh character, the first thing that comes to mind is pride. We are a very proud nation, and you can see that if you ever watch supporters at a rugby game, for example. The pride doesn't come from our success, as we more often than not lose, but from just being there, taking in the atmosphere and as we say 'hywl', which roughly translated means spirit. The Welsh seem to get very emotional and poetic about all sorts of things, but generally, it's over rugby! It's about the only occasion a small country like ourselves has to beat another country 5 times its size!

The Welsh are also known for choral singing, poetry and acting, and more recently have put ourselves on the map with success in the sporting field and music industry. Bands such as the Manic Street Preachers, Stereophonics and Catatonia have all made it big on the European and international markets. Also, I think it would be fair to say that the image towards the Welsh and the country has changed. Previously, it was known as one of the poorer areas of England where they spoke with a funny accent. Nowadays, in Britain at least, it is almost as popular to be Welsh as it is to be Irish. But, I think we seem to take it all in our stride and just believe that it's about time that we had some recognition as a nation and a country and above all a bit of independence from the English.

Our wish for more independence may have been granted, well, was set in motion in 1999 at least. On May 6th, British politics as a whole underwent a significant change. In Wales, the National Assembly was formed (and in Scotland too) and officially opened by the Queen. This Assembly means that for the first time in several hundred years, decisions on certain issues in Wales will be made outside of Westminster and back on Welsh soil in Cardiff, the capital. It has been slow to get off the ground but it is generally welcomed by all as a step forward, with many seeing it as the only way in which Wales and its people will start to get what they need as a nation, and not what the rest of Britain thinks best for it; taking control but at the same time not isolating ourselves from the rest of the British Isles. But that's not to say that Wales wants to be recognised independently from Britain, instead what we are looking for is recognition within it.

Generally, traditions have remained the same for hundreds of years. St. David's Day (our national day) is still celebrated with children wearing traditional Welsh costume and their parents wearing one of the two national emblems. The women tend to wear daffodils and the men, leeks. It's great fun to see people showing off their emblems which they grew themselves in their own back garden! Also, there's the Eisteddfod, another popular tradition, which takes place once every year. It can roughly be described as a competition involving a variety of artistic activities from poetry recital to music performance to dance, where many different nations from across the globe get together to compete and experience other cultures and customs. Talking about customs, as for Welsh food, typical meals such as cawl which is a type of meat broth and cockles and laverbread – a type of chopped seaweed, can be found in homes especially across the south. Not forgetting the most popular accompaniment to the cup of tea, the Welsh cake, a type of scone but a little sweeter. There isn't one single recipe as families seem to have their own preferred and sometimes secret one passed down from generation to generation!

The Welsh also believe very strongly in community spirit and the family, not just immediate but the larger family too. Sundays are often spent in a crowded sitting room, the women chatting about this and that with a neighbour that has popped in for a cup of tea and the men generally agreeing, paying more attention to the sport on the TV or to falling off to sleep.

I often get asked when abroad why I don't say that I am English to save confusion and a lot of explanation. My usual reply is that I am not English and that I'd rather take the time to explain and let them know where I come from because after all we are different nations, so why not make the contrast between ourselves. (I sometimes also ask people if they would be happy to be called something that they weren't.)

But I feel that the only way which you can really experience Wales and Welsh hospitality is to experience it first hand. So, if you can put up with the unpredictable weather, go on, pay us a visit, you're always welcome! Croeso i Gymru!

*By Charlotte Trew, Bristol, 1999.*

**Looking at links to Britain**

*1. a) to increase competition by creating an alternative to ferries • to reduce transport fares and shorten transport time • to stimulate trade and tourism*

## 2  A British jigsaw

b) People involved in the ferry industry in Kent and those depending on it, e.g. shops, garages and hotels, saw the tunnel as a threat to their businesses. • People were concerned about the safety/danger of fire in the tunnel. • People saw this first "land link" to Europe as a possible threat to national security. • People were concerned about the danger of importing animal diseases, such as rabies, which are endemic on the continent but have died out in Britain.

2. a) plane, ferry, train

b) Other practical means of getting to Britain are by hovercraft or jet-foil. Other possibilities are: private yacht, helicopter, private plane. Still more fanciful options include hitchhiking, hot-air balloon, swimming the channel, etc.!

c)

|  | plane | ferry | train |
|---|---|---|---|
| convenience | • quick<br>• comfortable | • relatively slow<br>• allows you to travel by car and remain flexible | • relatively slow<br>• comfortable (for tourists with cars) |
| cost | • expensive (but getting cheaper) | • less expensive than plane | • similar price to ferry |
| environment | • creates air pollution<br>• noisy | • pollutes the channel with waste and fuel | • creates the least pollution<br>• transports a lot of people at one time |
| employment | • creates jobs at airports and on airlines | • creates jobs on board the ferries, and at the terminals | • creates few jobs directly, but … |
| business & economy | • business people can travel, e.g. to meetings, quickly (and return the same day) | • good for tourism near the coast<br>• bad for supermarkets, etc. in Kent, but good for supermarkets in France: British people go on one day shopping trips to Calais and fill up their cars with cheap French products! | • … better links with Europe are expected to stimulate trade and other business. |
| Other | • danger/fear of crashing | • sea-sickness, danger/fear of sinking | • danger/fear of accident/fire in the tunnel |

3. –

→ You are: a student travelling alone to visit a friend in Wales • a family going on holiday to Cornwall • a business person going to a meeting in Birmingham • a school class going on a trip to London. Which form of travel would you choose and why?

→ Consider the possibilities of 'virtual travel' via the Internet, reading books about Britain, watching TV documentaries, etc. In what situations and for whom might this kind of 'travel' be advantageous?

**Useful websites for further information:**
Channel Tunnel:
http://www.raileurope.com/us/rail/eurostar/channel_tunnel.htm
http://www.elec.rdg.ac.uk/staff_postgrads/academic/sjs/ctr.html
http://uk.dir.yahoo.com/Business_and_Economy/Transportation/Tunnels/Specific_Tunnels/Channel_Tunnel
http://www.channeltunnel.co.uk/
Air travel to the UK:
http://uk.dir.yahoo.com/Recreation/Travel/Air_Travel/
http://www.traveloverland.de (for current fares)
Sea crossings:
http://www.poferries.com
http://www.irishferries.ie
http://www.hoverspeed.com/eng/index.asp

## The British way of life     SB S. 24–25

The following is a 19 year-old British student's comment on what young people in Britain are interested in at the start of the new millenium:

Sport, especially football, is as popular as ever. Everyone supports a local team and often goes to home matches.

Celebrities are football player David Beckham (for marrying Posh Spice) and Vinnie Jones (for starring in 'Lock Stock and Two Smoking Barrels', 'Gone in 60 Seconds' and 'Snatch', which are very popular cinema films about London gangland.

It is almost obligatory for young people to wake up to Sarah Cox on BBC Radio One – who entertains with lots of bright and inconsequential chat and plays all the latest releases and chart hits. Chris Moyles in the afternoon is quite funny as well as (or because of) being scathing and sarcastic.

Young people (16 to 19 year olds) go out to pubs and clubs (!). The really 'cool' clubs are 'Cream' in Liverpool, 'Home' in London and 'Gatecrasher' in Nottingham.

DJs are now famous in their own right – especially Fatboy Slim, Paul Oakenfield, Carl Cox, Dreem Teem. Lots of young men aspire to becoming famous DJs – when they're not planning on becoming pop stars! Lots of youngsters join a band: there are pubs and clubs in the Midlands, for example, that support young bands by providing venues and amplifying equipment. (s. auch Ross Noon's 'Personal Statement', SB, S. 44, ll. 36 – 46) There are annual competitions (the Battle of the Bands) to bring young talent to the fore.

Main role models for young people are Robbie Williams, Craig David, Spice Girls.

The TV phenomenon BIG Brother (British version!) was immensely popular in the summer of 2000. It became the main talking point at any gathering of under 25s. Another popular TV show is 'Friends' (even if it is American!) and everyone watches a soap. 'Eastenders', set in London's East End, is the most popular, but the Australian 'Neighbours' also has its addicts.

# A British jigsaw 2

FHM (For Him Magazine) is one of the most popular teen/twen magazines, aimed at boys but also read by girls.

Most young people have a part-time job (in shops, coffee bars, pubs, restaurants) to feed their appetite for fashion. Brand names such as Voi, Duffer and FCUK are especially popular. Many people gather in shopping centres at weekends to go shopping and then get a coffee.

The mobile phone is becoming an essential accessory and is the main means of communication locally. Social arrangements are nearly always made by mobile phone at the last minute.

E-mail and use of the Internet is growing, but is not universal. Everyone has access to the Internet in school for educational purposes, but the use of websites for leisure has not really taken off (in 2000) amongst teenagers. However, once young people get to University and get an e-mail address they often use it to keep in touch with friends at other universities and (occasionally!) with home.

 **CC:1/4 / CD1:4  The new Brits: single, …**  SB S. 24–25

*Dieser Text fasst die demografischen, wirtschaftlichen und sozialen Änderungen zusammen, die am Ende des 20. Jahrhunderts in Großbritannien statistisch festgestellt wurden. Das hiesige 'Handbook' kann man/können S bestellen. (s. Adresse, SB, S. 24)*

## Comprehension

1. a) Social, economic and demographic factors have affected family life. Due to improved communication technology, e.g. mail, fax or phone, distances between family members can easily be bridged. Many people lead their own lives. Family life has become less important. Families are smaller today with an average of 2.4 people. That means there are more families with only one child, and more single-parent families. People are also having their children later, and divorce has become more common. (People prefer cats as pets.)
b) People spend more money on leisure pursuits such as eating out, going to the cinema, TV, fitness. Men enjoy snooker and pool and women do yoga. TV is the most popular leisure activity at home, but people also enjoy reading: over 500 million books are borrowed from libraries each year.
2. a) Social changes: singles/living alone, single-parent families, later marriages, more women in paid employment, more divorces, less children. Economic changes: financial cautiousness, greater spending on leisure activities.
b) Examples of demographic change: increasing number of old-age pensioners, declining birth rate.
3. *S. machen eine Tabelle mit einer Spalte* Germany *und einer* Britain. *Zu den Begriffen* Social changes, Economic changes *und* Demographic changes *tragen sie relevante Informationen ein, vergleichen diese und diskutieren über die Veränderungen.*

→ *Interessant wäre an dieser Stelle ein Vergleich mit den Veränderungen in Deutschland. Grundlegende Daten wie Bevölkerungswachstum, Familiengröße und Durchschnittseinkommen liefert das Statistische Jahrbuch des Statistischen Bundesamtes. Ebenfalls sehr nützliche Informationen befinden sich in den Jugendstudien der Deutschen Shell GmbH.*
*Nähere Informationen zu Schlagworten wie Politikverdrossenheit, Zukunftsängsten (und -hoffnungen) befinden sich im Internet unter:*
http://www.shell-jugend2000.de *(Shell Jugendstudie),*
http://www.bib-demographie.de/
http://www.jugendforschung.de/ *(Statistisches Bundesamt).*
http://www.ida.his.se/ida/~gerrit/anita/node6.html#SECTION0003
1200000000000000

## Asking questions

*(S. 'Skills files', SB, S. 125, 131, 140.)*
1. Do you (go to) work? • Have you got any children? • When did you go back to work after having your child/children? • What do you do?/What's your job?
2. a) *S erfinden Fragen wie:* Do you get more than DM 20,- pocket money per week?/Did you get more than 20,- DM per week two years ago? • Do you do any sports?/Do you play football/tennis?/Do you belong to a sports club? Do you do more/less sport now than two years ago? • Have you got a video recorder?/Did you have a video two years ago? • Do you ever borrow books from a library? • Do you ever go to church?/Do you go to church every week? • Have you got a pet?/Do you own a dog/cat?/Did you have a pet two years ago? • etc.
b) *Fragen an Tafel/OHP schreiben. S geben per Handzeichen Antwort. Antworten sammeln. Bei umfangreicheren Fragebögen können pro Fragenkomplex Arbeitsgruppen gebildet werden.*
c) *S organisieren die Ergebnisse in Absätzen (wie im Text). z. B.:* Students in our class are financially well off, two thirds of the class get more than 20,- DM pocket money each week. We are spending more on clothes, CDs and mobile phones than we did two years ago. (etc.)

## Vocabulary

*(S. 'Skills file', SB, S. 133.)*
1. a) a meal bought in a restaurant but eaten at home: a takeaway (Col. 1. l. 2) • a special service which records messages for you and which you can call and listen to at a suitable time: a voicemail service (Col. 2, l. 16)
b) household (Col. 1, l. 19): group of people (usually family) who live together • breakdown (Col. 1, l. 26): falling apart of s.th. which had functioned well • workforce (Col. 1, l. 35): total number of people in paid employment in a country, region, company, etc. • answerphone (Col. 2, l. 15): a machine for recording messages when people ring you and you can't take the call • voicemail (Col. 2, l. 16): device that records and sends messages over the telephone
2. <u>to increase in number</u>: to overtake (Col. 1, l. 14/15); to rise (Col. 1, l. 22); to grow (Col. 2, l. 25); to be on the rise (Col. 2, l. 27)
<u>to decrease in number</u>: to decline (Col. 1, l. 10/11); to be/go down from/by (Col. 1, l. 19/20); to tumble (Col. 2, l. 41)

## Grammar

*Evtl. S in Gruppen aufteilen, die jeweils alle Beispiele nur einer der angegebenen Zeitformen im Text finden. Anschließend vgl. in der Klasse. Die häufige Verwendung vom* present continuous, *um die Aktualität der Trends zu unterstreichen, könnte hier erwähnt werden. (S. auch 'Grammar files', SB, S. 142–145, 150.)*
1. <u>simple present</u>: *Die Beispiele vom* Simple Present *im Text sind zu zahlreich, um diese hier im Einzelnen aufzulisten! Beispiele aus dem ersten Absatz:* They are both single; He lives alone; She juggles care; both have jobs; neither belongs to.
<u>present continuous</u>: Family life is declining (Col. 1, l. 10); People are eschewing (Col. 1, l. 13); They are still bumping (Col. 1, ll. 29/30); Both men and women are marrying later and living longer (Col. 1, l. 36/37); age and gender are becoming (Col. 1, l. 42/43); we are getting married/having/reducing/living (Col. 2., ll. 7–10); Other traditions are tumbling. (Col. 2, l. 41)

# 2 A British jigsaw

*present perfect:* Both have taken drugs (Col. 1, l. 5); cats have overtaken dogs … (Col. 1, l. 14/15); the proportion has risen (Col. 1, ll. 21/22); social, economic and demographic changes have downgraded (Col. 2, ll. 1–3); Communications technology has revolutionised (Col. 2, l. 13/14); We have become (Col. 2, l. 20); Spending has grown (Col. 2, ll. 24/25);
*present passive:* She is divorced (Col. 1, l. 3); households made up of (Col. 1, l. 21); with less of our lives taken up by other people (Col. 2, ll. 11/12); dogs are now outnumbered by 8 million cats … Col. 2, l. 45/46);
*simple past:* the Office for National Statistics found (Col. 1, l. 39); and had three kids … (Col. 2, l. 5); people had three kids (Col. 2, l. 5); a huge chunk was (Col. 2, ll. 5/6);
2. a) Examples: "Spending on …" (Col. 2, l. 24); "Eating out …" (Col. 2, l. 26).
b) Nowadays travelling long distances is no problem for people anymore.
Playing snooker regularly is the only physical exercise one in five men do.

### Understanding the cartoon

1. He is probably talking to people who rarely go to church, since the clergyman assumes they might not even remember the Lord's Prayer.
2. Col. 2, ll. 41–44: "Only one in ten Britons regularly go to church, half never or scarcely ever do." The cartoon reflects the fact that British people don't go to church very often.

### Your view

● Possible reasons for changes:
People want to have more fun and spend more time on their own leisure pursuits and interests. • We are living in the age of consumerism, in which having a lot of money is more important than other values • People today have become more selfish and want less responsibility, so they marry later (if at all) and have fewer children. • People have become more cynical (i.e. more divorces, not going to church). • Women now have careers and earn their own money and don't want or need to be dependent on men.

## Notes from a small island  SB S. 26–29

*An dieser Stelle folgen drei Abschnitte aus der gleichnamigen Erzählung von Bill Bryson. Bill Bryson gelingt es, ein persönliches aber auch durchaus repräsentatives Bild von Großbritannien in seiner Erzählung abzugeben. So lernt man auf unterhaltsame Art Land, Leute und die britische Mentalität kennen. Das Buch wurde inzwischen verfilmt und als Serie im englischen Fernsehen gesendet.*

[i] Bill Bryson was born in Des Moines, Iowa in 1951. He lived in England for twenty years, where he worked for *The Times* and *The Independent*, and wrote for many major British and American publications. His books include the travel memoirs *Neither Here nor There*, *The Lost Continent*, and *Notes From a Small Island*, as well as *The Mother Tongue*, *Made in America* and *Notes From a Big Country*. He now lives in Hanover, New Hampshire, with his wife and four children.

See also:
http://www.smallisland.co.uk/test.html
http://www.januarymagazine.com/profiles/bryson.html

 CC:1/5
CD1:10 **Part 1: Marmite and village fêtes**  SB S. 26

*In diesem Abschnitt, der sich am Ende von 'Notes from a small island' befindet, erzählt Bryson, was aus seiner Sicht Großbritannien so liebenswürdig macht. Viele Eigenschaften werden hier angesprochen, die typisch (stereotypisch) britisch sind.*

### While you read

● Elements illustrated: country lane • milk bottles on doorstep • Ordnance survey map • seaside pier • drizzly weather • cricket • view from a hillside

### Language & comprehension

1. a) drizzly (Sundays), l. 6 • wondrous (place), l. 7 • crazy, l. 7 • adorable, l. 7 • benign, l. 20 • enlightened (way), l. 20 • far-seeing (welfare-state), l. 20 • best (place) l. 22 • odd, l. 10 • mighty (empire), l. 19 • chronic (failure), l. 21/22
b) The adjectives Bill Bryson uses describe Britain as a country full of contrasts and contradictions. There are many opposites: mighty empire & chronic failure, enlightened & benign/crazy, wondrous & odd. Bill Bryson shows distance, admiration, respect and love for the country and the people.
2. *Advantage:* As a foreigner he can probably provide a more objective view as he sees the British from an outside perspective. The details he notices are not biased by education and familiarity. He is able to see the things that set the British apart from other nationalities. As an American he will find a lot of his own country's traditions reflected in British culture.
*Disadvantage:* As a foreigner he may not understand the significance of certain cultural details, prejudices and ideas, because he does not have enough background knowledge.

### Looking at style

(S. 'Glossary', SB, S. 153.)
Rhetorical and literary devices: humour, ll. 8 ff • irony, ll.18–22 • hyperbole (extreme statements, superlatives), ll. 2, 22 • rhetorical question ("What other nation …?"), l. 14 • enumeration ("… milk in bottles, beans on toast, …"), ll. 2–6 • parallel sentence structures (second paragraph: What a wondrous …/What other country …/What other nation …/) ll. 7–16 • allusion (referring to something indirectly: Nelson's dying wish) l. 12 • personal style (e.g. "Suddenly … I realized …"), l. 1 • generally short sentences (e.g. "None, of course."), l. 16.

### Over to you

● (S. 'Skills file', SB, S. 129.) <u>Ordnance Survey maps</u>: detailed maps of the landscape very useful for hikers.
http://www.davidmorgan.com/CATALOGS/DM/dm39/dm43?992157 59475204973103465287 12
<u>Cricket</u>: game played with bat and ball and two teams of 11 players.
http://www.uk.cricket.org/
<u>Lord Chancellor</u>: The Head of the House of Lords sits on a stool called the woolsack. Sometimes the term woolsack is also used as a synonym for the office of the Lord Chancellor.
http://www.open.gov.uk/lcd/lcdhome.htm
<u>William Shakespeare</u>: born 1564 in Stratford-upon-Avon, died 1616; most important writer of Renaissance, still influential today; famous works include: Macbeth, King Lear, The Merchant of Venice, As You Like It, Hamlet, Romeo and Juliet, Julius Caesar.

http://www.smsu.edu/English/eirc/shpag.html
http://www.shakespeare.org.uk/
<u>Sir Christopher Wren:</u> *born 1632, died 1723 in London. Wren was an architect, designer, astronomer, and geometrician. Most famous building: St. Paul's Cathedral.*
http://www.encyclopedia.com/articles/14014.html
http://www.groups.dcs.st-and.ac.uk/~history/Mathematicians/Wren.html
http://www.spartacus.schoolnet.co.uk/ARwren.htm
<u>Open University:</u> *British experiment in higher education for adults, opened in January 1971. No academic prerequisites. Courses are conducted by various means, including television, correspondence, study groups, and residential courses.*
http://www.open.ac.uk

CC:1/6
CD1:11  **Part 2: A lonely island**          SB S. 27–28

*In diesem zweiten Abschnitt wird das Inseldenken der Briten näher betrachtet.*

### While you read

🖉 *Similar in many respects: use of personal style, irony, humour, hyperbole, etc.*
*Differences: less enumeration, fewer rhetorical questions; use of personal anecdote to make his point. Also in this extract Bill Bryson sets himself distinctly apart from the British: he makes prominent use of his "otherness" in order to make his point.*

### Comprehension                          SB S. 28

*1. <u>Britain itself:</u> "… Britain is a big place." (l. 7). Although Britain is actually comparatively small, the British think it is very big. Even when making a comparatively short trip, e.g. from Surrey to Cornwall (approx. 250 kms) the British make preparations as if they were going on a long journey. This is especially surprising for an American who is used to travelling great distances.*
*<u>Britain and Europe:</u> The British do not consider themselves to be part of Europe and think of Europe and even countries like France which are geographically very near as being a long way away.*
*<u>Britain and the rest of world:</u> The British have a close political relationship with the USA, and also feel closer to America in terms of 'emotional geography'. Bill Bryson implies that the British are ignorant in terms of world geography: they don't know (or care) where many countries are, even some European ones. Countries that are or were linked to Britain (e.g. Australia, India, as part of the Commonwealth) are considered to be geographically closer than they really are.*
*2. a) Great Britain is an island. The British understanding of geography seems to be largely governed by the quality of the relationship the country has (had) towards the nations concerned. Britain's Commonwealth links and the link to America as another English-speaking nation are still more important and embedded in history than Britain's links with Europe.*
*b) <u>Yes:</u> It is not unusual to identify more closely with people of one's own culture, who speak the same language, etc. There is nothing wrong with such a strong feeling of national identity. It doesn't necessarily mean one can't cooperate with other nations.*
*<u>No:</u> The British should try to be more European. Britain should try to identify more with Europe. This attitude might prevent Britain joining whole-heartedly in European projects (e.g the Euro).*

### Language

*1. to plan to do s.th. = to intend to do s.th. (l. 9)*
*that's expecting too much of s.th. = that's a tall order (l. 14/15)*
*a long serious talk about s.th. = a protracted discussion (l. 15)*
*to be influenced totally by s.th. = to be shaped entirely by s.th. (l. 24)*
*to be very surprised = to be astounded (l. 34)*
*2. … think about travelling and what is a long or short journey in a completely different way to most other nations.*
*… the majority of the people I work with were convinced that this was not the truth.*
*… as though I was being too precise and making unimportant distinctions.*

### Translation

*Beim Versuch, Bill Bryson's Stil nachzuahmen, soll nicht übertrieben werden: Die Anweisung zielt auf den persönlichen, plauderhaften Ton, nicht auf die sprachlichen Formulierungen. Schwierigkeiten können sich v. a. durch die Länge der Sätze ergeben. Da im Deutschen keine Partizipialsätze möglich sind, ergibt das manchmal lange, verschachtelte Nebensätze. Man soll als Ausgleich alle vorhandenen Kürzungsmöglichkeiten wahrnehmen. Eine weitere Hürde kann die häufige Anwendung von Gleich- und Vorzeitigkeit (past perfect) darstellen. Diese müssen im Deutschen nicht immer wiedergegeben werden. S können zusammenhängende Satzteile markieren, um so die Übersicht über Haupt- und Nebensätze zu bewahren. (S. auch 'Skills file', SB, S. 122 & 123.)*

*Ich erinnere mich, nachdem ich ungefähr ein Jahr in Bournemouth gelebt und mein erstes Auto gekauft hatte, wie ich am Autoradio herumdrehte und überrascht war, wie viele der empfangenen Sender auf Französisch waren. Als ich auf der Karte nachsah, staunte ich noch mehr, als mir klar wurde, dass ich näher an Cherbourg als an London war. Das erwähnte ich am nächsten Tag im Büro und die meisten meiner Kollegen wollten es nicht wahrhaben. Auch als ich es ihnen auf der Karte zeigte, runzelten sie voller Zweifel die Stirn und sagten Dinge wie: „Na ja, im rein physischen Sinne mag Frankreich vielleicht schon näher sein," als ob ich Haarspalterei betreiben würde und als ob man ein völlig neues Verständnis für Entfernungen benötige, sobald man sich in den Ärmelkanal hineinstürze – und natürlich hatten sie ja gewissermaßen Recht damit.*

CC:1/7
CD1:12  **Part 3: Two nations**          SB. S. 28–29

*Schwerpunkt dieses dritten Abschnitts ist das Nord-/Südgefälle in Großbritannien. Folgende Fragen könnten als Einstieg dienen:*

→ Look at the map of Britain at the front of the book. Compare the North of England (North of Sheffield) with the South-East in terms of roads and motorways, National Parks, towns and cities. What conclusions can you draw from your observations? • Look at the position of Liverpool, Manchester and London and say why you think these cities developed here. • The title of the extract is 'Two nations'. What do you think it might be about?

### Comprehension

*1. The landscape of the north is physically different. The North has more open countryside, old villages, etc. (ll. 2–4)*
*The people in the north speak with a different accent and use different words. They are also more direct than people in the south. (ll. 5/6)*

## 2 A British jigsaw

There is a "sense of economic loss" about the North because the North has suffered much more greatly from unemployment due to the closing down of factories and industries (ll. 15–25).
2. (S sollen plausible aber eigene Antworten geben, z. B. :) Many of the people in the houses are probably out of work. Maybe they spend their time watching TV, sleeping, meeting friends and sometimes going out to the local pub. The children will probably have to leave home and go to a different part of Britain (the South?) to get jobs.

**Creative writing**

● (S. 'Skills file', SB, S. 124.) Die Abbildung zeigt einen verlassenen und heruntergekommenen Wohnblock im Norden Englands. Als Stützhilfe könnte man folgende Fragen in Form von 'Key words' geben: Where is the row of houses? Who once lived here? What did they do? How long have the houses been empty? Who goes there now? What has happened?
Possible scenarios: a crime • returning home • leaving home • site for a new leisure centre • now and then

**Looking at style**

1. First person narration, present tense, short sentences, figurative language (cf. adjectives, listing of examples), humour, rhetorical questions, direct speech.
2. He uses different styles to make the text more interesting and varied. He uses factual style for making more serious or critical points and light-hearted style to make the text funny and entertaining.
3. –

**Over to you**

● Diese Aufgabe könnte sinnvollerweise in Zusammenhang mit dem Fach Wirtschaftsgeographie/Erdkunde gemacht werden. S evtl. in Gruppen mit der Beschreibung (auf Englisch) einer Region in Deutschland beauftragen. Vorteilhaft wäre Kontaktaufnahme mit einer Schule in der jeweiligen Region, z. B. per e-mail, möglicherweise im Rahmen einer Klassenpartnerschaft. S sollten zuerst ihre Eindrücke von der jeweiligen Region darstellen und diese dann mit den Fakten und weiteren Informationen, die sie entdecken, belegen oder ggf. verbessern. Websites zu den meisten Regionen Deutschlands findet man per Suchmaschine.

### The two Ashingtons SB S. 29

Die Informationen in der Tabelle und der Karte stammen aus einem Bericht in The Guardian vom 6. März 1997, der als Klausurtext für dieses Kapitel aufbereitet wurde. (s. CD ROM und Kopiervorlage, TRB, S. 40).

**Comprehension**

1. In Ashington, W. Sussex far more people own a car than in Ashington in Northumberland, where nearly half the households haven't got a car.
In Ashington, Northumberland there is over three times more low rent housing than in Ashington, W. Sussex.
In Ashington, Northumberland there are many pubs and clubs but in Ashington, W. Sussex there are only two.
In Ashington, Northumberland Labour is the most popular party whereas in W. Sussex most people vote Conservative.
Unemployment is five times higher in Ashington, Northumberland than it is in Ashington, W. Sussex.

2. In terms of the standard of living, people in Northumberland are not as well off as people in West Sussex. This can be seen by the number of households without a car as well as by the number of people living in low rent housing. The sociability and friendliness of Northerners is reflected in the number of pubs and clubs there. The North is traditionally more working class because of the traditional industries and the past strength of the trade unions. People in the south are much more conservative.

**Role Play**

An dieser Stelle wird schwerpunktmäßig 'Small Talk' geübt, d. h. Rücksichtnahme, Vermeidung heikler Themen, Einsatz von verbalen Verstärkern, etc. (S. 'Skills file: Small Talk', SB. S. 128.) Ggf. eine Videoaufnahme der S machen und danach analysieren. Dabei nicht nur sprachliche Richtigkeit, sondern auch Höflichkeit und Körpersprache beachten.

### City streets SB S. 30–31

### Revealed: Britain's filthiest air SB S. 30

**Comprehension**

1.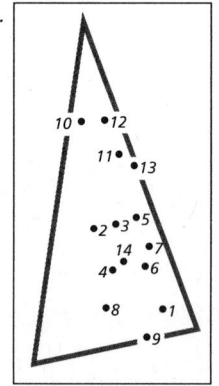

| 1 London | 7 Nottingham |
| 2 Liverpool | 8 Bristol |
| 3 Manchester | 9 Portsmouth |
| 4 Birmingham | 10 Glasgow |
| 5 Leeds | 11 Newcastle |
| 6 Leicester | 12 Edinburgh |

Tipp: S legen Transparentpapier über die Karte am Anfang des Buches und zeichnen GB als Dreieck ab. Städte dann an entsprechenden Stellen markieren. Ggf. auch geografische Eigenschaften markieren, z. B. Berge, Flüsse.

2. Problem: Pollution caused by traffic is making the air dirtier in many British cities, and particularly those in the south like London. Consequence: More and more inhabitants suffer from illnesses like asthma, lung disease and viral infections.
Solution: Reduce traffic by making people pay for using their car in the city, by putting a tax on company car parking and by improving the system of public transportation.
3. The results were surprising because in the past the older industrial regions of the North were more heavily polluted. However, factory closures in industrial towns like Newcastle mean that these towns are now cleaner than many southern non-industrial towns, where there are more cars on the roads.

**Vocabulary**

Words for topic web: polluted (l. 1), dirtiest (l. 4), cleanest (l. 5), heavily polluted, air quality (l. 8), Minister of the Environment (l. 15), smog (l. 17), particle level, nitrogen dioxide (l. 18), ground-level ozone (ll. 19–20), emissions, gas (l. 22), pollution targets (l. 26), environmentalist (l. 27), Friends of the Earth (l. 28), traffic (l. 29)

### Greening of the Midlands grime SB S. 31

Further information can be found at:
http://www.go-wm.gov.uk/towns.htm

## A British jigsaw 2

### Talking about the photo

*Green city?*
No, because: picture shows a wide road, there is little green, no trees, no plants.
Yes because: there is public transport. Picture shows a bus passing by. There is a ring road. That means less traffic in the town centre. There is not much traffic. There are several signs for public car parks.

### Comprehension

*Queen Victoria refused to visit the town.*
*Wolverhampton was once a dirty industrial town with a bad reputation; now it is on the green list.*
*John Young can't believe that Wolverhampton is said to be the cleanest city. He is a flower seller and is 62 years old.*
*Mander Shopping Centre is grey and was built in the 1960s.*
*Gerard Kells is 40 years old, writes plays and campaigns for the environment. He was brought up in London, but moved to Wolverhampton, where the air is cleaner, to escape London smog.*
*Sonia Colabella has a 16-month-old baby and is married to a man suffering from asthma. She enjoys the cleaner air in Wolverhampton and was considering moving away but now that the air is better she wants to stay.*

### Grammar: adverbs

a)/b) Adverbs of time: once (col. 1, l. 1) = previously • at first (Col. 1, l. 10) = initially • lately (col. 2, l. 9) = recently
Adverb of manner: safely (col. 3, l. 9) ≠ dangerously

### Sentence structure

1. Translation: „Je reiner hier die Luft, desto glücklicher bin ich."
2. The heavier the traffic, the more polluted the air. • The closer people live to busy roads, the more likely they are to suffer from asthma. • The cleaner the air in Wolverhampton, the better the reputation of the town.

### Over to you

PA oder GA. Die Kopiervorlage auf TRB, S. 74 sowie auf der CD-ROM, Chapter 4, enthält Tipps zum Schreiben eines Zeitungsartikels.

### Focus on Birmingham        SB S. 32–35

*i* In the 6th Century Birmingham was a small settlement in a forest. The name derives from the home (ham) of the tribe (ing) of a leader called Birm or Beorma.
In 1086 Birmingham was a hamlet worth 20 shillings but thanks to its geography became Britain's centre of manufacturing in the 20th century. Whilst it was a dry site there was a good supply of water from Deritend Ford and the River Rea. The area had easy access to coal, iron and timber.
Smithing and metal working also became established in Birmingham in the 16th century. In 1538 there were 1500 people in 200 houses, one main street with a number of side streets, markets and many smiths who sold goods all over England. Birmingham gained a strong reputation as a metal working centre by supplying the Parliamentarians with swords, pikes and armour in the English Civil War (1642–46).
By 1731 the population had grown to 23,000 and the manufacturing business had started to thrive. By the time of the Industrial Revolution, Birmingham was already the industrial and commercial centre of the Midlands.

Further information:
http://birmingham.gov.uk/epislive/citywide.nsf

### Preparation

Folgende Wörter sind evtl. unbekannt bzw. sollten zum aktiven Sprachgebrauch der S gehören:
population • pensioner • household • one parent household socio-economic • employment • employee • manufacturing • services • part-time • self-employed • government training scheme • unemployment • unemployed
total number • % (percentage) of

### Expressing figures

1. A comma separates thousands and is used after every three digits, e.g. 1,000 (one thousand) • 42,244,244 (forty two million two hundred (and) forty four thousand, two hundred (and) 44. A decimal point is used to show tenths of units, e.g 1,564.98 (one thousand five hundred (and) sixty four point nine eight). So, in English a comma is used where a point is used in German, and vice versa.
2. a) 21,793: twenty-one thousand seven hundred (and) ninety-three (AE: no 'and').
b) 86.4%: eighty-six point four per cent.
3. –
4. Working as an accountant, stock-broker, in trade (pronouncing quantities correctly), using order forms, talking about results of surveys, etc.

### Drawing conclusions

1. S sollen berechnen und dann auf Englisch erklären, wie sie zu ihrem Ergebnis gekommen sind. Dabei brauchen sie evtl. folgende Verben: to add (together) • to subtract (from) • to multiply (by) • to divide (by) • to equal/to be equal to
*Add together the figures for Birmingham in Table 1 to find the total population of Birmingham: 1,017,400. Multiply this by 100 and then divide the result by 58,395,000 (total population of GB). The answer is 1.74%.*
2. a) percentage of Indian, Pakistani, Bangladeshi • percentage of Black Caribbean African & other • more households without cars • (the employment figures) • the number of employees in manufacturing • twice as many government training schemes • long-term unemployment is higher
b) *Birmingham is a multicultural city with a large Indian, Pakistani and Bangladeshi population. A relatively high number of people probably do not have the financial means to own a car, indicating an underlying level of poverty. This is also suggested by the long-term unemployment figures, which could cause social problems and are probably a result of structural change from manufacturing to service industries.*
3. *The cost of living is probably high in terms of rent and housing prices because there are so many people in such a small area. Living conditions are likely to be difficult: problems with waste disposal, traffic (e.g. traffic jams and lack of parking space), small houses, blocks of flats, few recreational areas.*
4. a)/b) Die Tabellen geben z. B. keine Informationen über: Sport, Kultur, Freizeitmöglichkeiten (für junge Leute), Ein- und Auswanderung, etc.

# 2  A British jigsaw

5. a) Central location in the Midlands, only approx. 100 miles north of London and south of Liverpool and Manchester, linked by major motorways to the North and South. Unlike other major cities in England Birmingham is not situated on the coast or a river.
b) The water routes and major motorways make the transport of goods easier. There is easy access to coal, iron and timber. Birmingham is near the capital. Birmingham is near many other major cities.

### Over to you

● S sollen diese Aufgabe in Einzelarbeit zuerst schriftlich vorbereiten und dann kurz vortragen. Eine Erweiterung dieser Aufgabe als Referat über Birmingham befindet sich auf SB S.35 unter 'Working on the Internet'. (S. auch 'Skills file', SB, S. 129.)

### Quick & Quirky: Facts about B'ham    SB S. 34–35

*Diese 'Fakten' sind der offiziellen Website von Birmingham entnommen (Website-Angabe auf SB S. 34). Manche Angaben können angezweifelt werden, z. B. die Angaben zu x-ray photography (Röntgen?), oder weisen mangelnde internationale Kenntnisse auf, z. B. die Angabe von Bonn statt Berlin bei "How many miles is it from Birmingham to…".*

*Folgender Einstieg wäre möglich:*
⟶ Can you find any facts which you think are wrong? Are any of the facts out of date in your opinion?

● *Evtl. unbekannte Wörter:*
quirky • x-ray, x-ray photography, to take an x-ray • to invent • cottage • foundary • domestic building • steam engine • forerunner • light bulb • pneumatic tyre • to sweep • to be founded

⟶ *Quick Quiz: Als Lernspiel nach dem ersten Durchlesen um „skimming" zu üben: Kurze Fragen zu den Fakten vortragen, die S in PA möglichst schnell beantworten müssen. Fragen dabei immer nur einmal und in kurzen Abständen (ca. 10 Sekunden) vorlesen. Evtl. in Form eines 'Best of 3' Quizes durchführen: 2 S stehen vorne und beantworten Fragen per TA. Wer 2 Fragen richtig und am schnellsten beantwortet, bleibt stehen und bekommt einen neuen 'Gegner'. Der andere scheidet aus, bis ein Class Champion ermittelt wird.*
*Beispiele für geeignete Fragen:*
Which town is 983 miles from Birmingham? • Who or what are 'the Bullets'/'the Baggies'? • How many litter bins are there in Birmingham?

⟶ *Übersetzung: Die kurzen Abschnitte eignen sich gut als Übersetzungs- bzw. Dolmetscherübungen, die in PA ausgeführt werden können. 1. 'A' liest Abschnitt vor, 'B' übersetzt bei geschlossenem Buch ins Deutsche (simultan). 2. 'A' übersetzt bei offenem Buch einen Abschnitt ins Deutsche. 'B' gibt bei geschlossenem Buch die englische Version wieder mit Kontrolle durch 'A'.*

### Comprehension

1. a)/b) Possible headings: inventions, population, education, location, twin towns, sports, economy, industry, famous people, international relations, etc.
2. Possible answers: bands • music • night life • kinds of schools • traffic and transport
3. –

### Grammar

(S. 'Grammar file', SB, S. 147.)
1. a) (active ➞ passive:) George and Richard Cadbury's factory was moved from Bull Street to Bourneville in 1879.
b) (passive ➞ active:) Alex Issigonis designed the Mini and (passive ➞ active:) the Longbridge factory workers started production of it in 1959.
c) (passive ➞ active:) Major John Hall Edwards invented x-ray photography; (active ➞ passive:) the first x-ray photograph was taken (by him) in Birmingham in 1896.
d) (active ➞ passive:) The steam engine was developed by James Watt at the Soho Factory in Birmingham and the letter copying machine was also invented by him there.
e) (active ➞ passive:) Gas lighting was invented in Birmingham at the end of the 18th century by William Murdock.
f) active ➞ passive:) John Dunlop invented the pneumatic tyre in Birmingham in 1888.
g) (passive ➞ active:) In Birmingham 1,300 miles of road are regularly swept by council cleaners.
2. The passive is used to put emphasis more on the invention or action than on the agent. Generally, the passive is used in more formal style. The passive is also used by writers or speakers in order to express things more tactfully.

### Working on the internet

*S können in EA oder PA arbeiten. Die Website ist sehr ausführlich. L kann ggf. bestimmte Rubriken vorschlagen, die nachgeforscht werden sollen, z. B.*
http://birmingham.gov.uk/epislive/whatson.nsf/ (events)
http://birmingham.gov.uk/epislive/citywide.nsf/ (night life)

### Round Britain game, questions, crossword

 *Kopiervorlagen 2, 3, 4: TRB, S. 36 – 39/CD-ROM*
*Lösung zu 4: TRB, S. 135*

*Zur Wiederholung und Festigung des Inhalts dieses Kapitels befinden sich im TRB sowie auf der CD-ROM drei Kopiervorlagen, die an dieser Stelle eingesetzt werden können:*
*KV 2 & 3: Ein Würfelspiel mit dazugehörigen Fragekärtchen. Trifft man auf eines der folgenden Felder: "Miss x turns" oder "Go back x spaces", hat man die Möglichkeit, die Strafe abzuwenden, indem man ein Fragekärtchen zieht und die Frage richtig beantwortet.*
*KV 3: Kann auch als Fragespiel in PA verwendet werden.*
*KV 4: Ein Kreuzworträtsel zum Thema 'Großbritannien'.*

### Project: Presenting a town/region    SB S. 35

*Das Projekt versammelt die wichtigsten Aspekte, die in diesem Kapitel behandelt wurden, und erstellt einen direkten Bezug zum Lebensraum der S. Projekt sollte in GA bearbeitet werden.*
*Zusätzliche Hinweise zur Projektarbeit: TRB, S. 5 – 7 und 'Skills files', SB, S. 139.*

### Test: Two towns and two nations

 *Kopiervorlage 5: TRB, S. 40/CD-ROM (Aufgaben)*
*Lösungen: TRB, S. 135, Vokabeln: TRB, S. 142*

# Listening comprehension

## A British jigsaw 2

## Wales and the Welsh

**Gaelic** [ˈgeɪlɪk] Celtic language in parts of Ireland and Scotland
**Joe Bloggs** [blɒgz] name standing for any ordinary person
**to spring to mind** when a thought comes into one's mind spontaneously
**to ban** to forbid
**to punish** *bestrafen*
**work force** a group of workers

**compulsory** [kəmˈʌlsrɪ] (in school) required
**to make it big** *(fig.)* to become popular
**to take s.th. in stride** accept s.th. calmly
**to set in motion** to start
**daffodil** [ˈdæfədɪl] a flower *(Osterglocke)*
**leek** a vegetable *(Lauch)*
**cockles** [ˈkɒklz] a kind of shellfish (seafood)
**laverbread** [ˈlɑːvəbred] a type of seaweed eaten on toast

You will see the sign above in a certain part of Britain. What language is it in?
What do you think the words on the sign mean?

## Comprehension

1. When you hear the three words below, write down the speaker's explanations for them:
   a) hywl
   b) cawl
   c) Eisteddfod
2. Listen to the first part of the talk ending with *"... independence from the English"* again and answer the following questions:
   a) Why does only a fifth of the nation speak Welsh fluently?
   b) In which ways have attitudes changed towards the Welsh language?
   c) What word does the speaker use to describe the Welsh character?
   d) Why is rugby so important for the Welsh?
3. Listen to the next short section ending with *"... recognition within it"* and answer these questions:
   a) What happened on 6th May 1999?
   b) Why was this event so important?
4. Listen to the rest of the talk. Choose one of the traditions described, and say whether you would/wouldn't like to see/taste/experience it. Give reasons.
5. What do you think the speaker's main intention in giving this talk was?

## Language

Indicate the stressed syllables for the words in the box below. Use the symbol ' for for a main stress and , for a secondary stress. For example: advantage = [-'--]    disadvantage = [,--'--]

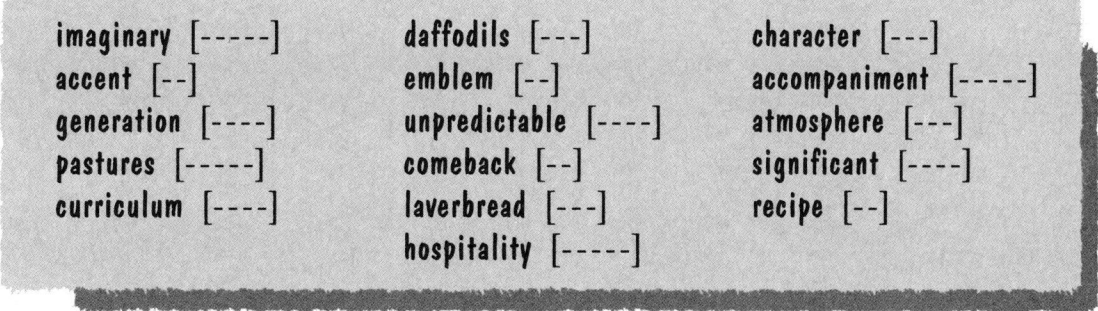

# Round Britain game

A British jigsaw 2

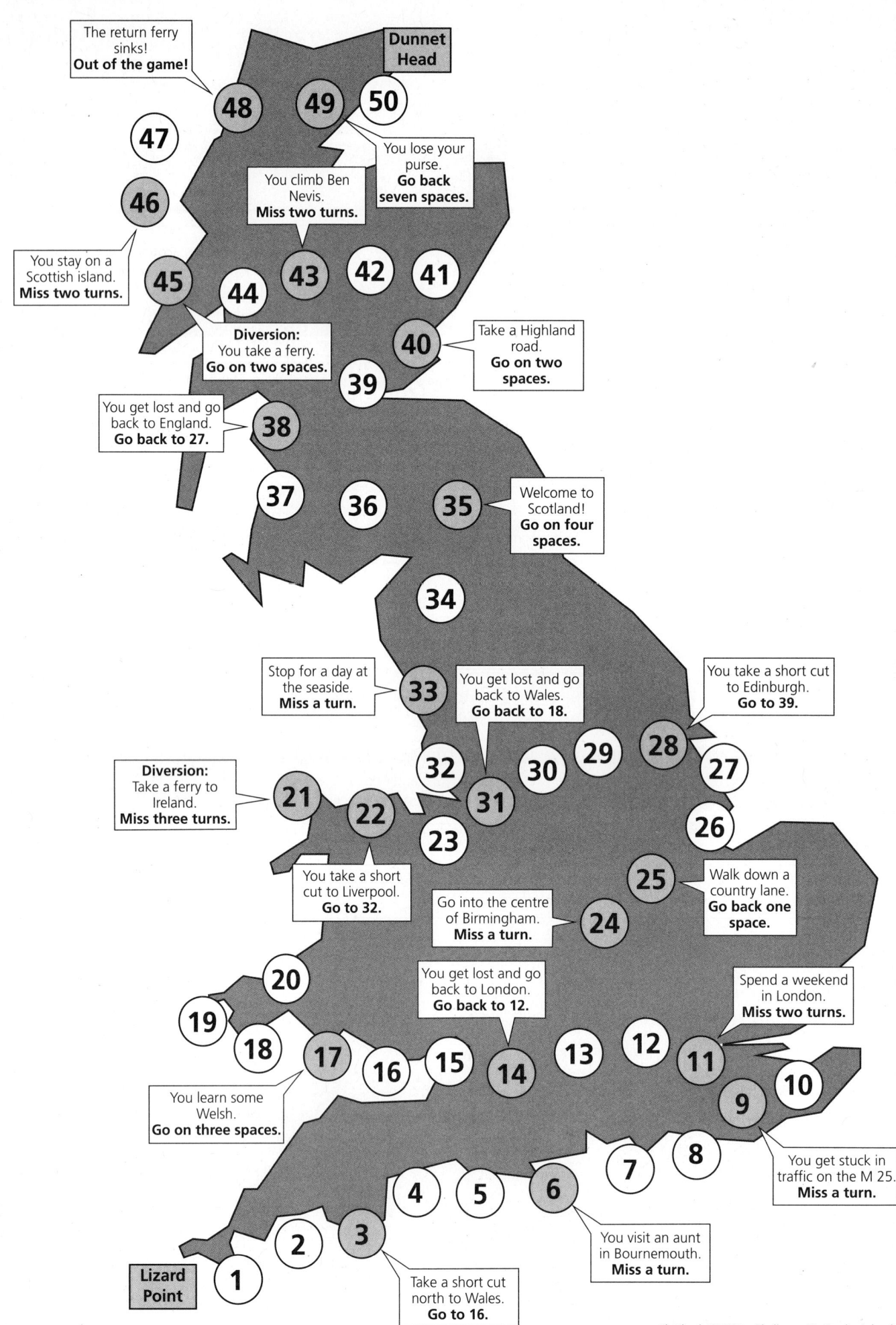

36

# Round Britain review questions (1/2) — A British jigsaw 2

---

**True or False?**

According to the article "The New Brits: Single, stoned, selfish", the New Brits are more likely to put responsibility before pleasure.

*(False, the other way round)*

---

**Geography:**

In which country is Ben Nevis located?

*(Scotland)*

---

**Geography:**

Which countries make up the United Kingdom?

*(England, Scotland, Wales, Northern Ireland)*

---

**Explanation:**

Is most of Britain's population rural or urban?

*(Mainly urban)*

---

**Multiple choice:**

How would you describe Britain's climate?
a) Cold and rainy.
b) Very extreme but mild.
c) Temperate and mild.

*(c)*

---

**Multiple choice:**

The Channel Tunnel joins:
a) Ireland and England.
b) England and Scotland.
c) England and Italy
d) England and France.

*(d)*

---

**True or False?**

More British people get married at an older age, and they tend to have more children than in previous years.

*(False, fewer children)*

---

**Explanation:**

What does Bill Bryson love about Britain?

*(All of it! Everything!)*

---

**Explanation:**

How does Bill Bryson describe the British sense of distance?

*(As "totally private")*

---

**Multiple choice:**

According to Bill Bryson, what most differentiates the North from the South of England?
a) the difference in climate.
b) the difference in the economic situation.
c) the different social customs.

*(b)*

---

**Geography:**

Name the town which can be found in both the north and the south of England.

*(Ashington)*

---

**Geography:**

In which town is air in England the dirtiest?

*(London)*

# Round Britain review questions (2/2) — A British jigsaw? 2

---

**Explanation:**

Why did Queen Victoria not even want to look at Wolverhampton as she passed through?

*(It was so dirty at the time.)*

---

**Geography:**

What is Birmingham's rank in terms of the largest cities in Britain?

*(second)*

---

**Multiple choice:**

The Midlands are in:
a) central England.
b) southern England.
c) central Scotland.
d) central Ireland.

*(a)*

---

**True or false?**

There is very little industry in Birmingham.

*(False, there is considerable industry)*

---

**Multiple choice:**

According to the statistics for Birmingham, the highest percentage of inhabitants are:
a) 0–4 years old.
b) 5–15 years old.
c) 16–44 years old.
d) 45 years and older.

*(c)*

---

**Multiple choice:**

In Britain the highest percentage of inhabitants are:
a) 0–4 years old.
b) 5–15 years old.
c) 16–44 years old.
d) 45 years and older.

*(c)*

---

**Multiple choice:**

One of Birmingham's partner cities in Germany is:
a) Stuttgart.
b) Leipzig.
c) Düsseldorf.
d) München.

*(c)*

---

**Multiple choice:**

Which is the name of one of Birminghams football teams?
a) the "Bulls".
b) the "Bubbles".
c) the "Beasts".
d) the "Baggies".

*(d)*

---

**Explanation:**

What is mainly responsible for air pollution in large British cities?

*(road traffic)*

---

**True or false?**

Decreasing numbers of British go to church.

*(True)*

---

**Multiple choice:**

What is the largest minority population in Britain?
a) White.
b) Black, Caribbean, African & Other.
c) Indian, Pakistani, Bangladeshi.
d) Chinese & Other.

*(c)*

---

**True or false?**

Wolverhampton's pollution problem has recently improved only slightly.

*(False, is has become a lot better.)*

# Round Britain crossword

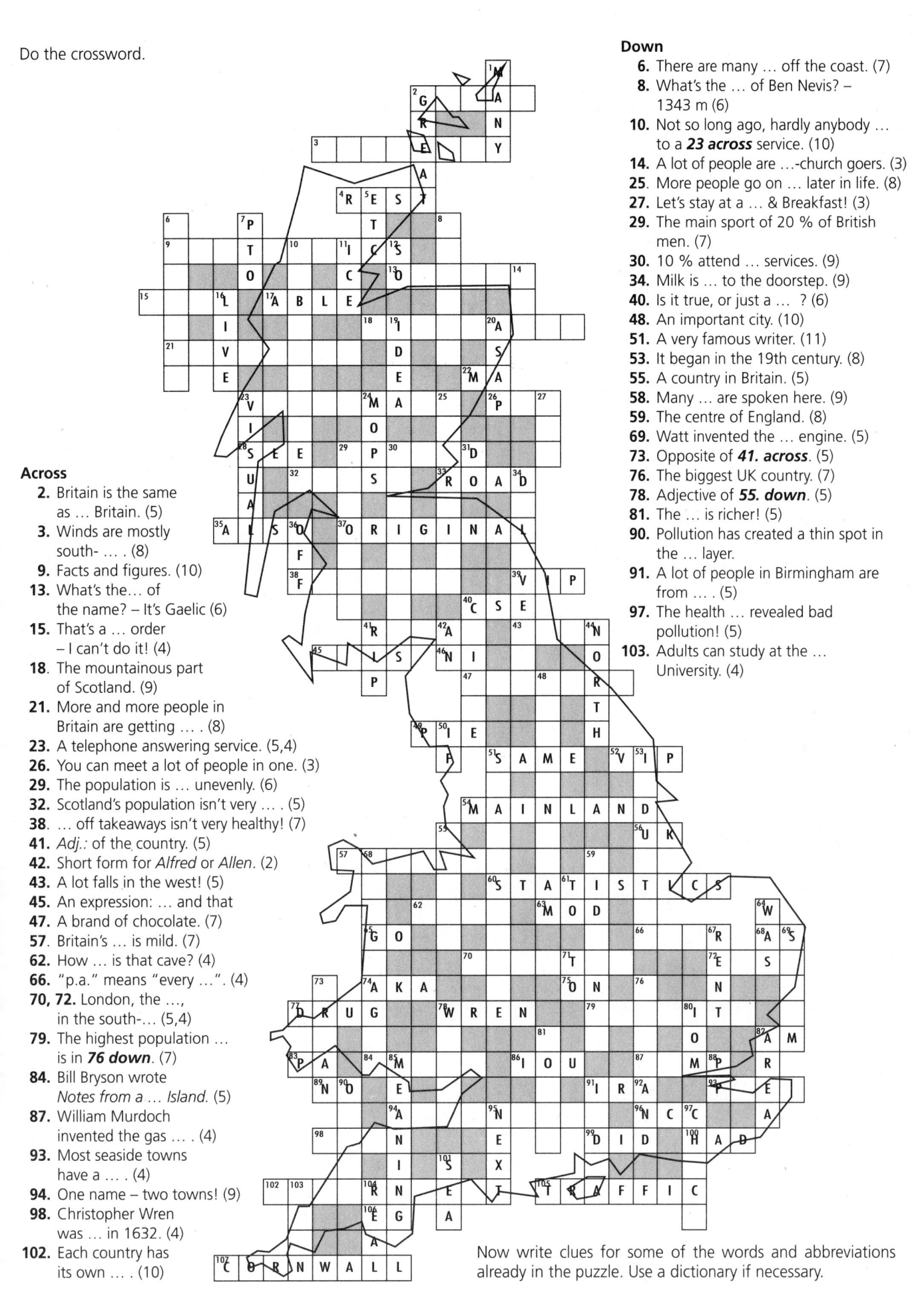

**A British jigsaw 2**

Do the crossword.

## Across
2. Britain is the same as … Britain. (5)
3. Winds are mostly south-…. (8)
9. Facts and figures. (10)
13. What's the… of the name? – It's Gaelic (6)
15. That's a … order – I can't do it! (4)
18. The mountainous part of Scotland. (9)
21. More and more people in Britain are getting … . (8)
23. A telephone answering service. (5,4)
26. You can meet a lot of people in one. (3)
29. The population is … unevenly. (6)
32. Scotland's population isn't very … . (5)
38. … off takeaways isn't very healthy! (7)
41. *Adj.*: of the country. (5)
42. Short form for *Alfred* or *Allen*. (2)
43. A lot falls in the west! (5)
45. An expression: … and that
47. A brand of chocolate. (7)
57. Britain's … is mild. (7)
62. How … is that cave? (4)
66. "p.a." means "every …". (4)
70, 72. London, the …, in the south-… (5,4)
79. The highest population … is in **76 down**. (7)
84. Bill Bryson wrote *Notes from a … Island*. (5)
87. William Murdoch invented the gas … . (4)
93. Most seaside towns have a … . (4)
94. One name – two towns! (9)
98. Christopher Wren was … in 1632. (4)
102. Each country has its own … . (10)

## Down
6. There are many … off the coast. (7)
8. What's the … of Ben Nevis? – 1343 m (6)
10. Not so long ago, hardly anybody … to a **23 across** service. (10)
14. A lot of people are …-church goers. (3)
25. More people go on … later in life. (8)
27. Let's stay at a … & Breakfast! (3)
29. The main sport of 20 % of British men. (7)
30. 10 % attend … services. (9)
34. Milk is … to the doorstep. (9)
40. Is it true, or just a … ? (6)
48. An important city. (10)
51. A very famous writer. (11)
53. It began in the 19th century. (8)
55. A country in Britain. (5)
58. Many … are spoken here. (9)
59. The centre of England. (8)
69. Watt invented the … engine. (5)
73. Opposite of **41. across**. (5)
76. The biggest UK country. (7)
78. Adjective of **55. down**. (5)
81. The … is richer! (5)
90. Pollution has created a thin spot in the … layer.
91. A lot of people in Birmingham are from … . (5)
97. The health … revealed bad pollution! (5)
103. Adults can study at the … University. (4)

Now write clues for some of the words and abbreviations already in the puzzle. Use a dictionary if necessary.

# Two towns and two nations

They might be in the same country and share a common name. But in every other respect – from house prices to unemployment – the two Ashingtons, separated by little over 300 miles, are poles apart.

"We're stuck at opposite ends of the country with little knowledge about life in the other half," says solicitor Brian Norton, who chairs the parish council of Ashington, West Sussex.

"We've got this great divide – everything north of Watford is almost foreign, and it seems a bit silly really."

Local Councillor and former miner Colin Parker, Chairman of the leisure committee in the old northern colliery town of Ashington, agrees. "It would be nice to know more about the south, although I would imagine there's a big difference in living standards – we've suffered terribly from pit closures up here."

Yesterday, in northern Ashington, they set about bridging that gap with a 10-week course to examine the English divide in microcosm, well-heeled West Sussex versus down-at-heel Northumberland.

Organised by the Workers' Educational Association, it aims to establish links between the two communities. [...]

The idea came from Bill Gale, an Ashington (Northumberland) community worker who recently stumbled across the West Sussex village of the same name on the A24 between Worthing and Horsham.

He eventually discovered a local historian, Daphne Norton, wife of the parish council chairman, who soon established a liaison group. They began writing to each other, and quickly agreed that both communities could gain from sharing experiences.

"While we cannot underestimate this great social divide, we want to break down taboos," Mr Gale said. "The only thing we seem to have in common, apart from the name, is that we're both close to the sea."

Mrs Norton, who lives in a 14th century farmhouse, finds it hard to visualise the other Ashington, although she thinks she may have passed through it 30 years ago on the way back from Scotland. "[...] We think twinning is a rather nice idea, although we all thought it was rather hilarious at first."

Ashingtonians (N) who turned up for the launch of yesterday's twinning course were told in a leaflet that they would "explore social, cultural and economic variations ... and reasons and perceptions behind the north-south divide".

Lecturer Ian Rushton said he thought people in the other Ashington were well aware of the fact that they lived in a "relatively well-off commuter-belt area".

"It will be interesting to see whether brown ale swilling ex-pitmen can be understood south of the Tyne," he joked.

(420 words)

*From the article by Peter Hetherington,* The Guardian, *March 6, 1997.*

## Content

1. Give two similarities and two differences between the Ashingtons.
2. What have the residents of the two towns agreed to do, and for what purpose?
3. How did the co-operation come about?

*(Your teacher will tell you which of the following tasks you should complete.)*

## Comment

1. Considering what you have learned about England, what reasons can you suggest for the differences between the two towns?
2. How can Germany be 'divided'? Describe this division and try to come up with explanations for it. In what ways is it similar to or different from the one described here?
3. Later in the article a resident of Ashington (N) comments, "People are much friendlier up here." Comment on whether you think there really is a correlation between friendliness and economic prosperity. Give examples to illustrate your point of view.

## Form

1. What features of this text are typical of newspaper articles?
2. Find examples of different uses of tone and register in the article, and compare their functions.

## Language

1. Explain in a complete sentence (without using the underlined words).
   a) "... the two Ashingtons ... are poles apart." (ll. 3–4)
   b) "Yesterday ... they set about bridging that gap ... ." (ll. 17–18)
   c) "Mrs Norton ... finds it hard to visualise the other Ashington." (ll. 36–37)
   d) "... people in the other Ashington (are) well aware that they (live) in a relatively well-off commmuter-belt area." (ll. 46–48)
2. Find synonyms for the following words.
   a) well-heeled (l. 19)        c) stumbled across (ll. 24)
   b) down-at-heel (l. 19)       d) swilling (l. 49)
3. Provide the correct verb forms by using the past or the present perfect (simple or progressive).
   a) Tim (do) research lately about towns with identical names.
   b/c) I (call) him yesterday to hear what he (learn).

# The British political system XtraFile

## Didaktische Hinweise

In beiden XtraFiles handelt es sich um die Vermittlung eines faktischen Basiswissens, vor dessen Hintergrund dann in den Jahrgangsstufen 12 und 13 die Themen ‚Politik im Vereinten Königreich' sowie die ‚Politik in den USA' vertieft werden sollen. Die XtraFiles werden durch eine gewisse Reduzierung dem Stellenwert des entsprechenden Themenbereiches in der Klasse 11 gerecht und ermöglichen daher eine zielorientierte Wissensvermittlung in ausgewogener Gewichtung.

Die stringenteste Bearbeitung ermöglicht das gemeinsame Lesen und die Zusammenfassung der Texte im Unterricht: nachdem der Wortschatz geklärt ist, können die wichtigsten Punkte des Inhalts in Stichpunkten an der Tafel aufgelistet werden.
Es wäre ebenfalls denkbar, dass sich die S im Vorfeld Karteikärtchen besorgen. Für die einzelnen Kärtchen werden dann gemeinsam im Unterricht Überschriften gefunden, unter denen dann die wichtigsten Stichpunkte auftauchen.
Zur Lernzielkontrolle dienen die Kopiervorlagen des TRB/der CD-ROM.

## Kopiervorlagen

*Kopiervorlage 1: TRB, S. 42/CD-ROM*
*Lösungen: TRB, S. 136*

Dies ist ein Fragebogen mit multiple-choice Fragen zum politischen System Großbritanniens. Um die Vorkenntnisse der S festzustellen, ist es sinnvoll, diesen Fragebogen vor der Bearbeitung des XtraFiles ausfüllen zu lassen. Zur Lernzielkontrolle kann der Fragebogen nach Durchnahme des XtraFiles ein zweites Mal eingesetzt werden.

*Kopiervorlage 2: TRB, S. 43/CD-ROM*
*Lösungen: TRB, S. 136*

Diese Kopiervorlage dient als Comprehension und Summary der Texte und sollte im Schüler-Lehrer-Dialog erarbeitet werden. Die Kopiervorlage soll während des Bearbeitens der Texte verteilt werden. Note taking/Note making erscheint hier sinnvoller, als Questions on the text, da es inhaltlich in erster Linie um Fakten geht, die es unsinnig wäre, mit eigenen Worten zu umschreiben.

Die Kopiervorlage ermöglicht ein zügigeres Vorankommen als der klassische TA, auf den hier ganz verzichtet werden sollte: die S sollen trainieren, eigenständig Notizen zu machen (aufgrund mündlicher Aussagen), ohne immer nur ‚sklavisch an dem zu kleben*, was an der Tafel steht' (* was ohnehin denjenigen, die sich nicht am Unterricht beteiligen wollen, dies noch erleichtert, da sie ja dem TA 'nebenbei' folgen können).

*Kopiervorlage 3: TRB, S. 44 & 45/CD-ROM*

Auf diesen Kopiervorlagen befinden sich Kärtchen mit Fragen (Bogen 1/2) und Lösungen (Bogen 2/2), die ausgeschnitten und als Memoryspiel gespielt werden können. Das Spiel kann am sinnvollsten nach Bearbeiten des XtraFiles eingesetzt werden, evtl. zu einem späteren Zeitpunkt zur Wiederholung/Auffrischung. Das Sortieren der Kärtchen wird erleichtert, wenn man farbiges Papier zum Kopieren verwendet: eine Farbe für die Fragen und eine andere für die Lösungen. Die Kärtchen sind nummeriert, damit S die Richtigkeit der Lösungen kontrollieren können.

## Klassenarbeit

*Kopiervorlage 4: TRB, S. 46*
*Lösungen: TRB, S. 136.*
Da die Thematik der politischen Systeme in erster Linie Vermittlung von Fachwissen ist, bietet sich hier die Herübersetzung besonders als Form der Klassenarbeit an.

Auf der CD-ROM befindet sich zusätzlich ein themenunabhängiger Übungstext, der allgemeine Schwierigkeiten bei Übersetzungen aufweist.

# Government in Britain quiz

**The British political system** XtraFile

How much (or how little) do you already know about government in Britain?

1. **Who is the British Head of State?**
   - a) the ruling Monarch (king or queen)
   - b) the Prime Minister
   - c) the Lord Chancellor
   - d) the President

2. **Which of the electoral systems described below is currently used in General Elections in Britain?**
   - a) Proportional representation:
     *The seats in parliament are divided between the parties according to the percentage of votes they win. For example, if a party wins 20% of the votes it wins 20% of the seats.*
   - b) Direct mandate or "first-past-the-post":
     *In areas known as constituencies one candidate per party can stand for election. The people who live in a constituency vote for the candidate of their choice. The candidate who wins the most votes is elected to represent that constituency in Parliament.*
   - c) Dual system:
     *In the dual system electors have two votes: one for a candidate who wins a seat by direct mandate and one for a party. These second votes are added together on a national scale and seats are divided proportionally.*

3. **Which are the main political parties in Britain?**
   - a) the Conservatives
   - b) the Republicans
   - c) the Liberal Democrats
   - d) the Labour Party

4. **After a general election which party forms the government in Britain?**
   - a) the party which wins the most seats
   - b) the party which wins two-thirds of the seats
   - c) the party which wins all of the seats

5. **Where do the Members of Parliament (MPs) in Britain meet?**
   - a) Buckingham Palace
   - b) The House of Commons
   - c) Big Ben
   - d) The Old Bailey

6. **Who lives at 10 Downing Street?**
   - a) the Prime Minister
   - b) the Foreign Secretary
   - c) the Home Secretary
   - d) the Chancellor of the Exchequer

7. **What kind of government has Britain most often had?**
   - a) single-party government with an absolute majority
   - b) two-party coalition government
   - c) minority single-party government

8. **The term 'devolution' in British politics means:**
   - a) modernization
   - b) decentralization
   - c) the opposite of evolution
   - d) development

9. **Parliament is made up of:**
   - a) the House of Commons and the House of Lords
   - b) the House of Lords and the Monarchy
   - c) the House of Commons and the Monarchy
   - d) the House of Commons, House of Lords and the Monarchy

10. **What happened during the first stage of the reform of the House of Lords in November 1999?**
    - a) Hereditary peers were no longer allowed to sit and vote in the House of Lords.
    - b) The hereditary peers abolished the ministers' right to sit and vote.
    - c) The hereditary peers were all recognized as life peers.
    - d) The automatic right of the hereditary peers to sit and vote in the House of Lords was abolished. They had to be elected in order to retain their seats.

11. **The Chancellor of the Exchequer is in charge of:**
    - a) domestic policy
    - b) foreign policy
    - c) economic policy
    - d) financial policy

12. **A government may stay in office for a maximum period of:**
    - a) 3 years
    - b) 4 years
    - c) 5 years
    - d) 6 years

13. **Which of the following have been Britain's Prime Minister?**
    - a) Winston Churchill
    - b) Oscar Wilde
    - c) Margaret Thatcher
    - d) Franklin Delano Roosevelt

# The British political system

*The British political system* XtraFile 2

Read pp. 36–39 in your book and fill in the information in note form. Use the back of the worksheet if you need more space.

## Parliament

| House of Commons (Lower House) | House of Lords (Upper House) | The Monarchy |
|---|---|---|
| Main tasks: | Main tasks: | Main tasks: |
| Number of members: | Number of members: | |
| Form of election: | Form of election: | Form of power: |
| The Speaker: | Reform: | |

## Government

Party which forms government:

Head of government:

Important cabinet ministers:

## Opposition

Party which forms opposition:

## The Political Parties (Name • Importance • Political leaning)

## Current electoral system

## Devolution

N. Ireland:

Scotland:

Wales:

# British politics game (1/2) — The British political system  XtraFile

| | | | |
|---|---|---|---|
| **1** How can the constitution be changed? | **2** Who is Head of State? | **3** Who is Head of Government? | **4** What is the Monarch's function? |
| **5** Where does Parliament meet? | **6** Name the three elements that make up Parliament. | **7** For what functions is the Chancellor of the Exchequer responsible? | **8** Who decides when exactly to hold a General Election, and within which period? |
| **9** How many members are there in the House of Commons? | **10** To which groups do the members of the House of Lords belong? | **11** What happens in the House of Commons? | **12** What is the main business of the House of Lords? |
| **13** Which party forms the government after a General Election? | **14** Which party forms the Opposition? | **15** Which voting system is used at a General Election? | **16** What is known as the Good Friday Agreement? |
| **17** Which parties have played the most decisive role in British politics in the twentieth century? | **18** When was the first election for the Scottish Parliament held? | **19** Which voting systems were used for elections to the Scottish Parliament? | **20** Which are the nationalist parties of Scotland and Wales? |

# British politics game (2/2) — The British political system

| 1<br><br>By Act of Parliament | 2<br><br>The Monarch | 3<br><br>The Prime Minister | 4<br><br>Formally appoints the Prime Minister and many other government officials |
|---|---|---|---|
| 5<br><br>The Palace of Westminster | 6<br><br>The House of Commons, House of Lords and the Monarch | 7<br><br>Financial and monetary issues | 8<br><br>The Prime Minister, within a five-year period |
| 9<br><br>659 Members of Parliament | 10<br><br>Bishops and archbishops of the Church of England, hereditary peers (who must now be elected) and life peers | 11<br><br>New laws are passed and the main business of government is done | 12<br><br>Has a mainly controlling and advisory function, but it can delay bills for up to a year |
| 13<br><br>The party which wins the most seats at a General Election | 14<br><br>The largest minority party in the House of Commons | 15<br><br>The simple majority or 'first-past-the-post' system | 16<br><br>The proposal for a Northern Ireland Assembly which was proposed on April 10, 1998 |
| 17<br><br>The Conservative Party (Tories) and the Labour Party | 18<br><br>May 6, 1999 | 19<br><br>First-past-the-post for 73 MSPs and proportional representation from party lists for 56 MSPs | 20<br><br>The Scottish National Party and the Plaid Cymru |

# Test: Translation

## Australia and the Monarchy

Australia used to be a colony, part of the British Empire and directly ruled from Britain. The earliest settlers were originally sent to Australia as convicts 211 years ago, because British prisons were overcrowded. Ever since, Australia has been ruled by a British king or queen. From 1793, people began emigrating to Australia of their own free will, attracted by the wealth of the country and the promise of land (as well as cheap labour by convicts). These settlers came from all over Europe, but most came from Great Britain and Ireland. [...] By the mid-19th century it was clear that Australia was no longer a big prison and needed its own government. [...] In 1901 the Commonwealth of Australia was established. [...] But even though Australia is now independent, it has kept a British monarch.

(136 words)

3 **convict** prisoner

*From the article 'Battle royal over republic' by Emily Moore,* The Guardian, *November 2, 1999.*

# Making the grade 3

## Didaktisches Inhaltsverzeichnis

| Title | Text type / Topic | Skills & Tasks | 💿📄 |
|---|---|---|---|
| **Education: What's the point?** (SB S. 40) | • college brochures (50 words)<br>• educational goals | • Reading: identifying key words and phrases<br>• Speaking: discussing priorities, finding consensus<br>• Writing: mission statement<br>• Project: designing a cover<br>• Vocabulary: glossary on education | |
| **16+** (SB S. 41) | • college brochure (256 words) | • Reading: for detail<br>• Speaking: interview (role play)<br>• Writing: short personal statement, profile page<br>• Grammar: tenses (review) | **1** TRB, S. 49 |
| **School life in Britain** (SB S. 42) | • fact files (805 words)<br>• British educational system | • Reading: for detail<br>• Speaking: asking and answering questions<br>• Vocabulary: organizing information in a mind map<br>• Grammar: question forms | **2** TRB, S. 57/58<br>**3** TRB, S.59 |
| **Personal statement** (SB S. 44) | • National Record of Achievement text (590 words)<br>• recording achievement, skills and experiences | • Reading: for detail and comparison; transferring information to a grid<br>• Writing: personal statement based on model<br>• Grammar: present perfect (simple, progressive forms) | **4** TRB, S. 60 |
| **Work experience** (SB S. 45) | • work experience (800 words) | • Listening comprehension | **5** TRB, S. 61 |
| **Academic Report** (SB p. 46) | • academic report<br>• recording academic progress | • Reading: for detail<br>• Writing: academic report<br>• Vocabulary: adjectives and verb-noun collocations | |
| **Single-sex education** (SB S. 47) | • photos<br>• provocative statement (24 words)<br>• co-education vs. single-sex schools | • Speaking: describing photos<br>• Project: survey on single-sex education<br>• Vocabulary: adjectives, similes | |
| **Regardless of sex, it's cool to do well** (SB S. 48) | • newspaper article (646 words)<br>• academic success and gender | • Speaking: describing trends<br>• Writing: summary<br>• Vocabulary: synonyms and antonyms | |
| **Them & Us** (SB S. 50) | • passage from a novel (555 words)<br>• teacher-pupil relationships | • Reading for gist and detail; identifying point of view<br>• Writing: list of 'dos' and 'don'ts' for pupils and teachers<br>• Grammar: reported speech | |
| **Fettes college** (SB S. 52) | • brochure extracts (160 words)<br>• independent schools | • Reading: for detail<br>• Speaking: telephoning (asking and giving information); discussing private education<br>• Vocabulary: phrases for telephoning, school subjects, activities and facilities | **6** TRB, S. 62 |
| **IT revolution ...** (SB S. 54) | • illustration/ key terms<br>• role of information | • Reading: for gist and detail; guessing new words<br>• Writing: listing pros and cons<br>• Vocabulary: computer terms | |
| **Laptop to oust books** (SB S. 55) | • newspaper article (254 words) | • Reading: for detail<br>• Writing/speaking: your view on the electronic classroom | |
| **Project: A new centre of learning** (SB S. 55) | | | |
| **Test: Real Life U** | • magazine article (365 words) | | **7** TRB, S. 63 |

47

# 3 Making the grade

## Introduction

The focus of this chapter is education in Britain, in particular education and training opportunities for young people after the age of 16. Throughout the chapter, pupils are encouraged to compare the opportunities provided in Britain with those of their own country, and to reflect on their personal achievements and educational/career goals.
While the US educational system is not included in the Student's Book, teachers may wish to ask pupils to do their own research in order to make comparisons. (Information on the US system is provided in the TRB.)

Topical and controversial issues are covered, such as single-sex education and gender differences in academic success. The importance of constructive teacher-pupil relationships is also explored.
Although the great majority of British pupils attend state schools, the aspect of independent schools has been included because of their importance in British society.
The last section deals with the increasingly important but controversial role of computer technology in education. The project 'A new centre of learning' rounds off the chapter.

## Education: What's the point? SB p. 40–41

[ *i* ] The Central College of Commerce in Glasgow is a college which offers vocational and academic courses for students aged 16 and over, and is therefore similar to the type of college students attend in Germany.

**Analysing language & illustrations**

1.

| key words | what they mean | how they relate to my education |
|---|---|---|
| ambition | desire to become rich, successful or powerful | my determination to work hard |
| career | working life | choosing my career path |
| direction | where one is heading | discovering what I enjoy/my talents, esp. in terms of my career |
| focus | what one concentrates on | specializing in career-related subjects |
| goal | aim or target | success in exams and extra-curricular activities |
| jobs | occupations, types of work | work experience |
| links to universities | connections to universities | Should I go on to university? |
| success | doing well, achievement(s) | getting good qualifications |
| work | what one does for a living, opposite of 'play' | homework, schoolwork, work experience |

2. The signs and compass suggest that the college offers students a number of possible career paths, and that the brochure will point the reader in the right direction.
3. a supportive environment • high quality career and personal development to enhance individual aspirations • reflect local, national and international needs
4. (See 'Project: A new centre of learning', SB, p. 55)

**Collecting words**

A glossary should be in alphabetical order. Relevant and important words can be collected during each lesson on a section of the board or OHP. Each lesson a different student can be given the task of recording words on a transparency, which is then displayed and the words copied down by all students at the end of the lesson. Students can arrange the words in alphabetical order and give English meanings (and German equivalents) for homework.
The following table provides topic-related examples to go with the suggestions in the skills file on p. 133.

| Recording vocabulary | Examples |
|---|---|
| English-German translations | vocational (adj.) – *beruflich* |
| German-English translations | *Verbraucher* – consumer |
| Synonyms or definitions in English | A levels – British university entrance qualifications (= *Abitur*) |
| Giving opposites | compulsory ≠ voluntary |
| Recording in word families | to obey (v.) – obedience (n.) – obedient (adj.) |
| Diagrams | e.g. mind maps, word forks |
| Verb-noun collocations | to carry out a survey, to tackle a problem, to do training |
| Adjective-noun collocations | a bright student, a light task |
| Words in context | We played football on a muddy pitch. |
| Uncountable nouns | no 'a'/'an' with: training, information, advice, … |

**Making the grade** 3

→ Suggest how you might record the following words from the article "The new Brits: single, stoned and selfish" on p. 24. stoned (in heading) • to be divorced (Col. 1, l. 3) • trade union (Col. 1, l. 7) • to be made up of (Col. 1, l. 21) • marital (Col. 1, l. 26) • consumer consultancy (Col. 1, l. 40/41) • to downgrade (Col. 2, l. 2/3) • chunk (Col. 2, l. 5) • leisure pursuits (Col. 2, l. 24) • to tumble (Col. 2, l. 41) • scarcely (Col. 2, l. 43)

*Further activities (group work):*
→ Find out whether your own college has a mission statement. If it has one, translate it into English. If not, devise one together!
Useful vocabulary: Our aim is to provide … • Our mission is to offer … • Our goal is to create … • a supportive environment • opportunities (for) … • a positive learning atmosphere • to give encouragement/guidance/support • to enhance/ to improve/to achieve • high quality/excellence • to have aspirations • to achieve an ambition/objective/goal/aim

→ Design a cover for a school brochure. Create a logo and a motto for your school. Brainstorm for keywords that express the goals, strengths, special features and general atmosphere of your school, and decide how to present them in a visual form. Bear in mind that your aim is to market your school, so make the cover as appealing as possible. *(See also 'Project', SB, p. 55.)*

**Class opinion**

● *It is important that class has an overview of the class ranking in order to contest it. To ensure this, follow these steps:*
*1. Appoint a student (S 1) to write the statements on the board while the other students are working in pairs. (Or use an OHP.)*
*2. After the pairs have agreed on their top five, they read out their choices and S 1 puts strokes next to the statements as they are mentioned.*
*3. S 1 numbers statements according to their popularity.*
*4. The class as a whole reviews the ranking, and tries to find consensus on a new 'top five'.*

**16+** SB p. 41

[*i*] *Like the Central College of Commerce in Glasgow, Eastbourne College of Arts and Technology is also a college which offers vocational and academic courses for 16+ students.*

→ Reading comprehension tasks:
Which student …
1. … praised the college's atmosphere?
*(= Richard – humorous, relaxed, informal, supportive)*
2. … discovered the importance of independent learning?
*(= Carla)*
3. … praised the college's equipment?
*(= Claire Hafernik – "printing facilities … particularly good")*
Which two students …
1. … are doing/have done science or technology courses?
*(= Richard and Carla)*
2. … have completed their courses at ECAT?
*(= Claire and Carla – they don't use the present tense)*
3. … found their courses demanding?
*(= Claire and Carla – both use the term 'challenge')*

→ Tenses: Look at the tenses each student uses and say what this tells you about when they studied at ECAT:

*Claire uses the simple past tense because her one-year course is over. Although she hasn't yet started studying again, some time has elapsed since she was at ECAT.*
*Richard is still studying and uses the simple present tense to describe general truths about his course.*
*Carla uses the present perfect tense, which suggests she has only just finished her studies. Perhaps she is still waiting for her A Level results.*

**Role play**

*Ask S to deal with each part of the interview in groups. Ask them to come up with suggestions for greeting the interviewer/ answering the interviewer's questions, etc. After each section, list the results on the board and then discuss which of the solutions would be most appropriate in this situation. (Pay attention to whether the solutions are polite enough/too abrupt/rude/etc.) Give S the following tips (board or OHP):*
• Use the simple past tense to talk about events that happened in a time now past. ("Which school did you go to before you came to ECAT?" "I went to …")
• Use the present perfect to talk about states/actions that happened in the past and have an effect on the present, or continue up to the present. ("So far I've found the courses really useful." "I think I've made the right decision.")
• Use the going to future to talk about plans, intentions and decisions already made. ("I'm going to do a degree course at the University of …")
• Use the will future/future progressive to talk about predictions/ expectations ("I'll do/be doing my military service in Bochum.")

*A model dialogue (copymaster 1), which can be copied and handed out to S is provided on p. 56 of this TRB.*

**Over to you**

*S use material practised so far in the chapter to complete this task.*

**School life in Britain** SB p. 42–43

*See the information boxes (copymaster 2) on TRB, pp. 57 & 58 giving details of the education systems in Britain and the US. These tables can also be used as solution to copymaster 3.*

**Collecting information**

*See mind map on CD-ROM.*
*S work in groups and find information to go with one category only. These can then be combined in a mind map via OHP.*

*1. Possible categories which should/could appear in the mind map: School subjects • extra-curricular activities • National Curriculum • examinations • post-16 qualifications • types of schools • further education colleges • independent schools • the school year/school day • vocational training • work experience • careers guidance*
*2. –*

**Fact finding & making questions**

*1./2. a)/b) These tasks introduce students to the idea of dealing with texts on their own.*

49

# 3 Making the grade

→ S design a multiple choice test or quiz cards using this information, which can be used for revision purposes.
E.g. GCSE stands for: a) Government College of Supplementary Education; b) Government Certificate of School Education; c) General Certificate of Secondary Education.

*Copymaster 3*: TRB, p. 59/CD-ROM
Solution: Copymaster 2, TRB, p. 57 & 58
S focus on identifying key differences rather than giving detailed information. The grid can be used as a structure for group presentations, each member of the group dealing with a different country or aspect.

## Records of achievement    SB p. 44–46

**CC:1/8 CD1:13 Personal statement**    SB p. 44–45

[i] The National Record of Achievement (NRA) was launched by the Government in 1991. Recording achievement is now an established part of pre- and post-16 education and training. It provides a national format for summarizing achievements in education, training and personal life, and aims to motivate individuals and encourage their further development. An individual's NRA consists of:
• Personal details: name, date of birth, address, brief summary of education and training history.
• Personal statement (updated each year): own view of your achievements to date and plans for the future.
• Qualifications and credits: Vocational and academic qualifications, or credits towards them, certificates.
• Achievements and experience: Summary of achievements, experience and interests, other than qualifications; for example, hobbies, voluntary work and youth clubs.
• Individual action plan: To help plan the next stage of one's development and take the steps needed to achieve one's goals.
• Employment history: Up-to-date record of full-time employment history, including part-time jobs or work placements.
• Continuation sheet: To record additional achievements or plans, or as extra space to add to any one of the sheets.

### Comprehension & comparison

*Copymaster 4*: TRB, p. 60/CD-ROM

Especially with large classes S can be given the personal data sheet (Copymaster; see above) on which they note down their answers. Discuss answers in pairs or small groups.
The answers/worksheet provide a basis for the S's own 'personal statement' (see 'Over to you', p. 45).
(Only the answers to a) are given. b) answers will be individual per S.)

1. a) four – A level subjects: History, English Literature, Sociology, General Studies
b) –
2. a) Ross finds the style of study more enjoyable. It is more thorough ("the more in-depth detail l. 13"), and involves more discussion. It has also improved his study skills (critical analysis, writing essays, conducting primary research and constructing arguments based on evidence, ll. 12–17).
b) –
3. a) He has learnt to work independently, and only ask his teacher for advice occasionally.
b) –
4. a) Ross went on work experience at the School of History at Birmingham University for a week at the end of Year Ten.
b) –
5. a) (as table, see SB p. 45)
**extra-curricular activities:** organizing charity events, e.g. Talent Contest; regular performances in concerts and revues at college
**other hobbies and interest:** music (has studied the clarinet, now plays the bass guitar); plays gigs in a local band; collects CDs and records (especially from the 60s and 70s); enjoys reading about the pop culture of the 60s; going out and spending time with friends; travelling and learning about other cultures; sport (football, cricket and swimming)
b) –
6. Ross is planning to go to university to study History.
7. –

### Grammar

1. a) "have been studying" (l. 8) = present perfect progressive, "have found" (l. 10) = present perfect
b) The tenses tell us that Ross is still studying the books he mentions.
2. a) –
b) Lynne and Helen have been learning German for three years.
c) Simon has been in a band since last summer.
d) Celine has been doing work experience/has been working in a retail store since Monday.

### Over to you

Draw attention to phrases in the personal statement that S can use. For example:
At present I am studying …; I enjoy … . This is because …; My (name of subject) course involves …; I find (that) these topics …/I have found …; I am also looking forward to …; The skill of … developed in … has been very useful in …; I have learned how to …; Because of my love of …, I hope to …; My other subjects have allowed me to … which I find extremely useful in my … studies.; At the end of … I spent … week's/weeks' work experience at …; I did …/I particularly enjoyed. …; During the week(s) I discovered …; As well as my studies, I …; As a hobby, I …/I am also an avid …/I also enjoy …; Through this, I have learned …; I consider myself well-suited to …

→ S can write a CV based on their personal statement.
See 'Skills file: Writing a CV' on SB, p. 138.
Discuss similarities and differences between a personal statement and a CV. Encourage S to give details about any work experience they may have had, including 'after-school' jobs and voluntary work.

### Listening comprehension    SB p. 45

*Copymaster 5*: TRB, p. 61/CD-ROM
Solutions: TRB, p. 137

**CC:1/4 CD:27 Work experience** (Transcript)

*Introduction:* Listen to a student at Rowan High School in London, talking about her work experience.

"I worked for a menswear company which has many shops around England, but most of the shops are in central London. My work experience took place in the store in Regent Street. This shop is the newest. It opened in January and is doing very well. As yet it is the only one like it in the country, but plans are being made for two more stores to open in Manchester and Glasgow. The shop is very big and very modern. A lot of money was spent designing and making it.

The night before my first day was very nerve-wracking. I couldn't sleep. I kept thinking of the people who I was going to work with. Would they like me? Would I get along with them? I didn't know what to think. The next morning I woke up really early. I set my alarm for 7.00 am and woke up at 6.30 am. I was just lying in bed for half an hour thinking about work and hoping everything would go smoothly.

I had seen the shop before I started, but only briefly from the outside. My expectations were very high of the actual shop, but when I went in and actually looked around I realised that the shop was really nice. It was big and I knew that I would enjoy working there. My first impressions of the people were good too. They all seemed really friendly.

My duties were basically what the other sales staff did, which was to make sure the shop always looked at its best, serving customers and stocking up. During the two weeks I did many things. Every day I had to do general duties. Sometimes I had to get altered suits from different branches. One time I went to the bank to cash in takings from the weekend. Sometimes I had to stock up new stock which had come in. One day a woman from Germany, who was a window dresser, came in and I helped her get the clothes and dress the windows.

I enjoyed working in the shop. But I never realised how hard it is being on the other side of the shop floor as a salesperson. Standing up all day isn't easy. I think that was the toughest part. Every night when I came home, I felt as though my legs would drop off. I liked the atmosphere of the shop though. Everyone was kind. And I liked working as part of a team. If anyone needed help someone would always be there. Meeting new people was fun, too. So many different types of people came into the shop. It was great.

The people I was working with were brilliant. I soon got to know everyone. I can't say everyone was perfect. There were one or two exceptions, but that's all part of the experience. You can't get along with everyone.

Everything went smoothly. Actually, one day, when we were not that busy I went downstairs where the suits and formal wear are. I went behind the cash desk and was asking one of the salesmen what all the funny buttons were. I think after a while he got fed up with me and wasn't paying much attention. There were two red buttons and as I asked him what they were, I pressed one. When he came around and saw what I had pressed he told me they were the panic buttons and the message went straight to the police station. I ran to the manager and told him. He was in a state. He ran to ring the police. When he came back he asked me if I'd pressed them both together. I said no. Thank God I hadn't pressed them both together or the police would have come straight away. I was really sorry and so scared. How could I have been so silly?

The one thing that quite surprised me was the money I made for the company. In the two weeks I was there I made £ 2,652, which I am proud of as I had no previous experience whatsoever. I sold most upstairs in the casual section.

I think I made a good impression as everyone got along with me fine. My report had mostly excellents on it and I have been asked to go back and do a Saturday job. I'm definitely going to take them up on the offer. Overall I had a brilliant time. I'm glad the staff liked me as much as I liked them. On the last day they stayed after work, got me chocolates and opened a bottle of champagne. I took pictures. I can't wait to go back."

*Staff and students of Rowan High School*

## Academic report SB p. 46

*If S ask whether Balvinder is a boy or a girl, ask them to say what they think, and explain why. (See also SB, p. 48, 'Looking at stereotypes', task 2.)*

### Comprehension & analysis

*1. Strengths: shows promise, is bright, capable, enthusiastic and pleasant. Weaknesses: does not prepare enough for exams.*
*2. a) Balvinder's report contains fairly detailed handwritten comments and advice. Information is given about Balvinder's potential, progress and attitude to work. Percentages are listed instead of grades. No class average is given. Balvinder is addressed directly and informally ("Bal, you have shown ...")*
*b) –*
*c) An employer may find the comments on Balvinder's character and attitude to work useful, even though they are subjective. A German-style school report is more objective, but only allows employers to see the academic standards reached.*

### Language

*1. a) Exam results: disappointing, superficial (knowledge).*
*Course work: encouraging, developing (understanding).*
*Contributions in class: valuable.*
*Type of student: enthusiastic, bright, capable, a pleasure to teach.*
*b) –*
*2. **to be** a little disappointing • **to improve** on the knowledge • **to make** an enthusiastic start • **to show** an understanding • **to keep up** your reading • **to prepare** tests • **to maintain** progress • **to show** enthusiasm • **to be** a bright and capable student*

### Over to you

*This task not only requires S to make use of the adjectives and verb-noun collocations in the text, but also encourages them to reflect on their personal strengths and weaknesses, and what they need to do to improve their performance.*
*As an alternative S chooses three other students to be their 'teachers', who then write information about them.*

## Single-sex education SB p. 47–49

### Talking about the photos.

→ *Before S answer the question "Do you prefer to work in single-sex or mixed groups", ask them to describe situations:*
• *where they have to work in single sex groups (e.g. certain sports).*
• *where they choose to work in single-sex groups.*
*To help S compare the atmosphere in each photo, the T can list pairs of opposite adjectives, e.g. competitive/cooperative, friendly/aggressive, noisy/quiet, disciplined/chaotic, playful/studious, easily distracted/focused. S decide which adjective goes best with which picture. (See 'Skills file' on SB, p. 130.)*

### Your view

*1. –*
*2. Possible reasons for: Different learning styles require different teaching styles. It is impossible for teachers to cater to the different needs of boys and girls, and this is impossible in mixed classes.*

# 3 Making the grade

*Statistics show that girls in particular do better in single-sex schools than in co-educational schools.*
*Possible reasons against: The statement over-generalizes, and is even misleading. Some girls benefit from tough discipline, and some boys respond better to gentle encouragement. The gender differences described may simply be due to conditioning, and single-sex schools perpetuate this. Once S leave school, they will have to work together. The sooner they learn, the better.*

**Language**

1. –
2. On the board, write the pattern (simile + relative clause) for S to copy and complete: "Boys are like _____ who _____ . Girls are like _____, who _____ ."
If necessary, suggest they start by using animals (rats, mice, sheep, wolves).

→ Ask S to explain the difference between similes and metaphors, or refer them to the glossary on pp. 152 & 153. Then have them write metaphors illustrating the difference between boys and girls.

**Class survey**

1.–6. (See 'Skills files', SB, pp. 140 & 141.) Alternative to all groups conducting similar surveys and present similar results: T divides the class into four 'research teams'. Each team tailors its questionnaire to one of the following target groups: teachers • • the general public • a partner school in Britain or America. Each group presents their findings, and the class then discusses reasons for differences in opinion between the target groups.

## Performance and achievement SB p. 48

**Looking at stereotypes**

1. Alternative: Write the following sentences (or similar) on the board (or dictate them) and ask S to complete them with 'boys' or 'girls'. Encourage S to give examples to justify their opinions.
" _____ are better at maths and science subjects."
" _____ are better at languages and humanities."
" _____ read more than _____ ."
" _____ are much better behaved in class than _____ ."
" _____ are more interested in sports than _____ "
2. Balvinder is a girl. The subjects she takes and the tone in which teachers write about her are influenced by this.

**Looking at charts**

1. Academic standards have shown an overall improvement, except in the case of English where standards have fallen for both boys and girls since 1994. Girls tend to do better than boys, especially in English, where the gap between boys' and girls' achievements has widened slightly. On the other hand, girls do only marginally better than boys in Maths and Science.
2. Possible reasons why overall standards have risen: the introduction of the National Curriculum • improvements in teaching methods • national league tables of schools' exam results
Possible reasons for the widening gap between boys' and girls' achievements in English: neurological differences predisposing boys to science subjects and girls to languages • boys at that age read less than girls for pleasure • teachers fail to take boys' interests into account in the choice of reading texts

→ S collect a set of current statistics on the ratio of boys to girls in various classes or courses at their college and examine the reasons for any strong imbalances, i.e. classes where there are hardly any girls/boys.

CC:1/9
CD1:20 **Regardless of sex, ...** SB p. 48–49

**Language**

1. a) Girls are <u>getting better results in examinations.</u>
b) At GCSE and A level, girls <u>have caught up in the subjects</u> of maths and physics, <u>which used to be considered the domain of boys.</u>/<u>girls are now competing successfully with boys in the formerly male-dominated subjects</u> of maths and physics.
c) The Qualifications and Curriculum Authority is preparing <u>a collection of material</u> for teachers to be sent out in the New Year <u>that will encourage boys to take more interest in English/that takes the special interests of boys into account/that will give English a greater appeal to boys.</u>
d) (...) there are still plenty of under-achieving girls who <u>go on to have children without any clear goals in life or employable skills.</u>
2. to win ≠ to lose • to do better ≠ to do worse • realistic ≠ fanciful • to borrow ≠ to lend • employment ≠ unemployment
3. certainly = no doubt, surely • level = standard • all at the same time = simultaneously • reports = case studies, accounts • the answer = one of the keys, the solution

**Summarizing**

1. The text is about differences in achievement and perfomance at school by girls and boys, the reasons for this and possible solutions.
2. (ll. 1–5) Girls are achieving higher results at all levels and catching up with boys.
(ll. 6–10) In a recent assessment of 14 year-old pupils, more girls than boys reached the expected standards in a wide range of subjects.
(ll. 11–15) Even in A level maths & physics girls are as good as boys. The problem of boys achievement must be tackled if government targets are to be reached.
(ll. 16–19) Part of the problem is that jobs requiring muscle power are disappearing and nothing can change that.
(ll. 20–22) Unlike boys, girls have always had a number of jobs at once, at home and employers like this.
(ll. 23–26) Boys also generally like reading less and read less than girls.
(ll. 27–29) Schools can help by choosing books that boys are interested in.
(ll. 30–38) The Qualifications and Curriculum Authority is going to send information to teachers about the type of material boys might prefer reading and writing about, e.g. non-fiction, football reports, etc.
(ll. 39–44) Things should not go too much in the this direction as this would be a disadvantage to girls. There are still many girls who leave school to become unqualified mothers. And it would not help boys improve in other areas, e.g. relationships.
(ll. 45–50) Schools are doing various things to improve the situation, e.g. short-term goals, extra help for weak pupils, better discipline and motivation.
(ll. 51–52) Both boys and girls need better teaching.
3. a) See the solution to c). The solution to task 1. can be used as an introduction.
b) –
c) The text is about differences in achievement and performance at school by girls and boys, the reasons for this and possible solutions.

*To begin with we learn that girls are achieving higher results at all levels and catching up with boys. For example, in a recent assessment of 14 year-old pupils more girls than boys reached the expected standards in a wide range of subjects. Furthermore, even in A level maths and physics girls are as good as boys.*

*Boys also generally like reading less than girls because they are not interested in the topics. So, the Qualifications and Curriculum Authority is going to send information to teachers about the type of material boys might prefer reading and writing about. Undoubtedly the problem of boys achievement must be tackled if government targets are to be reached.*

*One reason for boys' underachievement is the changing workplace. 'Male' jobs requiring physical strength are disappearing. In addition, girls have always had to do a number of jobs at once, at home and today this is often useful in the workplace.*

*Nevertheless, there are still many girls who leave school unqualified. And boys also need to improve in other 'female' areas. Judith Judd points out that schools are doing various things to improve the situation, e.g. short-term goals, extra help for weak pupils, better discipline and motivation.*

*In conclusion, she says that both boys and girls need better teaching, regardless of sex. (238 words)*

## CC:1/10 CD1:28 Them & Us          SB p. 50–51

[i] The English novelist, Evelyn Waugh (1903–66) published *Decline and Fall* in 1928. It is a satire on life in a boys' preparatory school (a private junior school) and was hugely successful. His other early novels, all social satires, include *Vile Bodies* (1930), *A Handful of Dust* (1934), and *Scoop* (1938). His later works were influenced by his conversion to Roman Catholicism in 1930. They include *Brideshead Revisited* (1945), *The Loved One* (1948), and his trilogy *Men at Arms* (1952), *Officers* (1955), and *Unconditional Surrender* (1961) based on his wartime experiences.

### Understanding & analysing the text

*The aims of these tasks are guided comprehension (1.), use of quotations to support arguments (2.), recognition of key points in literary texts (3).*

1. a) When Paul went into the classroom, the ten boys he was to teach were waiting for him expectantly. They started to greet him one by one until he told them to stop.
b) The crying was prompted by Paul telling the boys to "shut up". The other boys claim this is because of the boy's "Welsh blood" which makes him emotional and easily hurt.
c) When Paul asked for their names, several of the boys claimed to be called Tangent.
d) Paul bribed the boys by offering them half a crown for the longest essay and threatening to cane them.
2. a) False: Grimes told Paul not to try to teach them anything at first. ("Oh, I shouldn't try to teach them anything, not just yet, anyway. Just keep them quiet." (l. 3))
b) False: Paul was terrified by the prospect of his first lesson. He was "in panic" (l. 2) when he asked Grimes what he should teach the boys, and "dumb with terror" (l. 7) when he went into his classroom.
c) False: Paul later began to feel very warm, because of the way the boys were treating him ("He felt himself getting hot and red under their scrutiny." (ll. 24/25))
d) False: When Grimes came in, the classroom went quiet for a moment. ("… Grimes came in. There was a slight hush." (l. 43))
e) True. ("There will be half a crown … merit." (ll. 52/53))

3. a) The pupils start off being cheeky and lively. By the end, they are working in silence.
b) The turning point in the pupils' behaviour is when Grimes enters the classroom and gives Paul a walking stick. (And then again when Paul offers them money.)
c) Possible answer: Grimes intervenes at the right moment, just when the situation is getting out of control. Rather than taking over, which would undermine Paul's authority in the class and cause him to lose face, Grimes offers support in the form of the walking stick and a piece of useful advice. (The walking stick can be interpreted either as a theatrical gesture to shock the pupils into behaving, or as a real weapon for caning the boys.)

### Use of language

1. (Pupils should explain why the language is inappropriate, or suggest an alternative.)
- "Oh, shut up," (l. 14) More formal and polite would be: "Be quiet, please."
- "I suppose the first thing I ought to do is get your names clear." (l. 26) Paul comes across as too unsure of himself. He should ask the question in a more straightforward way, e.g. "Could you tell me your names, please?"
- "I don't care a damn …" (l. 47). 'Damn' is a swearword.
- "Then I shall very nearly kill you with this stick." It is unwise for teachers to threaten pupils with violence, even in fun.
2. –
3. Possible answer: It is important for teachers and pupils to use appropriate language with each other in order to create an atmosphere of mutual trust and respect.

### Grammar: Reported speech

*I went into the classroom and all the boys were sitting there and staring at me. Then each of them wanted me to say good morning to them individually, and in the end I told them to shut up. But then one boy started to cry and the others shouted out that I'd hurt his feelings because he was so sensitive. They said it was his Welsh blood; it made people very emotional. They even told me to say 'Good morning' to him or he wouldn't be happy all day. One serious-looking boy even suggested that perhaps he had been smoking cigars and didn't feel well. When I asked what their names were, three boys claimed that they were Tangent. So I asked if there was anyone who wasn't Tangent and four or five said they weren't. And then they all started fighting each other. It was terrible. Luckily Grimes arrived at that moment and gave me a stick and advised me to set them something to do. When he had gone I told the boys that I didn't care a damn what they were called, but if there was another word from anyone I would keep them all in that afternoon. Clutterbuck said that I couldn't keep him in because he was going for a walk with Captain Grimes. But I replied that I would very nearly kill them with my stick. I ordered them to write an essay on 'Self-indulgence' and promised a prize of half a crown for the longest essay, irrespective of any possible merit. From then on all was silence until break.*

### Your view

*Remind S that the emphasis is on improving pupil/teacher relationships, not creating a list of classroom rules. The task can be used as an opportunity to revise imperative forms (and modals expressing obligation/prohibition:*

# 3 Making the grade

- 'Dos': Always … Remember to … should, ought to, must, is/are to
- 'Don'ts': Never …, should not, ought not to, must not, is/are not (allowed) to

*S can also produce a humorous 'Code of Conduct', e.g. "Teachers should always speak to students in monotonous voice, so that students have the opportunity to fall asleep." "Pupils should always be late for lessons so that teachers have more time to prepare."*

**Text analysis**

*The story is told by a third-person narrator with the limited point of view of the protagonist, Paul. The narrator tells us what Paul sees, e.g.: "Paul watched him amble … " (l. 6), and feels, e.g.: "Paul felt himself getting hot and red under their scrutiny" (ll. 24/25); "Paul felt desperate." (l. 36).*

→ Write about a difficult situation between teachers and pupils. IIf you write about a true experience, you can change the names. You can write a sketch and act it out to the class or an account.
Possible scenarios: a student who always comes to class late; a teacher treats a student unfairly in a test; a student who is always talking out of turn, etc.

## Independent schools     SB p. 52–53

[i] Independent schools continue to be important in Britain as an alternative to state schools for those who can afford them. Academic results at independent schools, especially at A level, are generally higher and the number of students from independent schools who go on to University and particularly to Oxford and Cambridge is still disproportionately high. As a (logical) consequence, a disproportionately high number of top management and important political positions in Britain are held by people who once attended private schools. *(See also table on TRB. p. 57.)*

## Fettes College     SB p. 52–53

***Further information*** *about Fettes college can be obtained at the website address on SB, p. 53 or by writing to the school at the following address: Fettes College, Carrington Road, Edinburgh, EH4 1QX*
***Vocabulary:*** *See 'Additional tasks', task 1. below.*
***Additional annotations:*** *Accounting – Rechnungswesen; Young Enterprise – projects aimed at giving pupils a taste of what is involved in founding a company. Pottery – Töpfern; Netball – ball game played primarily by girls with some similarities to basketball; Public speaking – Rhetorik*

→ **Additional tasks**

1. Vocabulary: make an English/German vocabulary list of all the words given in the boxes. (see also 'Additional annotations' above)
2. a) Tony Blair, the British Prime Minister went to Fettes. Which subjects do you think he might have studied in the sixth form?
b) Judging by the subjects on offer, what other kinds of jobs do you think Fettesians may go on to do? Name the professions and the subjects that go with them.
3. Compare your college with Fettes College. Compare:
a) the number of students in the sixth form at Fettes and those studying for Abitur at your college.
b) the subjects taught to sixth form exam level at Fettes and those taught to the same level (Abitur) at your college.
c) the extra-curricular activities offered at Fettes and at your college.
d) the facilities at Fettes and at your college.
4. Judging by the information given, would you consider going to a school like Fettes if there was one in Germany:
a) as a paying student?
b) on a scholarship (i.e. without having to pay)?
Give reasons.

**Making a phone call**

*The task combines comprehension and practise in asking questions. T may want to revise indirect questions forms beforehand, for example: "Could you tell me how many …?" "I would like to know whether …" "I'd be interested to know why …"
S should first complete the task orally. If possible, S should work in pairs sitting back to back: this is an effective way of simulating the situation of not being able to see the person you are speaking to. If possible, if your college has an internal phone system, practise the conversation by telephone!*

📄 *A model dialogue (copymaster 6), which can be copied and handed out to S is provided on p. 62 of this TRB.*

→ Phrase book for phone calls:
a) Ask S to pick out expressions and phrases in the text which are useful for telephoning.
b) S suggest further alternatives of their own.
c) S list additional useful phrases in German and suggest English equivalents.
*The following headings could be given:*
- Offering help
*(Can I help you?/I'd be pleased to send you …/May I help you?/Would you like me to …?)*
- Expressing regret that you cannot help
*(I'm afraid …/Unfortunately, …)*
- Responding to 'Thank you'
*(You're welcome./Don't mention it./Not at all/My pleasure.)*
- Asking a caller to wait
*(Would you hold the line please?/Would you mind waiting a moment, please?)*
- Telling a caller she/he is about to be connected
*(I'll put you through./I'm just connecting you.)*
- Checking understanding:
*(Sorry, I didn't quite catch that./Did you say …?/Could you repeat that, please?)*
*S should add to their phrase book whenever they come across new phrases.*

## Talking about the photos     SB p. 53

Pupils at Fettes College:
*A very close look will show that the girls are wearing tartan skirts. (One can assume that girls are not allowed to wear trousers.) Judging by the photo boys have to wear trousers (not jeans), jackets and ties. The differences in the boys' jackets could indicate the year group or the house the students are in.*
Fettesians playing rugby:
*A rugby ball is very similar to an American football (i.e. it is oval). There are 15 members in a team. The game has some similarities with American football. However, the players do not wear lots of padding, protection or helmets. The aim of the game is to score*

Making the grade **3**

tries (like touchdowns) and conversions/goals between H shaped posts.

→ Write a letter or an e-mail to Fettes College requesting additional information. (Postal address: See Fettes College, Further information, TRB, p. 54. Internet addresses:
Fettes College website: http://www.fettes.co.uk
E-mail address: postmasteratfettesedin.sch.uk

→ With a partner practise a telephone call in which a student from a British college calls your school asking for information for a project on vocational colleges in Germany.

### Your view

Task 1 parts a) and b) should be completed in writing as preparation task in No. 2.
1. Possible advantages: wide range of facilities • parents can choose a school that meets the special needs and interests of the child • exclusivity (children are with the 'right' social class) • boarding facilities • possibly a better education and/or more sheltered environment than at the local comprehensive
Possible disadvantages: expense • socially divisive (children have less opportunity to mix with other social classes) • perpetuates snobbery • children at private schools are given an 'unfair advantage' over children of state schools • private schools drain resources (e.g. good teachers) away from the state system
2. Before the discussion divide the class into groups according to the opinions given in task 1. Group 1 = S who would prefer to go to a private school/who think private education should be available to those who can afford and want it; Group 2 = S who prefer to go to state school/who think that fee-paying schools are not justified. If necessary allocate pupils to group 1 or 2 in order to create a balance of opinions. Each group discusses further arguments before the duscussion with the opposite group begins.

→ After the discussion, list arguments on the board/OHP and discuss them with the aim of finding a class consensus.

→ Find out about opportunities for private education in Germany (e.g. Salem) and write a short article comparing the role of private education in Germany and in Britain.

## Schools of the future    SB p. 54–55

### IT revolution in the classroom    SB p. 54

Further information on IT in education can be found at the Department of Education website: http://www.dfee.gov.uk

### Your view

• S give own opinions, which will vary from college to college. In general schools in Britain are currently better equipped with computers, etc. than schools in Germany and S should consider the consequences of this in terms of their education and future careers.

### Comprehension

a) home-based learning: learning at home via PC/Internet
b) live links: direct communication on-line, e.g. being able to listen to university lectures or take part in seminars
c) paper-free learning: learning using software or material from the Internet instead of books, and by writing and sending assignments to teachers on disk or per e-mail, without needing to print anything out.
d) palm-top computer: computer small enough to hold in your palm (Handfläche)
e) virtual access: enables you to communicate via Internet/video-conferencing with someone as if you were speaking to them face-to-face

### Laptop to oust books    SB p. 55

### Comprehension

1. Books and the blackboard will no longer be necessary. They will be replaced/ousted by computers.
2. Each S will have his/her own computer. Teachers will have access to them via a main computer and be able to concentrate on them individually. Instead of having to use reference books when setting course material, teachers will have access to data banks on the Internet.
3. S will be able to work at their own speed, not that set by the teacher. They will be able to e-mail their work to their teacher to be marked/checked, or have it marked by their own computer. They will be able to do research using the Internet. Their home PC can be linked to the class computer, so if they are ill at home – but still able to work – they can continue to take part in lessons.
4. S are able to work more independently – at their own speed, checking their work without always having to rely on a teacher to do so. Teachers can receive pupils' (home)work online, reducing the need for paper. Both pupils and teachers have easier access to material needed for research purposes. Pupils can continue working even if they cannot go to school.

### Your view

Positive aspects: Work at own pace • less dependence on the teacher • less waste of paper • easy access to Internet for research purposes • good preparation for use of technology at work • learning can be done at home, if necessary • etc.
Negative aspects: Computers do not (yet) offer value for money (costs outweigh benefits) • over-dependence on technology is dangerous: computers often malfunction, health problems due to bad posture, possible side-effects from electro-magnetic radiation, eye strain, headaches • S will suffer from lack of human contact • S will be denied the learning benefits of group activities • etc.

→ Write a report on the the use of computers and IT at your college which should include the following aspects:
Number of computers with/without Internet access at your college • who can/does use computers (staff/students/subjects) • what they are used for (secretarial work/projects/research/fun) • school home page? • your opinion

### Project: A new centre of learning    SB p. 55

Additional suggestions for project work: TRB, pp. 5–7 and 'Skills file', SB, p. 139.

### Test: Real Life U

Copymaster **7**: TRB, p. 63/CD-ROM (exercises/questions)
Solutions: TRB, p. 137, vocabulary: TRB, p. 142.

# 16+ Role play

Making the grade 3

## Model answer (SB, p. 41)

INTERVIEWER AND STUDENT (AT MORE OR LESS THE SAME TIME): How d'you do?/Pleased to meet you.
INTERVIEWER: Do sit down.
STUDENT: Thank you.
INTERVIEWER: Right, well it says here that your name is … Is that right?
STUDENT: That's right. (or: No, actually it's … . )
INTERVIEWER: Good. (or: Oh, I am sorry. I'll just correct that.) Well, let's get started, shall we? I'd like to ask you a few questions that can be included in our next college brochure. But before we begin, would you mind if I recorded the interview?
STUDENT: No, go ahead. That's fine by me.
INTERVIEWER: And do you think you could provide us with a photo to use in the brochure?
STUDENT: Yes, of course. What size photo do you need?
INTERVIEWER: Oh, just a passport photo.
STUDENT: OK and would you prefer colour or black and white?
INTERVIEWER: It's a colour brochure, so colour would be nice, but black and white would do.
STUDENT: I'll see what I can find. I can bring one tomorrow if you like.
INTERVIEWER: Thanks, that would be great. Right, first I'd like to know a bit about your education: Which school did you go to before you came to ECAT?"
STUDENT: I went to … (name of school).
INTERVIEWER: And what do you think of the college courses here?
STUDENT: Well, so far I've found them really interesting and useful, and everything is very well-organized.
INTERVIEWER: Well, that's nice to hear. And what about the lecturers?
STUDENT: They seem very competent, and also very friendly and approachable.
INTERVIEWER: So you're satisfied with the college on the whole, are you?
STUDENT: Yes, I'm really glad I chose to come here. I had my doubts at first, but now I'm sure that it was the right decision.
INTERVIEWER: Well, I'm very pleased to hear that! Now, I'd like to move on to your plans for the future. Have you decided what you want to do when you leave college yet?
STUDENT: Yes, I'm going to … /I'll be …-ing …
INTERVIEWER: Right, well, that's all of my questions. Is there anything you'd like to ask me?
STUDENT: No, not really. (or: Yes. When will the brochure be coming out?)
INTERVIEWER: (It should be out by the end of October, I hope.) Well, thank you for coming to the interview.
STUDENT: My pleasure! Thank you for inviting me!
INTERVIEWER: Goodbye.
STUDENT: Goodbye!

# The school systems in Britain & America (1/2) — Making the grade 3

|  | **Great Britain** | **United States** |
|---|---|---|
| **School day** | Usually from 9 am to 3/or 4 pm.<br>Classes are never cancelled. If teachers are ill, either other members of the staff 'cover', or 'supply teachers' stand in for them. | Usually from approx. 7.30 am to 3/4 pm. Classes are never cancelled. If a teacher is absent a 'substitute teacher' is called in. The majority of students take part in extracurricular activities (e.g. school sports teams) after school. |
| **Years of compulsory education** | Age: 5–16 years | Age: 5–16 years. In practice most students leave high school at the age of 17 or 18. |
| **Curriculum** | The National Curriculum sets down the subjects to be taught during four 'key stages', and the standards to be achieved at each stage. | Schools are the responsibility of the state and local governments or school boards. Each state sets its own requirements. The school boards, which oversee the schools in their districts, establish curricula that fulfill these requirements. |
| **Types of schools** | Publicly funded **state schools** are attended by over 90% of pupils.<br>Years 1–6 (ages 5–11) = infant/junior schools.<br>**Secondary schools**<br>**Comprehensive schools** Years 7–11/13 (ages 11–16/18) = majority of secondary schools; all ability entry; usually some mixed ability and some streamed teaching.<br>**Grammar schools** Years 7–11/13 (ages 11–16/18) = still exist in some counties (mostly with conservative local authorities); admission by selective test at end of junior school (11+ exam).<br>**Further education colleges** Years 11–13 (16+)<br>For students and adults who have completed compulsory education and who wish to continue their education but not attend a school sixth form. Further education colleges offer a range of academic, vocational and day release courses usually lasting approximately two years.<br>**Private schools**<br>= fee-charging schools; attended by about 7% of pupils. Also known as 'independent' and 'public' schools (see below). Many private schools are **boarding schools** (*Internat*), or combined day/boarding schools. Independent schools claim to have the highest academic standards. Some of the larger independent schools are known for historical reasons as public schools. Famous schools are Eton and Harrow, which have a long tradition of preparing pupils academically for higher education, typically at the universities of Oxford and Cambridge. | Around 90% of students attend state-run neighbourhood **public high schools**. The most common form is the **comprehensive high school**, which includes mostly general academic courses but also some commercial, trade, and technical subjects. There are also **specialized schools**, e.g. agricultural schools, business or commercial schools, trade or vocational schools and **schools** which focus on the arts. **Private high schools** (fee-paying and/or grant-aided) offer primarily academic courses to college-oriented students. Private schools with religious affiliations are known as **parochial schools.** Most of the students attending public and private schools are college and/or university bound. |
| **School qualifications** | **GCSEs** (General Certificate of Secondary Education): certificate awarded at the end of year 11 (Key Stage Four of the National Curriculum). Pupils take GCSEs in English, Maths, Science and between three and seven other subjects. Final results are based 20% on course work and 80% on examination performance. The exams are set centrally. They take place in May/June, and results come out in late August. Grades awarded are: A, B, C (= Good pass), D, E, F, G (= Pass) and U (= Fail).<br>**GCE 'A' Levels** (General Certificate of Advanced Education): These courses normally involve two years' study (years 12 & 13). Students generally take two or three subjects only. Assessment is by centralized examination at the end of the course. GCSEs in five subjects and a minimum of two A Levels are the standard university entry requirements. | Students usually graduate from high school when they have finished 12th grade at the age of 17/18 with the **High School Diploma**. This is awarded according to a combination of 'credits' from coursework and grades achieved in exams. In some cases students must also complete a special project or do community work before they can graduate. It is the basic requirement for entry to university or further education, though students are usually required to take additional tests and/or entrance exams. |

# The school systems in Britain & America (2/2) — Making the grade 3

| | Great Britain | United States |
|---|---|---|
| **Vocational training** | There is no statutory vocational training in Britain. Both students and employers can choose programmes which suit their requirements and interests if they wish. There are government-sponsored training schemes for the young and especially the unemployed but the government does not provide any direct training for people in work. | Vocational training and education is available on a voluntary co-operative basis between schools and employers. In some high schools students can opt to take part in programs which involve spending time on practical experience in a work environment. |
| **Vocational and other qualifications** | There is a wide range of vocational qualifications, e.g.: **NVQ** (National Vocational Qualification) vocational equivalent to a basic GCSE pass. **GNVQ** (General National Vocational Qualification) vocational equivalent to an A level. **BTEC** (Business and Technology Education Council), **RSA** (Royal Society of Arts) **City & Guilds** equivalent to an A level in a business field **HNC** (Higher National Certificate) vocational qualification equivalent to the GCSEs **HND** (Higher National Diploma) vocational qualification equivalent to A level. | In addition to the high school diploma, most students who wish to apply to university take standardized tests like the **SAT** (Scholastic Aptitude Test). This is a test written by an independent central organization. It is taken on set dates in the US or abroad and students pay a fee to take it. Universities often set a minimum score that students must achieve in order to be accepted to study. |
| **Higher education** | All higher education institutions are now known as **universities**. There are universities in most larger towns. Some are more academically oriented (the traditional and older universities) some are more vocationally oriented or specialize in certain fields of study. The two most famous universities in England are **Oxford** and **Cambridge**. Entry requirements for university vary according to the institution (Oxford and Cambridge have their own entrance exam), the course of study and the prospective student. The most basic entry requirement is a minimum of five good GCSE passes and two A levels. Students on a first degree course are called **undergraduates**. Undergraduate degree courses usually last 3–4 years. | Academic post-high school institutions are called **universities** and **colleges**. The most prestigious and famous US universities are together known as the **ivy-league universities**, and these include Yale, Harvard, Princeton, the Massachusetts Institute of Technology, Stanford and the University of Chicago, Illinois. Entry requirements to universities vary according to the institution, and sometimes also according to the course of study the student wishes to pursue. The basic entry requirements are the high school diploma, a certain gradepoint average (the average of the grades earned in high school), and a certain SAT score. Other common requirements can include the completion of entrance essays, proof of involvement in extracurricular activities and/or community service, and entrance interviews. **Community colleges** offer two-year degree courses for students who have successfully completed 12th grade at high school. These students may end their studies after two years, or they can choose to continue at a four-year university or college. |
| **Higher education qualifications** | At the end of a university course usually lasting between 3 and 4 years students graduate and are awarded a degree: **BA** (Bachelor of Arts); **BSc** (Bachelor of Science), **BEd** (Bachelor of Education), etc. Post-graduate qualifications include **PGCEs** (Post graduate certificate in education, a teaching qualification for graduates); 'Masters' degrees (**MA, MSc**, etc.) and 'doctorates' (**PhD**). | **Associate's Degree**: after successful completion of a two-year college course. **University or College Degree**: after successful completion of a university course. After four to five years, students generally earn a bachelor's degree (**BA** = Bachelor of Arts, **BS** = Bachelor of Science). Higher degrees include 'Masters' degrees (**MA, MS**, etc.) and 'doctorates' (**PhD**). |

# Educational systems

*Making the grade* 3

|  | Great Britain | United States | Germany |
|---|---|---|---|
| **School day** |  |  |  |
| **Years of compulsory education** |  |  |  |
| **Centralization and national government control** |  |  |  |
| **Types of schools** |  |  |  |
| **Exams** |  |  |  |
| **Qualifications** |  |  |  |
| **Vocational training** |  |  |  |

# Personal data sheet

**Personal details:**

Name:  
Marital status:  
Telephone number:  

Date and place of birth:  
Nationality:  
E-mail:  

**Name of school:**

Subjects:


Personal skills developed during my studies so far:


Relevance of these skills to my future career:


**Other skills I would like to learn:**


**Work experience:**


**Extra-curricular activities:**


**Other hobbies and interests:**


**Future plans:**

**Listening comprehension**  Making the grade 3

# Work experience

**expectation** [ˌekspekˈteɪʃn] *Erwartung*
**to stock up** *here:* to resupply the shop with items that are running out
**altered suit** [ˈɔːltəd] a suit that has been fitted to a customer
**branch** *here: Zweigstelle*

**takings** money made
**window dresser** person who decorates shop windows
**cash desk** *Kasse*
**manager** *Filialleiter(in)*

Listen to the text and give the information about the student's work experience in note form.

Employer/type and location of company: _____

Length of stay: _____

Feelings before starting work: _____

First impressions: _____

Normal duties: _____

Additional duties: _____

Good points of the job: _____

Bad points of the job: _____

Achievements: _____

Listen to the text again and complete the sentences.

1. She was in the suits department because _____

2. She pressed one of the red buttons, so _____

3. When she told the manager, he _____

4. If she had pressed both of the buttons, _____

## Vocabulary

Match the expressions from the text on the left with their synonyms or definitions on the right.

1. nerve-wracking
2. to go smoothly
3. briefly
4. altered
5. tough
6. to be in a state
7. previous
8. casual

a) to panic or be agitated
b) opposite of formal
c) former, last
d) hard, difficult
e) fitted
f) causing anxiety
g) to run without problems
h) for a short time

## Writing a letter

After listening to the student talk about her experience, you decide to apply for a placement at the same company. Write a suitable letter to the employer in which you inquire about the position. Remember to mention how you heard about this placement, why you would like to work for this company, and why you would be suitable for the job.

Klettbuch 510511 – *Challenge 21, Teacher's book*
© Ernst Klett Verlag GmbH, Stuttgart 2001.

# Making a phone call

Making the grade 3

## Model answer (SB, pp. 52–53)

| | |
|---|---|
| SECRETARY: | Good morning, Fettes College. Can I help you? |
| YOU: | Yes, my name is … .I'm calling from … in Germany and was wondering whether you could give me some information on your school. It's for a school project we're doing on independent schools. |
| SECRETARY: | You need to speak to Andrew Norton, our PR manager. Would you hold the line, please? I'll put you through. |
| ANDREW NORTON: | Good morning, can I help you? |
| YOU: | Yes, my name is … .I'm calling from … in Germany and was wondering whether you could give me some information on your school. It's for a school project we're doing on independent schools. |
| ANDREW NORTON: | What exactly would you like to know? |
| YOU: | Well, first of all, could you tell me what your fees are, please? |
| ANDREW NORTON: | That depends on whether you are a full boarder, a weekly boarder or a day pupil. |
| YOU: | What's the difference between a full and a weekly boarder? |
| ANDREW NORTON: | As a full boarder you stay at the college all term and only go home in the holidays. Weekly boarders, on the other hand, can go home at weekends. |
| YOU: | I see. And how much are the fees for full and weekly boarders? |
| ANDREW NORTON: | Full boarding costs are between £3,245 and £4, 735, and weekly boarding costs are from £3,205 to £4,690, including meals and all activities, of course. |
| YOU: | Thank you. I'd like to know how many pupils there are at your school, too. |
| ANDREW NORTON: | At the moment we have 375 full boarders; that's 228 boys and 147 girls, and we have 103 day pupils; that's 56 boys and 57 girls. |
| YOU: | And what about in the Sixth Form? |
| ANDREW NORTON: | At the moment we have 99 boys and 78 girls in the sixth form. |
| YOU: | Right. Thanks. I'm studying … and …… at the moment. Can students at Fettes study these subjects as well? |
| ANDREW NORTON: | Yes, we teach a full range of subjects including … and … <br> Well, we do teach … but I'm afraid we don't teach … <br> No, I'm afraid we don't teach those subjects but we do offer … (similar subjects). |
| YOU: | Thank you. I'd also like to find out more about the kind of sports activities that you offer, if you don't mind. |
| ANDREW NORTON: | At Fettes we are very lucky to have excellent sporting facilities. We have athletics, badminton, cricket, fencing, lacrosse, sailing, you name it, so you can really do any sports from canoeing to shooting. |
| YOU: | That sounds brilliant. I'm also very interested in computers and new technology, so I was wondering what sort of opportunities there are in this area. |
| ANDREW NORTON: | New technology is very important nowadays in all areas of life: at school, at work and at home. Here at Fettes, we have a CDT centre, we run extra curricular activities in computers and IT, and of course there are courses to up A level in Design and Technology. |
| YOU: | Well, that's all I wanted to ask you. Thank you very much for your help, Mr Norton. |
| ANDREW NORTON: | You're welcome. I'd be pleased to send you a school brochure if you'd like to give me your name and address. |
| YOU: | Yes, of course. It's (…). |
| ANDREW NORTON: | Sorry, I didn't quite catch that. Could you spell your name for me, please? |
| YOU: | (…) |
| ANDREW NORTON: | Thanks very much. And don't forget, we also have a school website on the Internet. The URL is fettesedin.sch.uk |
| YOU: | That'll be very useful. Thanks once again for all your help, Mr Norton. Goodbye! |
| ANDREW NORTON: | Goodbye! |

# Real Life U

When Elizabeth, 17, leaves school, she is going to work at Disney World. "I've never been interested in college. I want to try out for a musical group and dance. And why go to college when you can get a job doing something you really love?"

It's easy to think Elizabeth is the only one asking that question. Wherever you turn, it seems, the message is deafening: About eighty percent of high school seniors plan to attend college in the fall. Enrolment is at an all-time high and growing. Competition to get into the best schools is tougher than ever; American students are told they must have a college education if they expect to succeed in the 21st century. And yet, though college can, of course, be a wonderful and valuable experience, it isn't for everyone. A closer look at statistics from the U.S. Department of Education reveals a startling fact: While most high school seniors say they intend to go to college, in 1998 only about 37 percent of 18-to 24-year-olds were pursuing an associate or bachelor's degree. In other words, more than half of the people in the age group had either decided not to go to school or had taken time off. […]

Even if your heart isn't set on a particular dream like Elizabeth's, you may find that there's another decision you can make about college: putting it off. In fact, skipping or postponing another four years of school may even be a wise decision. "I think we're wasting (a college education) on kids," says Rae Siporin, director of undergraduate admissions at UCLA, where enrolment is skyrocketing.

"Many of them are great students, and they've done an incredible job of preparation. But they're much more interested in what this degree is going to get them than they are in getting on a lifelong path of broadening their minds. They all ought to go into the military or do community service or God knows what and become more mature. Some of the best students have done exactly that and have come back. At that point they know what they want. They are committed. They just want to get at it and learn." (365 words)

*From "Real Life U" by Sean Smith, Seventeen Magazine, February 2000.*

## Content
1. To what extent is Elizabeth typical of American high school seniors?
2. What evidence is given that shows that American high school students change their minds about a college education?
3. Describe Rae Siporin's view of his students.

*(Your teacher will tell you which of the following tasks you should complete.)*

## Comment
1. "They must have a college education if they expect to succeed in the 21st century." (ll. 10–12)
   Say whether you agree or disagree with the statement, and explain why.
2. "They all ought to go into the military or do community service or God knows what and become more mature." (ll. 32–33)
   Discuss the pros and cons of compulsory military or community service, both for those having to do it, and for society as a whole.
3. Imagine: *either* a) You are going to meet Elizabeth's parents and you have to defend her decision. What would you say to them?
   *or* b) You want to persuade Elizabeth to go to college. What would you tell her?

## Form
1. What techniques have been used in this text to convince the reader that it is justified for young people to decide either not to go to college or to postpone going?
2. What other techniques does the author use to engage the interest of his audience?

## Language
1. Replace the underlined participles with relative clauses.
   a) "… when you can get a job doing something you really love?" (l. 4)
   b) "… Elizabeth is the only one asking that question." (ll. 5–6)
2. Give the opposite of the following words.
   a) tougher (l. 10)   b) reveal (l. 15)   c) skyrocketing (l. 27)   d) mature (l. 33)
3. Explain the following expressions.
   a) "Wherever you turn, it seems, the message is deafening." (ll. 6–7)
   b) "Enrolment is at an all-time high …." (l. 8)
   c) "… a startling fact." (l. 15)
   d) "… of broadening their minds." (l. 31)
4. Copy and complete the table.

|    | Verb       | Noun        | Adjective |
|----|------------|-------------|-----------|
| a) |            | competition |           |
| b) | to succeed |             |           |
| c) |            |             | valuable  |
| d) |            |             | committed |

# 4 Meet Britain's press

## Didaktisches Inhaltsverzeichnis

| Title | Text type/Topic | Skills & Tasks | 💿📄 |
|---|---|---|---|
| **Meet the press** (SB S. 56) | • quiz (183 words) • facts and statistics about the press | • Grammar: gerund/-ing forms/tenses | |
| **Mail on Sunday …** (SB S. 58/59) | • newspaper article (202 words) • sales figures and facts | • Speaking: giving a presentation • Vocabulary: qualifiers, comparative forms | **1** TRB, S. 73 |
| **News coverage in quality and popular papers** (SB S. 59) | • front pages of newspapers | • Speaking: comparing and analyzing elements • Vocabulary: comparing and analyzing language and writing styles | |
| **Mystery of crash …/ 7 minutes from safety** (SB S. 60–62) | • newspaper articles (552/571 words) • plane crash | • Writing: comparing styles of journalism; devising headlines and articles. | **2** TRB, S. 74 |
| **Top Ten Stories** (most popular articles) (SB S. 63) | • newspaper article (212 words) | • Reading: for gist; finding main ideas • Vocabulary: categorizing information under key terms | |
| **Paparazzi!** (SB S. 63) | • photos • freedom of the press | • Speaking/Writing: giving an opinion; researching | |
| **Headline News** (SB S. 64) | • song (497 words) | • Listening: content analysis • Discussion: Right to privacy or right to know? | **3** TRB, S. 75–76 |
| **A journalist's day** (SB S. 66) | • report (729 words) • work of a journalist | • Reading: analyzing the text • Writing: translation; analyzing style • Vocabulary: working with key terms | |
| **Working on a regional newspaper** (SB S. 67) | • interview (1550 words) • work of an editor | • Listening comprehension | **4** TRB, S. 77 |
| **Further assignments/** (SB S. 68) | • tasks | • Writing: writing a feature • Research: contacting British schools; finding out about newspapers; comparing newspapers | |
| **Project: A comparative study of British newspapers** (SB S. 68) | | | |
| **Glossary** (SB S. 69) | • glossary (592 words) • cartoon | • Vocabulary: using a glossary | |
| **Test: Talking in Whispers** | • novel excerpt (324 words) • freedom of the press | | **5** TRB, S. 78 |

# Meet Britain's press 4

## Einleitung

*Mit diesem Kapitel sollen drei Dinge inhaltlich geleistet werden:*
*a) Die S sollen einen Überblick erhalten über die wichtigsten britischen Tages- und Wochenzeitungen.*
*b) Die Unterschiede zwischen* quality *und* popular papers *sollen deutlich werden, einschließlich der dazugehörigen stilistischen Aspekte.*

*c) Ethische Aspekte bei der Berichterstattung (Paparazzi) sollen am Beispiel eines Songs und dem persönlichen Erfahrungsbericht eines Journalisten thematisiert werden.*
*Das Interview auf TRB, Seite 71 wurde live aufgenommen: etwaiige Unregelmäßigkeiten in den Formulierungen wurden nicht korrigiert!*

---

## Meet the press   SB p. 56–57

[i] The facts and figures published in the multiple choice questions on p. 56 and in the tasks on circulation and readership on p. 57 are taken from information brochures issued by *The Sun* and *The Times* from 1998. (NEWS INTERNATIONAL plc, P.O. Box 495, Virginia Street, London E1 9XY. Telephone: 0044/ 171/7826000). The information can be updated via Internet at the websites given in the chapter.

### Introduction

● *Diese Aufgaben sind geeignet, das Vorwissen der S auf diesem Gebiet zu aktivieren. Die Antworten auf die ersten beiden Fragen werden sicherlich eher oberflächlich ausfallen, dürften aber erste Hinweise auf wesentliche Unterschiede zwischen* quality *und* popular press *enthalten (z. B.: Größe der Überschriften, Auswahl und Größe der Fotos, etc.), ohne dass diese Begriffe hier vertieft werden müssen. Denkbar ist aber auch schon hier die Entwicklung von Kategorien im Unterrichtsgespräch, die auf Folie festgehalten werden können, und auf die im weiteren Verlauf der Unterrichtsreihe zurückgegriffen werden kann.*
*Bei der Beantwortung der dritten Frage dürfte u. a. der föderale Charakter der Bundesrepublik für die vergleichsweise große Bedeutung regionaler Zeitungen als Grund genannt werden.*

### Test yourself   SB, S. 56

*1./2./3. Die Antworten hierzu befinden sich auf S. 64 des SB.*

### Quality and popular press   SB, S. 57

*1. a) Die Antwort auf diese Frage ist eher offen gehalten; bei der Beantwortung sollte aber der Hinweis nicht fehlen, dass die* quality press *eben für Qualität in jeder Hinsicht steht („Nomen est omen"). Der Begriff* popular press *steht dagegen nicht etwa von vornherein für mangelnde Qualität, sondern sagt eher etwas über den Verbreitungsgrad einer Zeitung aus. Die begriffliche (und oft eben auch inhaltliche) Nähe zu 'pop music' könnte in diesem Zusammenhang durchaus erwähnt werden.*
*b) Mögliche Antworten könnten sein:*
Popular press: sensational, subjective, one-sided, manipulating, colourful, eye-catching
Quality press: neutral, objective, informative, investigative
2. Popular: The Sun, The Express, Daily Mail, The Mirror
Quality: Financial Times, The Guardian, The Independent, The Daily Telegraph, The Times
*3. a) Es ist davon auszugehen, dass die meisten S aufgrund der inhaltlichen Gegenüberstellung zu* quality press *entweder auf den deutschen Begriff 'Boulevardzeitung' oder möglicherweise auf die englische 'yellow press' verweisen. Die Frage eröffnet aber auch die Möglichkeit, auf die Etymologie des Begriffs 'tabloid' einzugehen:*

"Tabloid originated as a trade-name for a brand of tablets of condensed medicine […] It was an alteration of tablet […] This originally denoted a 'slab for writing on or inscribing'. Such slabs would have been flat and often quite small, and in the late 16th century the term came to be applied to a 'flat compressed piece of something' – such as soap or medicine. The notion of 'compression' or 'condensation' underlies the use of tabloid for newspapers of small page size and 'condensed' versions of news stories, which emerged at the beginning of the 20th century."
(John Ayto, *Bloomsbury Dictionary of Word Origins*. Bloomsbury, London, 1990, p. 518.)

*b) (Folgende Vorteile könnten genannt werden:)* easy to hold • easy to read and understand • big headlines, not much text (body of the article) • many photographs • aims to entertain more than inform (= infotainment!)
*c) ('Tabloids' gibt es in der Bundesrepublik kaum, und wenn überhaupt, höchstens als Regional- (meist Sonntags-) Ausgaben. Die wichtigste überregionale 'popular newspaper' ist sicherlich die Bild-Zeitung, aber auch die* Bild am Sonntag *oder das* Hamburger Abendblatt *könnten hier genannt werden. Darüber hinaus gibt es natürlich die Vielzahl regional begrenzter Boulevardzeitungen.)*
*4. a) The FT is printed on pink paper. It does not have as many photographs on the front page and shows the headlines of the most important articles in small print under the masthead. It is the only British newspaper that concentrates on one area (namely business and finance). It is famous for the FT-Index, the British equivalent to the American Dow Jones Index and German DAX, which gives information on current dealings on the stock exchange.*
*b) The readership is made up mainly of businessmen, bank employees, brokers and other professionals who work in the 'money market'.*
*c) A German version of The FT is now available. Another comparable publication is the magazine 'Das Capital'.*

### Circulation & readership

[i] *Die* circulation figures *stammen aus den oben erwähnten Veröffentlichungen von* News International *und wurden ergänzt durch statistisches Material der Monatsschrift* Press Gazette. *Aktuellere Zahlen können telefonisch angefordert werden unter 0044/181/5654200.*

→ *Es wäre denkbar, als begleitende oder anschließende Übung einen entsprechenden Vergleich zwischen zwei deutschen Zeitungen vornehmen zu lassen und diesen evtl. in Quizform den Mitschülern zu präsentieren oder von ihnen präsentieren zu lassen.*

1. a) are • b) live • c) is • d) was • e) has been printed • f) bought • g) are written • h) have
*2. (S versuchen Sätze zu schreiben, ohne die gegebenen Prozentzahlen zu verwenden:)*

# 4 Meet Britain's press

a) This newspaper has 10% more male readers than female readers. / Over half of this newspapers readers are men.
b) More than 50% of MPs read this newspaper. More MPs read this paper than any other paper.
c) Almost two thirds of the readers of this newspaper are under 45 years old and almost half are between 15 and 34.
3. a) S könnten diese Frage entweder auf der Grundlage der in Aufgaben 1 & 2 erworbenen Informationen beantworten, oder – besser noch – durch einen unmittelbaren Vergleich von zwei zuvor gekauften Zeitungsexemplaren.
1. a) The Times: professionals and senior managers want to read serious news.
1. b) The Times: A high proportion of management jobs are in London and the S. East.
1. c) The Times: Surprising because you might expect younger people to prefer a less serious paper.
1. d) The Sun: Bingo games are more likely to be found in a tabloid. (Though many quality papers now offer 'sophisticated' lotteries and games.)
1. e) The Times and The Sun: Both papers are national dailies and both are printed in a number of places.
1. f) The Times: Rupert Murdoch owns major newspapers and media concerns around the world.
1 g) The Sun: The Sun runs an Agony Aunt page which attracts large numbers of letters.
1. h) The Times: These people are most likely to go on to senior management.
2. a) The Sun: The Sun is male orientated (sexist) in its news coverage (lots of sensationalism and football), and illustrations (topless pin-ups on the notorious page 3)
2. b) The Times: The Times is THE British quality newspaper with a long tradition and history.
2. c) The Sun: Younger people want infotainment.
b) –

## Over to you

● Diese Umfrage erstellt einen ersten Bezug zu der eigenen Erfahrungswelt der S. Für die Umfrage zu den Lesegewohnheiten sollten S zuerst einen Fragebogen entwickeln. Denkbare zusätzliche Elemente eines Fragebogens könnten sein:
- distinction between dailies and weeklies
- distinction between papers and magazines
- sex, age, number of brothers and sisters
- possible changes in reading habits over the last years
- money spent on papers and magazines, etc.

Die in Teil 2 zu erstellenden Statements sollen die Satzstruktur der Sätze in 'Circulation and readership' widerspiegeln. Z. B.:
53% of the students in this class read a newspaper daily.
Over 80 % of the female students spend more than 20,- DM per month on magazines.
Only 3 people in this class have ever written a letter to a newspaper.

→ Die Umfrage zu einem fächerübergreifenden Projekt erweitern: Die genauen Fragestellungen und Durchführungsmodalitäten in Absprache mit (S und) Kollegen etwa folgender Fächer festlegen: Deutsch, Politik, Religion / Ethik oder auch Wirtschaftslehre. Möglicherweise könnte auch der Mathematikunterricht für die Erstellung von Statistiken mit einbezogen werden.

→ Die Umfrage zu einem interkulturellen Vergleich erweitern, u.a. um den direkten Bezug zum Fach Englisch zu erhöhen, indem hiesige S Studenten an einer Partnerschule / Partnerschulen per Internet / e-mail befragen.

→ In Zusammenarbeit mit einer Partnerschule die Darstellung des eigenen Landes in den Zeitungen des Partnerlandes untersuchen.

## Sales figures  SB p. 58 – 59

### Mail on Sunday climbs ...  SB p. 58

In diesem Text geht es um die Wichtigkeit von Absätzen. Sprachlicher Schwerpunkt ist das Vokabelfeld 'Talking about figures and statistics'.

Kopiervorlage 1: TRB, S. 73 / CD-ROM
Lösungen: TRB, S. 137

Diese Kopiervorlage kann als Einstieg (Vorentlastung) vor dem Lesen des Textes eingesetzt werden, nach Bearbeitung der 'Language'-Aufgabe b) (SB, S. 58) oder zur Festigung nach Bearbeitung des Abschnittes.

### From text to table

S sollen zuerst relevante Informationen aus dem Text notieren und dann erst eine entsprechende Tabelle erstellen. Z. B.:
The Mail on Sunday: 2nd biggest Sunday paper; +5%; has overtaken Sunday Mirror
Sunday Mirror: now overtaken by Mail on Sunday
Daily Mail: catching up with Mirror; difference 21,000; +7%
The Mirror: -3,5 %
The Sun: -5%
Daily Star: -7%
FT: biggest growth of quality dailies
Independent: -11.6%
Independent on Sunday: -8.4%
Sunday Times: highest sales for 16 years

| Biggest gainers | Biggest losers |
|---|---|
| 1. FT | 1. Independent |
| 2. Sunday Times | 2. Independent on Sunday |
| 3. Mail on Sunday | 3. Daily Star |
| 4. Daily Mail | 4. The Sun |
|  | 5. Mirror |
|  | 6. Sunday Mirror |

### Language

Diese Aufgaben dienen als Vorbereitung für die anschließenden Aufgaben 'From table to text' und 'Giving a presentation'. Die Wörter und Redewendungen sollten / könnten von S in einem Glossar zum Thema 'Statistics' festgehalten werden.
a) strange, unusual = freakish (Col. 1, l. 1) • because of = due to (Col. 1, l. 2) • a sudden increase = a jump (Col. 1, l. 3) • has been probable = has been on the cards (Col. 1, ll. 5/6) • selling less and less = in decline (Col. 1, l. 7) • to pass = to overtake (Col. 1, l. 9) • an increase over the last year = a year-on-year rise (Col. 1, ll. 10/11) • the difference between two figures = the gap (Col. 1, l. 14) • a fall = a drop (Col. 2, l. 1) • increase = growth (Col. 2, l. 6) • to have difficulties = to struggle (Col. 2, l. 9) • on the other hand = in contrast (Col. 2, l. 14)
b) Increase: a jump; a rise; growth • Decrease: in decline; less and less; a fall; a drop; • Comparison: to overtake; to pass; the difference; the gap; in contrast; on the other hand

**Meet Britain's press** 4

## From table to text

*S sollen zuerst einfache Sätze anhand der Information in der Tabelle und erst danach Vergleiche mit dem entsprechenden Vokabular erstellen. Z. B.:*
The Daily Telegraph sold 1,081,876 copies daily on average in December 1997. • The Daily Telegraph sold 1,098,440 copies daily on average in the six mths to Dec 1997. • This is a decrease of 16,564 or 1.5% on the average.
The Times sold 783,359 copies daily on average in December 1997. • The Times sold 792,151 copies daily on average in the six mths to December 1997. • This is a decrease of 8,792 or 1.1% on the average.
The Observer sold 407,306 copies daily (Sundays) on average in December 1997. • The Observer sold 439,573 copies daily (Sundays) on average in the six mths to December 1997. • This is a decrease of 32,267 or 7.3% on the average.
The Guardian sold 389,376 copies daily on average in December 1997. • The Guardian sold 403,999 copies daily on average in the six mths to December 1997. • This is a decrease of 14,623 or 3.6% on the average.
Daily sales of the Daily Telegraph are far higher than daily sales of any of the other papers. • Sales of the Observer showed a drop/fall of 7.3% in December. • The gap between the Times and the Daily Telegraph was slightly lower in December than in the last six months. • In contrast, sales of the Guardian declined by over 3.5%. • More than twice as many copies of the Telegraph are sold daily than of the Guardian.

## Giving a presentation

*1./2. Die Lösung dieser Aufgaben hängt von den Fähigkeiten der S ab. Falls die 'Skills file: Giving a talk or presentation' auf S. 129 im SB bislang noch nicht vorgestellt und bearbeitet wurde, wäre dies eine gute Gelegenheit. In jedem Fall könnte aber noch einmal auf die Ergebnispräsentation von der 'Over to you'-Aufgabe von SB, S. 57 zurückgegriffen werden.*
*Für schwächere S wäre es sinnvoll, die qualifiers und comparisons noch einmal als Folie während der Bearbeitung dieser Aufgabe zu präsentieren (s. Kopiervorlage 1).*

## Average sales figures ...    SB p. 59

## Abbreviations

● dy • Mon./Tues./Wed./Thurs./Fri./Sat./Sun. • yr • Jan./Feb./Mar./Apr./May/Jun./Jul./Aug./Sept./Oct./Nov./Dec.

## News coverage ...    SB p. 59–62

*Als Einstieg dient der Vergleich der ersten Seite einer tabloid (The Mirror) und einer quality paper (The Guardian), die abgebildet sind. Der Textinhalt der Berichte ist hier unwichtig. Es geht nur darum zu erkennen, wie die Zeitungen mit bestimmten Nachrichtentypen (sensational news: hier ein Flugzeugabsturz) in Wort und Bild umgehen.*
*Auf den folgenden Seiten (SB, S. 60 & 61) befinden sich Berichte zum Absturz aus den Zeitungen. Der Aufgabenapparat dazu befindet sich auf S. 62.*
*Da die Texte recht lang sind, sollten auf jeden Fall neue Wörter zur Vorentlastung erläutert werden. Das Vorspielen der Texte, die auch stilgerecht aufgenommen wurden, von CD/Kassette ist hier besonders empfehlenswert.*

## Before you read

● *Die Unterschiede zwischen den beiden Zeitungen sind offensichtlich und repräsentativ für popular und quality papers. Selbst wenn den S diese Unterschiede noch nicht bekannt sind, sollten sie in der Lage sein, folgende Aspekte zu benennen:*
a) space on front page:
**The Mirror:** the article covers the whole page.
**The Guardian:** the article is relatively small and certainly doesn't catch your eye.
b) headline (size, style, content)
**The Mirror:** very big (about one third of the page), participle-construction, alliteration, no informative details
**The Guardian:** relatively small, full sentence containing important facts about who and what
c) photos & text
**The Mirror:** about four times as much space for photos as for the body of the article
**The Guardian:** no photos at all

CC: 1/11+2/1
CD1: 29+33    **Mystery ... / 7 Minutes ...**    SB p. 60–61

## Comparing styles of journalism    SB, S. 62

**1. Headlines**
a) The front page headline referring to the crash ('229 die in plane crash') is objective and informative; it gives the most important facts (plane crash, number of dead). The front page headline in The Mirror ('Smashed to smithereens') is pure sensationalism with no attempt to be informative. The headlines of the articles also reflect this trend. (Although the Guardian headline 'Mystery of crash pilot's last message', whilst not being sensationalist, is clearly intended to arouse the reader's interest in finding out what the pilot said.
b) Both headlines are effective in attracting the reader's attention and making them want to find out more. The Mirror headline plays on the readers' emotions, whereas the Guardian headline is more likely to attract more serious readers, who want to find out facts.
**2. Layout**
a) Both newspapers show large photos from the scene of the crash and both also have illustrations showing how/where the crash occurred. However the Mirror also shows photos of the dead pilot and co-pilot as well as of relatives grieving. These aim to attract readers by playing on emotions and exploiting other people's loss (and could be considered to be gratuitous and superfluous). The main headline in the Mirror is in huge bold print followed by a subheading in large bold print, which is also underlined. Subheadings are also used within the article to maintain the readers attention. The Guardian has one main headline (see above). The subheading is in fairly small print and states facts.
b) Both newspapers make good use of the elements – in accordance with their target groups: The Guardian aims at readers who are more interested in learning facts and background. Mirror readers are less interested in facts and more interested in sensational news.
c) The function of these elements is the same in both newspapers: to attract readers.
**3. Use of quotations**
a)/b)
**eye-witnesses**
The Mirror: residents in Blandford • Edie Boyle • Alberta Martin • Darrel Fralick

67

# 4 Meet Britain's press

*The Guardian:* Edie Boyle • Claudia Zinck-Gilroy • Alberta Martin
Bob Gordon, reporter
**officials**
*The Mirror:* airport worker • ground control, Boston • Swissair chief, Brugisser
*The Guardian:* Swissair spokesman
**experts**
*The Mirror:* BA captain, Moody • Swissair pilot, Stuessi
**crew-member**
*The Mirror:* Captain Zimmermann
*The Guardian:* Captain Zimmermann
**relatives**
*The Mirror:* elderly couple • Lidia Picco

c) The Mirror article makes more use of quotations altogether: far more people are quoted than in the article in the Guardian. Both newspapers primarily quote eye-witnesses.

d) In both articles the eye-witness quotations have the effect of making the text more personal and interesting. They bring the news 'to life'. They give the impression of being factual, although in fact most of the quotations are more emotional/sensational. The Mirror article quotes so-called experts and officials, with the intention of making the article seem more serious and well-researched. Quotes from relatives in the Mirror serve no purpose but to play on the emotions of readers.

4. **Language and style**
<u>More factual:</u> The Guardian (lack of persuasive and evocative language). • <u>More persuasive:</u> The Mirror ("heroic battle", Col. 1, l. 3; "doomed airliner", Col. 2, l. 18; weeping relatives are described and interviewed). • <u>More evocative:</u> The Mirror ("... almost made it", caption; "distraught relatives", Col. 1, l. 22; "choking with emotion", Col. 2, l. 13; "had no chance", Col. 3, l. 12; "weeping relatives", Col. 3, l. 31; "she sobbed", Col. 3, l. 42). • <u>More dramatic:</u> The Mirror ("struggled", Col. 1, l. 11; "raced to the shore", Col. 2, ll. 37/38; "slammed", Col. 3, l. 4; "... desperately trying", Col. 3, ll. 5/6; "chances were non-existent", Col. 3, l. 18; "horrendous", Col. 3, l. 23; "... oh my God", Col. 3, l. 37). • <u>More serious:</u> The Guardian ("in difficulty, but not in jeopardy", Col. 1, l. 16; "situation had deteriorated", Col. 1, ll. 32/3; "descended", Col. 1, l. 36; "no indication of crisis", Col. 1, l. 44; "normal emergency procedure", Col. 2, l. 3; "become critical", Col. 2, l. 5; "point of impact", Col. 2, l. 29). • <u>More vivid:</u> The Mirror (more frequent use of quotations; more dramatic and evocative.
*(Selbstverständlich gibt es auch Beispiele in der jeweils anderen Zeitung, die aber im Sinne der Aufgabenstellung hier unerwähnt bleiben.)*

## Over to you

📀 *Kopiervorlage 2 : TRB, S. 74/CD-ROM*

*1./2./3. Diese Aufgaben bieten die Möglichkeit, die erkannten Punkte in den vorangehenden Aufgaben in die Praxis umzusetzen. Man könnte auch ein geeignetes gegenwärtiges Thema aus den Nachrichten für diese Übung verwenden.*
*Bei der Lösung der 3. Aufgabe sollte vor allem auf die in der Aufgabenstellung geforderte Kürze des Artikels Wert gelegt werden. Darüber hinaus sollte darauf geachtet werden, dass die Artikel jeweils einen einleitenden Satz oder Abschnitt haben.*

→ Project: Collect 'news' about events in your school/home/town for a week. Produce a front page of a quality or tabloid newspaper featuring your news. Pay attention to headlines, typefaces, use of illustrations, etc.

## What makes the news? SB S. 63

*In diesem kurzen Abschnitt geht es darum, die verschiedenen Themenkategorien zu erkennen, die international am interessantesten sind und in Zeitungen am häufigsten vorkommen. Insofern ist die Aktualität der Ereignisse nicht von besonderer Bedeutung.*

### Before you read

🖎 Successful stories at international level could include:
stories about world-famous sports events, e.g. the Olympics • stories about the Royal family • stories about international economic crises • stories about wars • stories about environmental disasters, e.g. oil tankers sinking, nuclear power stations leaking radiation • climatic problems: hurricanes, floods, earthquakes, etc.

## Top Ten Stories SB p. 63

### Comprehension

1. The article suggests that creating interesting news for the global market is what Britain is good at (in the same way that the Germans are good at making cars!). Globalisation has affected the news market and the British have "strong, highly competitive media" (Col. 2, l. 3) which are good at making "slick, appealing news for international consumption" (Col. 2, ll. 4/5). Even political news – such as the election of Tony Blair as Prime Minister – was turned into "an interesting parcel of information" (Col. 2, ll. 13/14) and became as attractive as any other product on the market (alcohol, music or cars).
2./3. News item/category: Princess Diana's death/Tragedy/Royal Family • Handing over of Hongkong, British election results/British politics • Cloning of Dolly the sheep, Pathfinder landing on Mars/Science • Murder of Gianni Versace/Crime, Fashion
4. Possible other categories: Sports, local, international, economy and finance, business, arts, environmental, gardening, radio and TV, entertainment, weather, travel, children's page, crosswords, letters to the editor, etc.

### Over to you

*Hier ist es wichtig, dass S möglichst viel miteinander auf Englisch reden! S auf die 'Skills files: Having a discussion' und 'Useful phrases for discussions' auf S. 131 & 132 verweisen.*

→ Project: What makes the news?
Step 1: Agree on the three most important topics currently in the news.
Step 2: Agree how long to follow the coverage of these three topics in the news. (minimum 1 week)
Step 3: Divide class into groups and allocate a particular newspaper or newspapers to each group.
Task: How much importance is placed on the three topics during the agreed period? How does reporting on the topics change during the period?
Step 4: Present your results to the class and discuss similarities, differences and developments and reasons for these.
*(Falls am Wohnort der S englischsprachige Zeitungen nicht erhältlich sind oder von der Schule nicht abonniert werden, könnten die homepages verschiedener Zeitungen (s. SB, S. 64) die Vergleichsgrundlage bieten, wenngleich dies sicherlich nur die zweitbeste Lösung ist.)*

Meet Britain's press 4

## Paparazzi! SB S. 63

*Hier und in dem nachfolgenden Popsong wird das Thema 'Freedom of the press' behandelt. (Das Problem der Verantwortung von Medien insgesamt wird im Kapitel 7 im Zusammenhang mit dem Romanauszug von Ben Elton's 'Popcorn', SB, S. 117 diskutiert.)*
*Mögliche Antworten auf die Fragen zu den Fotos:*
*Judging by the expressions on the faces of the photographers (calm, relaxed) and the way they are grouped together, they are taking photographs of a social or sporting event or an arranged photo-shooting session (rather than an accident, etc.). The photographers could be taking a photograph of a famous sports person/event, a pop star arriving at an airport, a member of the Royal family, a political meeting, e.g. President of the USA and the Prime Minister, etc.*
*Folgende Situationen könnten L auf OHP/Tafel als Anregung für eine Diskussion anschreiben:*
*A famous sportsman is photographed in a club with a woman who is not his partner. • After an accident a victim is shown with his head severed. • Whilst on holiday on a private yacht a famous female pop singer is photographed sunbathing in the nude on deck.*
*Im zweiten Foto heißt es "We are photographers not assassins". Die Aufgabe sollten S in GA oder EA selbstständig mit Hilfe von Archivmaterial (aus dem Internet) erarbeiten und präsentieren.*

## The right to know SB, S. 64–65

**CC:2/2**
**CD2:1 Headline News** SB S. 64–65

*Dies ist ein älteres Lied von Keith Hancock. Die Melodie und Art der Musik ist sicherlich nicht das, was die Mehrheit der heutigen S bevorzugt. Der Text ist jedoch genauso relevant und aktuell wie damals. Die Aufgabenstellung auf S. 65 beginnend mit 'Your view' greift diese Tatsachen auf und führt die Behandlung des Themas fort, das bereits in Kapitel 1 (SB, S. 11 & 12) angesprochen wurde. (Ein Zusammenhang dazu könnte/sollte hier gezogen werden.)*

### Your view

*Bei dieser arbeitsgleichen GA sollen die S die Gelegenheit haben, ihren individuellen Musikgeschmack sowie ihre persönlichen Eindrücke von dem Text und der Musik mit einzubringen. Auch sollten S darüber diskutieren, weshalb Musikrichtungen sich im Laufe der Zeit ändern, und welche Bedeutung Liedtexte haben (s. auch Kapitel 1, SB, S. 11 & 12). Es sollten nicht mehr als vier Gruppen gebildet werden, damit der anschließende Vergleich sinnvoll bleibt. Die S sollten ihre Ergebnisse entweder auf einer Folie, an der flip-chart oder an der Tafel präsentieren. Um eine möglichst lebendige Diskussion zu erhalten, ist es wichtig, darauf zu bestehen, Gründe für die Einschätzung des Liedes zu benennen.*

→ Perform/record the song as a rap. Devise your own rhythm/melody or use the rhythm and melody of a song you know.

### Comprehension

1. According to the songwriter, journalists do the following things:
- give up their ideals (ll. 3/4);
- use up their last energy resources for the sake of getting a story (l. 5)
- kill people (l. 8)
- interview the participants of tragic accidents (ll. 9–11)
- find it more important to get a story than help for seriously injured people (l. 12)
- establish, be responsible for and then ignore mob law (ll. 13–16)
- act in a hypocritical way (ll. 17/18)
- take away the dignity of people (ll. 19–24)
- completely ignore the privacy of people (ll. 26–32);
- eventually lose self-respect (ll. 33–40)

2. The key words could be: greed, irresponsibility, no sympathy, hypocrisy, carelessness

3. a) In verse 1 the songwriter describes the journalist at the beginning of his career and says that he still has ideals and principles. But he warns him that he will become "Just like all the rest".
In verse 5 the journalist has become a successful 'hack'. The song writer wants nothing more to do with him, he has given up all his principles and ideals as predicted and is only interested in making money: "you're just like all the rest".

b) Rhetorical devices used are:
<u>parallelism</u> of the two stanzas as a whole
<u>parallel sentence structure</u>: "So you want to be ... So you want to earn" (ll. 1/2) • "You'll start ... you'll be (ll. 3/4) • "... you'd use ... you'd hunt" (ll. 5/6) • "You're always ... you always" (l. 7) • "You can take ... you can stick" (ll. 34/35) • "You're ... you're" (l. 36) • "Can you look ... can you get" (l. 38)
<u>use of personal pronouns:</u> (you, me, they)
<u>exaggeration:</u> "you'd use your dying breath" (l. 5) • "you'd kill to get a story" (l. 8) • "you never pay your dues" (ll. 39 and 43)
<u>similes:</u> (s. 'Language', Aufgabe 1)
<u>other images/metaphors:</u> "... dust has settled ... leeches are gathering ..." (l. 10) • "... a man lies butchered ..." (l. 19) • "... they've got their claws in you ..." (l. 27) • Can you look into a mirror ..." (ll. 38 and 42)

4. Judging by the tone of the text and the aggressive language used we can safely assume that the songwriter has no respect for sensational journalists and considers them to be leeches on society.

### Language

1. "like all the rest" (l. 4): Right from the beginning the songwriter is convinced that the new journalist will be the same as all other journalists
"like a Nero playing fiddle" (l. 14): He accuses all journalists of falsely accusing people and presenting them as sadistic mass murderers who even enjoy looking at their victims.
"like vultures on a carcass" (l. 22): Journalists are seen as the primitive animals who do not even go hunting themselves but live from left-overs. One could even say that they are accused of body-stripping without any respect for the dead.
"like all the rest" (l. 36): By now the individual journalist has actually become one of the group of "vultures", it is no longer a prediction but a description.

2. The use of similes vividly underlines the songwriter's point of view. Together with other rhetorical means used in this song (personification, exaggeration, repetition, etc.), the similes help to keep the reader's/listener's attention and make the text convincing.

3. For example: The way a journalist searches for news is like a pig digging for food. • A group of photographers trying to get a good picture is like a pack of hyenas surrounding an injured antelope. • Readers of a newspaper when there has been a disaster are like thirsty dogs at the sight of water.

### Explaining words

1. a) hack
b) you will start with good intentions
c) they will make him look guilty

# 4 Meet Britain's press

d) his wife will be abused
e) all that matters is the story
2. Possible answers:
a) you always pay a fair price and don't exploit people
b) the ringing sound or siren which tells the emergency services that there has been an accident
c) to earn money as a freelance (journalist).
d) people need to find out what is going on
e) to make a lot of money, to become very rich
3. Diese Aufgabe kann man beliebig erweitern, z. B. indem S Gegenstände im Klassenzimmer umschreiben, die ihr Partner dann benennen muss. S darauf hinweisen, dass diese 'skill' besonders wichtig ist, wenn man eine Fremdsprache spricht, da man häufig eine genaue Bezeichnung nicht weiß oder vergisst und dann umschreiben muss.

## Using a dictionary

1. Examples: back (part of body); give back (return); back away; answer back; etc.
2. "living off another man's back" / "get right off my back": See p. 135, Col. 2, ll. 5–7: to get off s.o.'s back: to tell s.o. angrily to stop criticizing you or putting pressure on you. So to live off another man's back means to make money by putting someone else unfairly under pressure. And get right off my back means leave me alone and stop criticizing me.
3. You've got your sweatshirt on <u>back to front</u>. • My brother really <u>got my back up</u> last night. • There was a golf course <u>at the back</u> of our hotel.
4. –

## Role play

Die folgenden zusätzlichen oder alternativen Rollen könnte man auch auswählen:
a) A journalist who respects people's right to privacy.
b) An up and coming pop star or film star who is interested in any kind of publicity including details of his/her private life.
c) A famous sportswoman who doesn't want to talk about her private life in an interview
d) A journalist talking to a sportswoman (see c) who is more interested in private matters than sporting achievements.

*Kopiervorlage 3 : TRB, S. 75 & 76 / CD-ROM.*

(Auf den Kopiervorlagen befinden sich role play cards, die für dieses Rollenspiel verwendet werden können.)

→ S write (letter or e-mail) to celebrities, newspapers and/or other organisations or institutions to find out about their opinion and policy on the 'right to know vs. the right to privacy'. The websites given in this chapter may be helpful.

### CC:2/3 CD2:2 A journalist's day        SB S. 66–67

### Before you read

S sollen auf jeden Fall folgende Punkte bedenken, die man an der Tafel/OHP anschreiben könnte:
Working hours? • Time spent away from home/in the office? • Different types of journalism?
Als Vorentlastung/Ergänzung könnte man das 'Glossary: The Press' auf S. 69 anschauen.

## Comprehension

1. The journalists radio pager goes off and he gets a message to ring the newsdesk. The reason is that some news had broken in Oxford and the journalist had to change plans and go there.
2. They are in the office to send out reporters at short notice to important events. They organize all operations.
3. They collect information by telephone; they leave the office during the day to witness and report on important events; they go to criminal courts or press conferences; they must be ready to rush to more important events leaving other jobs unfinished if that is required; they dictate their stories by telephone or send e-mails; they must listen to news bulletins presented in other media.
4. He feels guilty because he cannot keep the promise he obviously gave to his wife to join her at a banquet.
5. He gives the impression that it is a very professionally run newspaper. The journalist is proud of working for The Daily Telegraph. He speaks very positively about the paper and is even willing to sacrifice important private obligations if he is called to do an important job.

## Your view

Possible reasons for preferring short-term work: more variation in everyday work • meet a lot more people • avoid a lot of news-desk work • spend almost all of every day out of the office.
Possible reasons for preferring long-term work: get the more important jobs • have more responsibility • do in-depth research • become an expert in certain fields.

## Vocabulary

1. newsdesk (l. 4); reporter (l. 7) • quality newspaper (l. 8) • daily coverage of news (l. 9) • newspaper (l. 12) • journalist (l. 16) • news-room (l. 21) • press conference (l. 27) • headlines (l. 28); publishing (l. 41) • copy-taker (l. 46) • articles (l. 50) • sub-editor (l. 50) • edition (l. 51) • front-page (l. 52) • news bulletins (l. 57) • foreign editor (l. 62)
2. Unbedingt spätestens an dieser Stelle das 'Glossary: The Press' auf SB, S. 69 anschauen. Die 'Vocabulary'-Aufgaben auf S. 69 könnten ebenfalls an dieser Stelle gemacht werden.
*Copy-taker:* a person who writes down dictated texts. • *Foreign editor:* the editor who is responsible for foreign or "overseas" news. • *Correspondent:* a journalist who is – often permanently – stationed in an other town or even country to work for the paper. • *Freelance journalist:* a journalist who is not employed by one newspaper or agency, but who writes for and sells his articles to various newspapers or agencies. • *Publisher:* the owner of a newspaper. • *Sub-editor:* the person who edits the articles written by reporters and who gives them headlines.

## Translation

Beim Journalismus gibt es, wie in den meisten Berufen, tägliche Pflichten. Beim Telegraph gehören dazu die Überwachung der Nachrichtenbulletins aus Radio und Fernsehen, sowie die Zusammenstellung jener kurzen aber genau gelesenen Listen von Ernennungen zu Militärgeistlichen, Testamenten und den parlamentarischen Veranstaltungen der bevorstehenden Woche. Falls der Reporter, der gerade ausführlich auf die Karrierepläne von Pfarrern auf dem Lande eingeht, auch darauf brennt, zu Aufgaben gerufen zu werden, die herausfordernder sind, so liegt es daran, dass diese Aussicht allgegenwärtig ist.
An einem freien Tag klingelte mein Telefon zu Hause. Der Auslandsredakteur wollte wissen, ob es irgendwelche zwingenden

# Meet Britain's press 4

*Gründe gäbe, eine sofortige Reise mit der Königlichen Marine in den Golf nicht anzutreten.*
*Ich schaute schuldbewusst auf den Smoking auf der gegenüberliegenden Seite des Zimmers, den ich vor nur einer Stunde ausgeliehen hatte, um an einem Bankett teilzunehmen, zu dem meine Frau aus beruflichen Gründen eingeladen worden war, und sagte: „Selbstverständlich nicht".*

## Analyzing style

*1. In the objective passages the author describes the daily work of journalists and gives examples (ll. 19–39, 43–56). The subjective passages contain evaluative statements about the paper he works for (ll. 40–43), personal opinions about the radio pager (l. 14) or events related to his private life (ll. 66/67).*
*2. He uses a narrative style (ll. 1–6, 63–67), but most of the text is descriptive.*

## Listening comprehension          SB S. 67

*Kopiervorlage 4: TRB, S. 77 / CD-ROM*
*Lösungen: TRB, S. 137*

CC:1/5
CD:37  **Working on a regional newspaper** (Transcript)

CHALLENGE: Morning Roz, nice to meet you and thank you for giving me time today to speak to you about the regional press.
ROZ DODD (ROZ): A pleasure.
CHALLENGE: So the Birmingham Post is a paper for the Birmingham area?
ROZ: It's for the Birmingham area primarily but, we also have a lot of readers in the outlying areas. So the counties around Birmingham; Warwickshire, Worcestershire, Herefordshire, Shropshire, Staffordshire.
CHALLENGE: So it's actually quite a big region that this newspaper covers?
ROZ: It is, we do actually cover a very, very large region, yes.
CHALLENGE: Is that typical of a regional newspaper would you say, or regional newspapers do they tend to be for a smaller area?
ROZ: Some do, I mean, it does vary, but I think a lot of the regional newspapers that are based in a big city do tend to also appeal to people who live perhaps in the Shires surrounding the city and who come into working the city, so they still want to know what's going on in the city.
CHALLENGE: And do you only cover the regional news, or do you also cover national and international events as well?
ROZ: The actual paper covers both local, national and international news, but as far as the journalists who work on it are concerned, we tend to sort of concentrate on obviously the local news.
CHALLENGE: I see. Where do you get your national news from then?
ROZ: We get it from agencies. We rely very heavily on the press association for our national news, and Reuters for our international news.
CHALLENGE: I see, and you have people here that go out then for the regional news in Birmingham and around Birmingham?
ROZ: Yes, we have quite a big group of reporters who sort of, are out and about yes, and relying on their contacts, and various things. Obviously, there will be times when national stories break, and they happen to have a local slant or something very big will happen in Birmingham that the nationals are also interested in.

\* \* \*

CHALLENGE: That would be quite interesting to know as well, who is, who are you aiming at then, who is the readership of the Post, for example?
ROZ: Well, we very much aim at the business community and we have a very strong business section. We often have a lot of business coverage. So basically we are very business orientated. However it's not just the business community, we aim at sort of young professionals and we know that a lot of our readership are sort of older people, we're trying to sort of draw in a few more younger people as I say, sort of.
CHALLENGE: From what you're saying it's probably more male orientated, and a slightly older readership?
ROZ: Yes, I suppose so, but we are, that has been changing in recent years. The fact that I'm women's editor we tend to get quite a bit of sort of quite a few features in the paper that appeal to women and also younger people. We've taken on quite a few younger writers who sort of you know get a few funkier articles in so, we're trying to broaden it more than it has been over some of years.
CHALLENGE: What kind of thing do you think that younger people are interested in?
ROZ: Well, I think they want to know what's happening in Birmingham you know, where it's at. Clubs and that sort of thing. They don't just want to know what the CBSO are doing at Symphony Hall, you know, they want to know a bit more than that.

\* \* \*

CHALLENGE: Can I ask you a few things about your working day? What time do you start, what is a typical working day for you?
ROZ: I actually work very nice hours, 10:00 til 6:00 roughly, so that means that you don't have to get up too early, and at six-o-clock you've still got your evening, it doesn't sort of eat into your evening too much. Obviously if a story breaks, and 'cause I write features rather than stories, but if a big story breaks, and they need a feature to go with it, you know, it's part of the job that you stay on and do it you know. You don't say oh well I'm sorry it's time to clock off now. So it's um, and the hours are, as I say, they're fine. So, when I come in I mean like most people, I open my post, a lot of it will be press releases sent out by PR companies, I have to say, a lot of which goes straight in the bin. It's just blatant advertising, and it's not very interesting. Occasionally somebody will write to me saying I've got this very interesting friend, who's just climbed up Everest you know, with one leg, or whatever it might be, I think she'd make a great feature and then of course, there are press releases that are telling you about an event that's coming up which you think, ooh yes that might make a good feature and whatever, so as I say, a lot of the post goes in the bin but, some of it's useful. Then I have to basically, write at least a feature a day. So that means I've got to have thought up an idea, I mean sometimes obviously, my features editor or the editor will come up with an idea.
CHALLENGE: Do you actually, you work on your own, or do you work in a team do you?
ROZ: No, I really work on my own. So, we don't have a womens page as such, it's just a feature page which is headed 'Aspects', I'm the women's editor and a lot of people say to me, "You know, in today's, the way things are today why do you need a women's editor?", it's actually quite a sexist thing, isn't it, you know? They're trying to say. And I think actually it will start dying out. I think that sort of within the next ten years there won't be such a thing really, because, yes there is a sort of …
CHALLENGE: There's a stigma about it really isn't there? …
ROZ: Yes, there is. But having said that, I defend it by saying that there are still a lot of women's issues that I think might not be covered in newspapers, if there wasn't a women's editor to do them.
CHALLENGE: What kind of things do you actually cover?
ROZ: Well, I tend to do, I don't do, we have a fashion and lifestyle editor so I don't do fashion and beauty, I don't do anything like that.

# 4 Meet Britain's press

CHALLENGE: I was going to say, people tend to think of women, and think immediately of fashion so …
ROZ: No I don't do that. I tend to sort of cover issues so I mean, that could be anything from stalking or rape through to breast cancer or women in the boardroom, or you know, fast track promotion for women, whatever, anything that's sort of obviously a womens issue. But, then I will also interview personalities, so, and in fact, I often interview a lot of men so, again, it sort of doesn't mean …
CHALLENGE: Men that are supposed to be interesting for women?
ROZ:: Yes, a lot of men are interesting to women.

\* \* \*

CHALLENGE: Actually, what qualifications do you need for this kind of a job?
ROZ: You need really, I mean, it used to be the case that you'd, you know you'd leave school at sixteen and you'd be the tea-boy, and then you'd get into it, of course, with all sorts, that doesn't happen now. Not just in journalism but, in every profession. You only need A-Levels, I think, but again, increasingly, as with all professions, most people who come into it are graduates.
CHALLENGE: Graduates in what? Is that graduates in journalism?
ROZ: You can graduate in anything but, you then have to go on and either join a newspaper, an in-house training scheme, some papers, we have a s… we have one. We have one, and where I trained on the "Express and Star" in Wolverhampton, which is another big regional paper, they had their own in-house training scheme, which I was lucky enough to get on. So, instead of having to leave university and go to another university to do a year's post graduate in journalism, post graduate scheme in journalism, I was lucky enough to get onto a very intensive five months training course whereby, you end up with the same qualification. And then I've taken what is called the Journalism's Proficiency Test, so I have my Proficiency Test, once you've got that you're then classed as a senior reporter. You can still work before you've taken your Proficiency Test, you've got to have gone through some level of training. So, you're a trainee, then you become a senior reporter and then, some people want to stay in the news reporting, some people want to go to sport, some people want to go to business writing and some people want to do features.
CHALLENGE: Is that what you've always wanted to do, features?
ROZ: Yes, yes, yes.

*Interview with Roz Dodd, The Birmingham Post.*

### Further assignments  SB, S. 68

*Diese zusätzlichen Aufgaben sind alle als Projektarbeiten zu betrachten, die in EA aber besser noch in PA oder GA gemacht werden können. L (oder S) können entscheiden, welche / wie viele der Aufgaben gemacht werden sollen.*

#### Writing a feature

Kopiervorlage **2** : TRB, S. 74 / CD-ROM

● *S sollen besonders auf einen passenden Schreibstil achten. Wenn möglich, englische Teen-Zeitschriften (zumindest im Internet) anschauen, um Ideen und Impulse zu bekommen.*

#### Finding out about British teenagers

*S auf 'Skills file: Letter writing' (SB, S.136 & 137) und 'Skills file: Questionnaires & surveys' (SB, S. 140 & 141) verweisen so wie auf die 'Over to you'-Aufgabe auf SB, S. 57.*

### Looking at on-line editions

● *Die angegebenen websites sind:*
www. independent.co.uk – *The Independent (national, daily)*
www.standard.co.uk – *Evening Standard (London, regional, daily)*
www.londonstudent.org.uk – *London Student Newspaper*
www.economist.co.uk – *The Economist (specialist magazine)*
www.ft.com – *The Financial Times (international, daily)*
www.sundaymirror.co.uk – *The Sunday Mirror (national, Sunday, tabloid)*
www.bigissue.com – *The Big Issue (monthly, national, magazine sold by the homeless)*
www.thisisbristol.com – *Bristol evening Post (regional, Bristol, daily)*
www.aberdeen-indy.co.uk/ – *Aberdeen Independent (free Scottish newspaper)*
www.megastar.co.uk – *cyber newspaper, tabloid, sex*
www.cosmogirl.com – *Cosmo Girl (Teen magazine, monthly)*
www.nme.com/ – *New Musical Express (music news, weekly)*
www.sundaysun.co.uk – *The Sunday Sun (national, Sunday, taloid)*
www.theherald.co.uk – *The Scottish Herald (regional, Scotland, daily)*

### Project: A comparative study …  SB S. 68

*Um einen sinnvollen Vergleich machen zu können, werden ca. 6 unterschiedliche (tabloid und quality) Zeitungen vom gleichen Tag benötigt. In den meisten Städten bzw. Großstädten kann man am Hauptbahnhof internationale Zeitungen bekommen. Es ist aber im Prinzip nicht wichtig, ob die Zeitungen hochaktuell sind, und insofern könnte der/die L passende Zeitungen bei Gelegenheit im Voraus besorgen.*
*Zusätzliche Hinweise zur Projektarbeit: TRB, S. 5–7 und 'Skills files', SB, S. 139.*

### Glossary: The Press  SB S. 69

*Dieses Glossar dient sowohl als Lernmaterial zum Thema 'Presse' als auch als Beispiel für das Ansammeln von Vokabular in einem thematischen Glossar.*

#### Vocabulary

● *Erstellte Kreuzworträtsel einsammeln und zu einem späteren Zeitpunkt zur Wiederholung einsetzen.*
● *Gelungene Poster unbedingt im Klassenzimmer aufhängen!*

#### Looking at the cartoon  SB S. 69

*(S. auch 'Skills file', SB, S. 130.)*
1. *She is reading the obituaries.*
2. *Black humour (= very popular in Britain, and rarely understood elsewhere!)*
3. *(S auf kulturelle Unterschiede hinsichtlich Humor aufmerksam machen, und besonders auf die Schwierigkeiten, die entstehen können, wenn man einen vermeintlichen Witz falsch versteht oder er falsch ankommt.)*

### Test: Talking in Whispers

Kopiervorlage **5**: TRB, S. 78 / CD-ROM (Aufgaben)
Lösungen: TRB, S. 138, Vokabeln: TRB, S. 142

# Using statistics

**Meet Britain's Press 4**

1. List the words alphabetically. Put the correct nouns and verbs next to each other.

> boom • to boom • to not change • climb • to climb • constant • decline • to decline • decrease • to decrease • doubling • to double • drop • to drop • to explode • explosion • fall • to fall • to go up • growth • to grow • to hold • increase • to improve • improvement • jump • to jump • rise • to rise • to shrink • shrinkage • to stay • to stay constant • not to vary

| Increase → | | Decrease → | | No change ↔ | |
|---|---|---|---|---|---|
| Verb | Noun | Verb | Noun | Verb | Noun |
| • _____ | • _____ | • _____ | • _____ | • _____ | • _____ |
| • _____ | • _____ | • _____ | • _____ | • _____ | |
| • _____ | • _____ | • _____ | • _____ | • _____ | |
| • _____ | • _____ | • _____ | • _____ | • _____ | |
| • _____ | • _____ | • _____ | • _____ | • _____ | |
| • _____ | • _____ | • _____ | • _____ | | |
| • _____ | • _____ | | | | |
| • _____ | • _____ | | | | |
| • _____ | • _____ | | | | |

2. Sort the words into the correct categories in the table.

> about • almost • approximately • astonishing • dramatic • enormous • explosive • gradual • a great deal • just under/over • less than • linear • more than • nearly • progressive • rapid • remarkable • sharp • significant • slight • slow • stable • sudden • surprising • (un)expected

| Adjectives | | | Adverbs | | |
|---|---|---|---|---|---|
| • _____ | • _____ | • _____ | • _____ | • _____ | • _____ |
| • _____ | • _____ | • _____ | • _____ | • _____ | • _____ |
| • _____ | • _____ | • _____ | • _____ | • _____ | • _____ |
| • _____ | • _____ | • _____ | | | |
| • _____ | • _____ | • _____ | | | |

3. Complete the following questions with the following prepositions: *over • by • since • from • in • to • for • at • of*.

Have there been any dramatic changes in the readership of your local newspaper _____ the years? • Describe the pattern of readership for your town paper _____ 1999 _____ 2000. • Has there been an increase _____ the readership? If so, _____ what percentage has the readership increased? • _____ when has this increase been taking place? • _____ which year were the numbers either constant or rising? • Or have readership numbers been falling? • What is the lowest percentage _____ which they have fallen? • Or has the number _____ readers remained _____ a constant level? If so, _____ how many years has this been the case?

# Writing an article

**Meet Britain's Press 4**

## Tips for writing newspaper articles

1. Make sure that you understand the **topic** that you have been assigned to write about.

2. **Gather information** from a variety of sources. Interview people such as experts, witnesses, etc. for material that you can quote, or get necessary background information from the internet or from other sources. Mention your sources if you quote or paraphrase!

3. Organize your information under questions beginning with **who, what, when, where, why** (and possibly **how**).

4. Decide on a **guiding idea** for your article. This idea, which is found in the first paragraph (often in the first line) narrows down your topic and summarizes the point that you will make in your article. The sentence with your topic + guiding idea is often called a **topic sentence**. For example:
   Thanks to more residents using public transport, air pollution in East Bigtown will decrease by 10 % this year. (air pollution = topic / 10% decrease = guiding idea)

5. Now **organize your information** in short paragraphs. The first paragraph will contain your topic + guiding idea, as this is the most important information that you will be presenting. Organize subsequent paragraphs in the order of **most to least important facts and supporting details**.

6. Try to use **descriptive and vivid language** (not abstract words) for your supporting details.

7. Try to make your **writing style** fit with the publication for which you are writing your article. In general keep most sentences short and simple in structure.

8. Think of a **headline** that tells readers in as few words as possible what your article is about, and why this information is important to write about.

Write a newspaper article based on the excerpts from the text 'The Pressure Cooker' (SB pp. 15–19):
a) Organize information under the questions **who, what, when, where, why** (and **how** if necessary).
b) First identify your topic and then come up with a guiding idea.
c) Decide if this will be an article in a tabloid or in a quality newspaper.
d) Follow steps 5–8 and write your article.

# Role play cards (1/2)  Meet Britain's Press

## James Kimber — journalist

- 35 years old, married, no children
- has worked for the tabloid *The Moon* for four years
- knows "what the readers want"
- his boss does not want to know where the story comes from as long as it sells well
- is hoping to become sub-editor
- wants to impress his boss with a really good story about William Swain's love affair
- believes that the public has a right to know

## Anthony Caulfield — photographer

- 22 years old, single
- has worked for *The Moon* for two years
- has a three-year contract but is hoping to stay longer with the paper
- admires the work of James Kimber
- has co-operated with him several times already
- is convinced that the public have a right to know and see everything
- wants to impress his new girlfriend with really sensational photos

## Suellen Hall — film star

- 27 years old, married, one child (boy, 3)
- had a breakthrough one year ago when she got the main part in Steven Spielberg's latest film
- is very religious (Protestant)
- would not allow any photographs of her child to be in the press
- is convinced that there should be a clear distinction between private and public affairs
- does not like tabloid papers like *The Moon* but has to give the interview as part of her contract

# Role play cards (2/2)  Meet Britain's Press

## William Swain
### tennis player

- 22 years old, not married
- very successful, last year's winner at Wimbledon
- is going to get married in six months
- has never taken his girlfriend to any interviews
- does not answer any questions about his private life
- had an affair with a prostitute in New York last year
- beat a cameraman six weeks ago who tried to take photographs at his home
- believes that paparazzi have really gone too far in recent years

## Paul Willin
### journalist

- 21 years old, single
- has worked for the quality paper *The Press* for two years
- believes in journalistic ideals and regards Mary as an ally
- tries to keep a balance between the public's right to know and the right to privacy
- had been offered a job by *The Moon* but refused to take it
- has known Anthony Caulfield since school, but has never liked him, especially because Anthony now goes out with his ex-girlfriend

## Mary Phillips
### photographer

- 43 years old, single mother of two children
- has never worked for a tabloid paper
- is highly respected by her colleagues for her excellent photographs
- would never take or publish photos in the paparazzistyle
- hopes that Paul will stick to his principles
- believes that Suellen Hall is a very good actress and would like to take photographs of her

# Listening comprehension

Meet Britain's Press 4

## Working on a regional newspaper

**outlying** ['-,--] surrounding
**to appeal to** to be interesting (to s.o.)
**contact** *here:* s.o. who can give information for a news story ['--]
**slant** a certain way of thinking about a subject
**orientated** [ˈɔːrɪənteɪtɪd] *(also oriented)* that which is concerned with a particular person or thing
**funky** [ˈfʌŋkɪ] unusual
**where it's at** *(informal)* that which is popular and in style

**to eat into** *here:* to take up time
**to break** *here:* when a newsworthy event happens
**to cover** *here:* to report on a subject
**to stalk** [stɔːk] to follow s.o. in a threating way
**rape** *Vergewaltigung*
**promotion** [prəˈməʊʃn] *Beförderung*
**graduate** [ˈɡrædʒuət] s.o. who has successfully finished university
**training scheme** *Voluntariat*

The *Birmingham Post* is a regional newspaper published and sold in Birmingham and the West Midlands. Listen to Roz Dodd, the women's editor of the Birmingham Post, talking about the newspaper and her work.

## Listening for gist

Write either a title for each of the four sections of the interview that you hear, or write one sentence only summarizing what each section is about.

Section 1: _____   Section 3: _____

Section 2: _____   Section 4: _____

## Listening for detail

**Section 1:** Give information on each of the following:

a) Region covered by the newspaper: _____

b) Type of news covered: _____

c) Sources: where the news comes from: _____

**Section 2:** What has been changing over the years? How?

_____

_____

**Section 3:** Answer the questions.

a) How many hours per day does Roz usually work? _____

b) Why does she sometimes work longer hours? _____

c) What does she do first when she gets to work? _____

d) What does she say about press releases from PR companies? _____

e) How often does Roz have to write a feature? _____

f) What kind of issues does she cover? (Name at least two.) _____

**Section 4** (Write your answers on a separate sheet.)

1. Write a summary on how to become a journalist on a British newspaper. The key words below may be useful to you:

> *A-levels • graduates • in-house training scheme • post-graduate scheme in journalism • Journalism Proficiency Test • senior reporter*

2. "In 10 years time there won't be such a thing as a 'women's editor' anymore."
Why do newspapers have women's editors (but not men's)? Do we need women's editors? Comment on this statement and give your opinion.

Klettbuch 510511 – *Challenge 21, Teacher's book*
© Ernst Klett Verlag GmbH, Stuttgart 2001.

# Talking in Whispers

*The action of the novel takes place in Chile at the time when the military junta ruled under Pinochet. The teenager Andres, protagonist of the novel, is eyewitness to the transport of political prisoners into the stadium of Santiago. Suddenly he notices a tall man making his way through the crowd …*

He's a pressman. Andres felt a thrill of hope. Here comes the American cavalry! He was right behind the pressman. He shouted in Spanish:

"Give him room!" And then in a low voice only audible to the American: "The world's got to know what's happening here."

"You bet it has." The pressman took Andres in in one friendly – even grateful – glance. They were comrades. Together they breasted a way through the crowd.

"That's my friend – the tall one."

The last prisoners were being driven down from the truck. One was not fast enough to please his guards. He was hurt, hobbling, gripping his side in pain.

"Step on it, you red scab!"

The American's camera was in the air. A rifle butt swung against the stumbling prisoner.

Click-whirr, click-whirr – the scene was banked, recorded.

Braulio had turned, stepping out of line. He protested at the guard's action and immediately drew soldiers round him like wasps to honey.

Click-whirr, click-whirr. The toppling of Braulio was captured. Here was evidence for the time when villainy would be brought to justice.

Yet here also was terrible danger. The American photographer had himself been snapped by the eye of the officer commanding the troops. "Christ, they've spotted me!" He lowered his camera swiftly below the shoulders of the crowd. He shifted, half-face, towards Andres. He seemed paralysed by fear.

The American pushed the camera into Andres' hand. "Take this – I'm finished."

"But –"

"I beg you. The film in that camera …"

The officer and his men were clubbing a passage through the crowd towards the American. Andres ducked the camera through the open zip of his jacket. "Who shall I say?" He was being carried away from the pressman by the retreat of the crowd.

"Chailey – Don Chailey!" He yelled the name of his newspaper too but the words did not carry to Andres who found himself squeezed step by step away from the oncoming troops.

(326 words)

*From* Talking in Whispers *by James Watson, London: Victor Gollancz/Hamish Hamilton, 1983, pp. 39-40.*

## Content

1. How does Andres feel about the American coming through the crowd?
2. Why is this situation very dangerous for the American?
3. Write a summary of the scene as if it were an article for a quality paper.

*(Your teacher will tell you which of the following tasks you should complete.)*

## Comment

1. Based on the situation that you have read about in this text, would you have agreed to take the American's camera if he had handed it to you? Why or why not?
2. After the death of Princess Diana many people demanded restrictions for journalists, especially for the so-called "paparazzi". Discuss the importance of the freedom of the press against the background of the extract from 'Talking in Whispers'.

## Form

1. How do sentence structure and choice of words help to make the scene so exciting?
2. Find examples of similes and metaphors in the text and describe their effect on the reader.

## Language

1. Give a synonym for the following words.
   a) gripping (l. 13)   b) breasted (l. 9)   c) snapped (l. 25)
2. Give the opposite of the following words.
   a) friendly (l. 8)   b) comrade (l. 8)   c) yelled (l. 39)
3. Change the following sentences from the active to the passive or vice versa.
   a) Photographers must capture important news events on film.
   b) The prisoners were treated terribly by the guards.
4. In your own words, explain in complete sentences what the following expressions mean.
   a) thrill of hope (l. 1)   c) to be captured (ll. 21–22)
   b) audible (l. 4)   d) paralysed by fear (ll. 28–29)

# Welcome to America 5

## Didaktisches Inhaltsverzeichnis

| Title | Text type / Topic | Skills & Tasks | 💿📄 |
|---|---|---|---|
| **Photos of America** (SB S. 70) | • photos | • Speaking: describing pictures and geographic features<br>• Vocabulary: terms for describing locations | |
| **Physical features and time zones** (SB S. 71) | • geographic outines / map<br>• illustration | • Speaking/writing: examining distances and geographic features; describing cities; looking at time zones | |
| **A conference call** (SB S. 71) | • conducting a conference call in three time zones (832 words) | • Listening comphrehension | **1** TRB, S. 88<br>**2** TRB, S. 89 |
| **Hunting Mr. Heartbreak** (SB S. 72) | • travelogue extract (260 words)<br>• mobility and identity<br>• license plates | • Reading: for detail<br>• Speaking: role play (booking a motel room); describing license plates; talking about local and national identity<br>• Writing: slogans; a travel report<br>• Vocabulary: Synonyms and opposites<br>• Grammar: the present tense | **3** TRB, S. 90/91 |
| **Temperature, rainfall and snowfall** (SB S. 76) | • table of statistics | • Speaking: discussing and comparing weather statistics<br>• Writing: describing climate | |
| **Extreme weather conditions** (SB S. 76) | • picture<br>• headines | • Speaking: talking about extreme weather conditions | |
| **Hurricane wreaks havoc on battered Gulf States** (SB S. 77) | • newspaper article (395 words)<br>• effects of a hurricane | • Reading: for detail<br>• Vocabulary: the word group 'weather'<br>• Grammar: participles and translation | |
| **Population** (SB S. 78) | • map and statistics showing population trends | • Analysing statistics<br>• Writing/Vocabulary: using statistical vocabulary to complete a paragraph | |
| **West, South are building more population muscle** (SB S.79) | • newspaper article (296 words) | • Reading: for gist and detail<br>• Speaking: reporting findings for population trends<br>• Writing: a report on US population | |
| **Focus on the South** (SB S. 80) | • word collage<br>• photos | • Speaking: talking about pictures and words/phrases describing the South<br>• Writing: completing the mind map 'The South' | |
| **The southernisation of America** (SB S. 80) | • magazine article (1,044 words)<br>• Southern influence in the USA | • Reading: for gist and detail<br>• Writing: taking notes<br>• Vocabulary: definitions and word families<br>• Grammar: relative clauses | |
| **Sweet home Alabama** (SB S. 84) | • song (178 words) | • Listening comprehension | **4** TRB, S. 92/93 |
| **Project: Planning a trip to the US** (SB S. 85) | | | |
| **Test: Notes from a big country** | • newspaper article (365 words) | | **5** TRB, S. 94 |

## 5 Welcome to America

### Introduction

*The chapter opens with a collage of scenes and images suggesting the regional and cultural variety of America. Students are given a chance to describe what they already know about the country and their attitudes to it. Physical features and time zones are then studied more closely with the help of maps, and in the section 'Hunting Mr Heartbreak' the themes of mobility and identity are explored. Students then go on to examine climatic features and population trends, which also prepares them for the section 'Focus on the South' that follows.*

*The development of transferable skills plays an integral role in the chapter. For example, there are tasks which involve analysing statistics, interpreting maps, carrying out research using the internet, and report-writing. The chapter rounds off with a project in which pupils plan a (hypothetical) trip to the USA. This enables them to draw on the knowledge and skills they have acquired during the chapter, as well as discover more about those aspects they found especially interesting.*

---

### Photos of America  SB p. 70

#### Getting started

*Note: Watch out for mistakes with tenses when talking about previous trips to the USA, especially with the present perfect. After the initial 'conversation opener' using the present perfect ("Have you ever ...?") students should switch to the simple past when asking or answering questions about details 'in a time now past'. If the need arises, exemplify the function of the tenses through simple model dialogues, for example:*

A: Have you ever been to America?
B: Yes, I went there last summer.
A: Where did you go?
B: We went to the West Coast and then to Colorado.
A: Did you see the Grand Canyon?
B: Yes, it was amazing!

A: Have you ever been to America?
B: Yes, I've been there six times already. My grandparents live in Colorado.
A: When was the last time you went?
B: In December. We spent Christmas with them.
A: Have you ever seen the Grand Canyon?
B: Yes, several times. I've even camped at the bottom.

*Note: In weaker classes, ask students to describe each picture before saying which place they would most like to visit. The following vocabulary prompts could be given (via OHP/blackboard):* mountain range • suspension bridge • steamboat • harbour/port • neoclassical/Greek revival architecture • beach/shoreline • cattle • herding • gorge/canyon • mule, skyscraper • arch • hunter

#### Talking about the photos

1. *Note: harbor (AE), harbour (BE), center (AE), centre (BE), 'D.C.' stands for 'District of Columbia'.*
1 = the Sierra Nevada mountain range • 2 = San Francisco (Golden Gate Bridge) • 3 = Mississippi • 4 = southern home in Kentucky • 5 = Boothbay Harbor, Maine • 6 = Washington D.C. • 7 = Miami Beach, Florida • 8 = cattle herding in Montana • 9 = the Grand Canyon • 10 = World Trade Center, New York • 11 = the Arch in St. Louis, Missouri • 12 = Eskimo hunters in Alaska
2. *Note: According to the Bureau of the Census, the Midwest region includes Illinois, Indiana, Michigan, Ohio, Wisconsin, Iowa, Kansas, Minnesota, Missouri, Nebraska, North Dakota and South Dakota. However, some sources sometimes define this region differently. From the point of view of the early pioneers who moved inwards from the east coast, these regions lay to the west, hence the terms 'Mid-west' (or: 'Middle West'). Additional phrases for describing locations:*
… is a mountain range in eastern (+ name of state) • The … (river) rises in the … near …, and flows (north/south/etc.) to a delta on the … coast. • … is a state in the south-eastern US • … lies to the (east/west/etc.) of … • … is a gorge formed by the … in the (southwestern/northeastern/etc.) state of … • … in the extreme north-west of North America
1 *The Sierra Nevada is a mountain range in eastern California. (It is also a mountain range in southern Spain.)* • 2 *San Francisco is a city on the coast of California.* • 3 *The Mississippi river rises in the northern state of Minnesota and flows south to a delta southeast of New Orleans on the Gulf of Mexico.* • 4 *Kentucky is a state in the south-eastern US, lying to the west of the Appalachian mountains.* • 5 *Maine is a state on the north-east coast, just south of the Canadian border. Boothbay Harbor is on the coast of Maine.* • 6 *Washington D.C., the capital city of the USA, is on the east coast, between Maryland to the north and Virginia to the south.* • 7 *Miami Beach is on the south-east coast of Florida.* • 8 *Montana is a state in the western US on the Canadian border and lies primarily east of the Rocky Mountains.* • 9 *The Grand Canyon is a deep gorge formed by the Colorado River in the south-western state of Arizona.* • 10 *New York City is situated on the Atlantic coast in the north-eastern state of New York.* • 11 *St. Louis is a city in eastern Missouri.* • 12 *Alaska is the largest state in the US, in the extreme north-west of North America, with coasts on the Arctic Ocean, Bering Sea and the North Pacific.*
3. *The Rocky Mountains are on the west of the USA and stretch from Alaska in the north to New Mexico in the south.* • *The Appalachians are in the east of the USA and stretch from Alabama in the south and then northwards through Maine and to Canada.*

### Physical features and time zones  SB p.71

#### Describing locations & features

*Note: The aim of these exercises is to familiarise students with main geographical features in the USA and to give them an impression of the sheer size of the United States.*
1. a) Largest lake: Lake Superior; longest river: Mississippi
b) Rio Grande
2. a) Los Angeles to Jacksonville, Florida: approx. 18.5 cms = approx. 2,150 miles/3,440 kms • Lake Ontario to Miami: approx. 11 cms = approx. 1,225 miles/1,960 kms
b) If you travelled 3,440 kms east from the western border of Germany you would be in Belarus (Weißrussland), if you travelled 3,440 kms west from the eastern border you would be in Cornwall in England. If you travelled 1,960 kms north from the Zugspitze you would be in Sweden. If you travelled 1.960 kms south from Flensburg you would be in Modena in Italy.

# Welcome to America 5

3. a) *(This task should be carried out orally in pairs.)*
b) *(This task should be done in writing. It is important for students not to be too local: they should be aware of the fact that some Americans have no idea where Germany is, let alone any region of Germany!)*
4. a) *Judging by the illustration the USA is approx. 26 times the size of Germany; 40 times the size of Britain, roughly the same as Europe including Scandinavia.*
b) *Germany is bordered by nine countries: Denmark to the north, the Czech Republic and Poland to the east, Switzerland and Austria to the south, and France, Luxembourg, Belgium, and The Netherlands to the west.*
*The USA has only two international borders: Canada to the north, and Mexico to the south.*
c) *(Possible answer:)*
*Europeans might be less willing than Americans to travel long distances because travelling in Europe involves crossing international borders and entering countries with different customs and languages. Travelling also tends to be slower and more complicated because the population density of Europe is considerably higher than in America.*
*Americans might be more willing to travel because they have to travel long distances if they want to avoid isolation and visit other parts of their country. Energy is cheaper in America, so Americans are less likely to be conscious of the economic and environmental costs of long-distance driving. Within America there are no problems crossing borders in terms of language, currency and basic customs. America is less densely populated than Europe so travelling is usually quicker and less complicated.*

[ *i* ] **Size and population of USA and Europe**
Total area of USA is 9,372,610 sq. km.
The estimated population of the USA in 1998: 269,816,000.
Approx. USA population density: 2.88 persons per sq. km.
The total area of Europe: approx. 10,400,000 sq. km.
The estimated population of Europe in 2000: 729,000,000.
Approx. population density of Europe: 7 persons per sq. km.
(approx. 2 1/2 times that of the USA)

5. a) *A political border is a line between two countries or states that has been defined and agreed on by the two particular groups on either side (e.g. nations). A natural border is created by a geographical feature, e.g. a river, coastline or mountain range. (A country's political borders may be defined by its natural borders, as in the case of an island. Political borders that are not drawn along geographical feature may take the form of a straight line (see USA), especially if they have not been subject to territorial disputes in the past.*
b) *Germany has a political border with Switzerland in the south, and a natural border represented by the Baltic Sea in the north and the River Rhine between France and Germany in the southwest.*
c) *The political borders of the USA are with Canada and Mexico. The Great Lakes represent a natural border with Canada, and the Rio Grande forms half of the border to Mexico.*

## Looking at time zones          SB p. 71

*Note: These tasks are intended to show pupils what the consequences of America being so large are, especially in terms of business timing.*
1. a) *There are five time zones: the Alaska, Pacific, Mountain, Central and Eastern Standard time zones.*
b) *Three hours (four hours to Alaska). When it is two o'clock in Washington State, it is five o'clock in Maine.*
c) *Germany (Central European Time) is six hours ahead of USA Eastern Standard Time. Therefore when it is noon in Berlin, it is 6 am in Washington D.C. and Atlanta, and 3 am in Los Angeles.*
2. a) *The telephone rings for the New York colleague at 7 pm (+ 3 hours from Los Angeles) and in Frankfurt at 1 am (+ 9 hours from Los Angeles).*
b) *The short-haired woman is Tracy Grey. The man is the colleague in New York. The woman being woken up in bed is in Frankfurt.*

→ What do you think each person in the illustration is saying? In a group of three work out a short dialogue.

## Listening comprehension          SB p. 71

*Copymaster 1: TRB, p. 88 CD-ROM*
*Solutions: TRB, p. 138*

CC:2/1
CD:41    **Conference call**

*The transcript of this listening comprehension text appears as a copymaster on p. 89 of the TRB (copymaster 2). The transcript should not be handed out to students before they have done the listening comprehension tasks! The texts can then be used and adapted to practise telephoning skills.*

CC:2/4
CD2:9    **Hunting Mr. Heartbreak**          SB p. 72–75

*This is the first lengthy text which students are expected to work with in Band 1 in preparation for the level of studies in classes 12 & 13. The speaker on the recording of the text is British, as the writer, Jonathan Raban, is a Briton writing about his experiences of travelling in America. (Cf. The extracts from 'Notes from a small island' in chapter 2 in which the American Bill Bryson, writes about life in Britain.)*

*The following pre-reading exercises may be useful:*
→ Find the I-81 and I-40 on the map of the USA at the back of the book. Describe its route through America, saying which towns and states you pass through and what main geographical features you encounter.
*The I 81 starts in New York and goes southwest along the Appalachian mountains through the states of New Jersey, Pennsylvania, Maryland, Virginia, and Tennessee. At Knoxville in Tennessee it becomes the I-40 and turns westwards to Memphis, crossing the Mississippi into Arkansas. From the town of Little Rock it follows the Arkansas River for some kilometres before crossing into the state of Oklahoma and passing through Oklahoma City. The I-40 continues westwards across the border into Texas and then into New Mexico. It goes over the Rocky Mountains passing through Albuquerque, then through Arizona. The Interstate then crosses the Colorado River into Nevada and goes over the Sierra Nevada mountains to Los Angeles.*

## Comprehension          SB p. 74

1. a) *Although the author lists all the states the route (I-78, I-81 and I-40) passes through, starting in Canada, it is not clear from this passage that he starts his journey there. Assuming he does, he passes through 12 states: New York, Pennsylvania, Maryland, West Virginia, Virginia, Tennessee, Arkansas, Oklahoma, Texas, New Mexico, Arizona and California.*
b) *In ll. 8–10 ("It was an epic road ... wide loop") the writer describes how the road spans and joins together the whole of America.*

## 5 Welcome to America

In ll. 10–12 ("If such roads ... Novaya Zemlya.") he makes a comparison with Europe comparing the distance between places as far away from one another as London and Tehran.

2. As the number plates suggest (ll. 13–28), there are people from Minnesota (Land of 10,000 Lakes), West Virginia, Ohio, Florida, South California, Maine, Kentucky, New York (Empire State), Massachusetts, Michigan, Illinois (Land of Lincoln), North Carolina (First in Freedom), Texas (Live Free or Die), Idaho (Famous Potatoes), Alaska (The Last Frontier).

3. a) The author compares the U-haul trailers to covered wagons of the pioneers, so likening these people to the early pioneers travelling across America to embark on a new life.

b) The author's guess is that the elderly couple are heading south because the man's doctor has recommended he retire to a warmer climate. He thinks the blond man is on the move after having been thrown out by his pregnant girlfriend. He imagines the single woman to be on her way to a new job in Atlanta.

4. In ll. 43–48 ("If you live ... down the street.") the author says that travelling long distances is easier for Americans than Europeans because Americans do not have to cope with different languages, whereas in Europe language barriers tend to discourage mobility. Also Americans can feel at home in any state: wherever they go the same programmes are on TV and there are the same kinds of shops and fast-food restaurants, etc.

5. In ll. 65/66 the writer says ("... I went legal. Down to sixty, ...") so the legal speed limit must be 60 miles per hour (96 km p h).

6. Possible answer: The motels come across as seedy and bleak ("scabby advertising boards ... strung up in trees", (ll. 69/70)), ("cigarette burn in a too-thin coverlet ... slovenly solitude", (ll. 81–84)), with little more to offer than easy access to and from the freeway ("EZ-OFF EZ-ON", (l. 71)). They are indistinguishable from one another ("They were all one", (l. 74)), and their lack of charm and individuality is contrasted with the 'real hotel' the author chances upon in Virginia, where he is struck by the pronounced southern accent of the girl at the bar.

### Role play: Booking a motel room

1. Tourist: Do you have any vacancies/any rooms free? • I'd like a room for tonight. • A kingsize, please. • How much will that be? • Thank you.
Receptionist: Good evening, Sir/Madam. • Can I help you? • Would you like a single or a double room? • Would you prefer smoking or non-smoking? • Just a moment, Sir/Madam. • $39.95 plus tax. • Would you like to pay cash or by credit card?/How would you like to pay? • Here's your key, Sir/Madam. • Would you sign here, please? • Thank you. • I hope you enjoy your stay. • Have a nice evening, Sir/Madam.

2. Model dialogue:
Receptionist: Good evening, Sir. Can I help you?
Tourist: Yes, I'd like a room for tonight.
Receptionist: Would you like a single or a double room?
Tourist: A single, please, with a shower.
Receptionist: Just a moment, sir. ... Yes, we have a couple of vacancies left. Would you prefer smoking or non-smoking?
Tourist: Non-smoking, please. How much will that be?
Receptionist: $39.95 plus tax, Sir.
Tourist: OK, I'll take it. Do I have to pay now or later?
Receptionist: Now, if you don't mind, Sir.
Tourist: Do you accept traveler's checks? (BE: traveller's cheques)
Receptionist: Yes, sure. We just need proof of your identity.
Tourist: Here's my passport.
Receptionist: Thank you. Would you just fill out this form, please, Sir?
Tourist: Ok. Can I borrow your pen, please?
Receptionist: Sure, go ahead.
Tourist: Thanks.
Receptionist: And would you sign here, please?
Tourist: OK.
Receptionist: Right, well, here's your key, sir. You're in Room 293. You can park your car in the parking lot right out front. We serve free coffee and donuts here at the reception in the morning.
Tourist: Great, thanks a lot.
Receptionist: You're welcome. Enjoy your stay, sir.
Tourist: Thanks. Bye.

→ Perform the same role play, but take on the following roles: Make any necessary changes to the dialogue!
a) a tired and grouchy business executive and an impatient receptionist.
b) a hotel guest who has forgotten his/her wallet and a suspicious receptionist.
c) two newly-weds who are lost and a receptionist who is a "romantic" at heart.

Copymaster 3: TRB, p. 90/91/CD-ROM
Role cards for practising similar situations can be found on the worksheets.

### Language: Synonyms, opposites and definitions

1. similar ≠ different (l. 44), many ≠ few (l. 45), opened up ≠ shut down (l. 50), lead ≠ follow (l. 55), slowly ≠ fast (l. 55), accelerated ≠ slowed (l. 67), filling ≠ emptying (l. 74), intelligently ≠ stupidly (l. 94)
2. a) tied up = connected/bound/linked • plump = rather fat/rounded/tubby/corpulent/portly, • flip = toss/throw carelessly • glanced = looked quickly at • gathered = realized/understood • image = symbol • chronic = unrelenting/unending/unremitting • goods = belongings/possession • head = aim/go in the direction of
b) "It was an epic road, a three-thousand mile trans-American ribbon that bound the subcontinent in a wide loop." • "A stately, portly Winnebago ..." • "I watched him ... toss it out onto the median strip." • "By the expression on his face when he looked quickly back at me, I realised that a white Dodge Spirit ..." • " ... there could be no symbol more expressive of the unremitting restlessness ..." • " ... in which were stowed the drivers' worldly possessions." • " You'd better aim for the Sunbelt."
3. Definition of sunbelt: A strip of territory that receives a high amount of sunshine. (The Sunbelt: The region in the southern US stretching from California in the west to Florida in the east.)

### Grammar & use of language

1. Breezing south in my wicked Spirit, my eye is tuned to watching other vehicles on the road, while the landscape spools by far too fast for me to follow the story. It comes to me in totemic fragments, observed only after they are already miles behind. That bridge back there is the Mason-Dixon line, and it takes the slick new tarmac and trim white picket fences of Maryland to make me realize that Pennsylvania has, on the whole, been kept like an unkempt family back yard with bald turf, a vegetable plot and the children's tricycles left out to rust in the rain. Only the sudden deterioration in the road surface as I hit West Virginia makes me see Maryland, in retrospect, as a rich man's garden, with sprinklers playing on mown and rollered lawns, a pony in the paddock, rhododendrons, bronze Pan on a stone plinth.
In West Virginia, the freeway begins to twist and steepen, enclosed by darkening forest, and, unlike most of the residents of that dis-

reputable statelet, I go legal. Down to sixty, peering anxiously into the twilight, I feel abruptly tired and thirsty. I slow before each forthcoming exit to scan the board reading LODGINGS NEXT RIGHT by the beam of my headlights. Mac's Motel. (...) Their scabby advertising boards are strung up in the trees, and the best recommendation they can make for themselves is that they are EZ-OFF EZ-ON, as if the true afficionado of the freeway can sleep comfortably with the breaking of surf of overnight traffic in his ears.

2. a) *Possible answer:* The effect of the present tense is to involve the reader more closely. As in a running commentary, the events and images come across as more immediate because the author appears to be describing them while they occur.
b) Sometimes writers use the present tense even when talking about events from the past to make a scene more vivid.

## Creative writing                                              SB p. 75

→ Choose one or several scenes from one of your holiday videos. Write a travelogue, description or "running commentary" of what you saw or experienced. Show the scene to the class whilst reading your commentary.

## Further activity

1. a) S should type in the slogans listed (including quotation marks around them) with the words 'Nickname' or 'Slogan' into a search machine to find the following answers:
Massachusetts • Florida • New York • Illinois • North Carolina • New Hampshire • Idaho • Minnesota • Alaska
In case of a time shortage, this exercise can also be done as a matching exercise. T should give S the following clues in mixed-up order, and the S should match them with the slogans listed in the book. (The following clues are listed in the order that matches the order of the slogans mentioned in the text.)
Massachusetts is shaped like a stovepipe hat. • Florida is also known as the Sunshine State, and is shaped like a pistol. • George Washington once called New York "the seat of the Empire". • One of Illinois' most famous residents became president of the US. • North Carolina was the first colony to call for independence from Britain at the Second Continental Congress in 1775. • New Hampshire was the first colony to vote for the Declaration of Independence in 1776. • This slogan indicates Idaho's most famous crop. • Boat owners love Minnesota! • The US purchased the land that would become Alaska from Russia as late as 1867.
b) –
c) *Mögliche Antworten:* The Puritans settled in Massachusetts. • Florida is shaped like a pistol. • The Empire State Building is in New York, New York. • Abraham Lincoln lived in Illinois. • Freedom is very important for North Carolina. • The residents of New Hampshire would rather die than not live free. • Agriculture, and especially the farming of potatoes, is important in Idaho. • Minnesota has a lot of lakes. • There is still unsettled frontier land in Alaska.
2. a)/b) –

## Over to you

● *Possible answers:*
Most Americans are immigrants or are descended from immigrants, which in itself is an important unifying factor. No one group is made to feel excluded. Also, shared values of democracy, egalitarianism, and even the 'American Dream', can transcend ethnic differences. American schools consciously try to inculcate a sense of patriotism and civic pride in pupils (e.g. pledging allegiance to the flag). Perhaps the absence of a common cultural heritage (esp. in modern America) creates the need to foster one.

● –
● *Possible answers:*
Europe itself is difficult to define. The political, cultural and even geographical boundaries are not clear. Europeans are also more strongly rooted in their past. They are constantly reminded of it through their literature, art and architecture, and so may be more aware of what makes them different than what they have in common. The British may, for example, feel they have more in common with Americans than with the French, both because they share a language but also because of their so-called 'Anglo-Saxon' values. Europeans tend only to be conscious of a European identity when comparing themselves with non-Europeans. A stronger European identity may be created by the introduction of the common currency, (the Euro), especially if it has a positive effect on the economy. The perception of a common enemy or trading block that threatens 'fortress Europe' could also pove to be a unifying factor.

## Climate and weather in the USA                     SB p. 76–77

### Temperature, rainfall and snowfall              SB p. 76

**Understanding statistics**

1. –
2. Note: Work through the conversions for the first city, Atlanta, together with the whole class to ensure that everyone knows what to do. Then divide pupils into pairs/groups, with each pair/group dealing with a different city. Point out to students that in the USA (and in Britain) it is still common to talk about temperatures in Fahrenheit and precipitation in inches!
*Example conversions for Atlanta:*
Average monthly temperature in January: 41.9° Fahrenheit.
To convert to Celsius: (41.9–32) x 100/180 = 5.5° C
Average monthly temperature in July: 78.6° Fahrenheit.
To convert to Celsius: (78.6–32) x 100/180 = 26°C
Annual precipitation in inches: 115
To convert to centimetres: 115 x 2.54 = 292.1 cm
Annual snowfall in inches: 1.9
To convert to centimetres: 1.9 x 2.54 = 4.75 cm
3. Mary: Miami/Honolulu • Andy: Fairbanks • Jo: Buffalo/Denver • Marcia: Miami/Honolulu/Los Angeles • Davey: New Orleans, Miami, Atlanta
4. The USA has a whole range of climactic regions: Alaska (Fairbanks) in north-west has an arctic climate. It is the coldest region of the USA. The West Coast (Los Angeles) has a mild climate with not much rainfall. Texas (Dallas) has hot summers and cold winters. Nevada (Las Vegas) has very hot summers and mild winters. The south-east of the USA (Miami, New Orleans, Atlanta) is a warm humid region, with tropical summers and mild winters and a lot of rain. Some inland areas in the Northeast and Northwest also have a lot of rain.

### Extreme weather conditions                        SB p. 76

**Before you read**

● fires, floods, hurricane (storm)
● *Storm four times bigger than Hurricane Andrew*
● *These types of weather conditions occur in Germany, but fires and hurricanes are rare. Germany seldom experiences very long dry periods that could lead to forest fires, and it is not in the path of the kind of tropical air streams that are conducive to hurricanes.*

# 5 Welcome to America

● The USA has a wide variety of climates and geographical characteristics, i.e. mountains, desert regions, etc. As a result of this, at certain times of the year and in certain areas there are widely varying temperatures and moisture levels in the air, causing weather fronts which collide with each other and cause extreme weather.

→ Ask pupils to suggest further examples of natural disasters (e.g. tornado, earthquake, tsunami, landslide, avalanche, drought, volcanic eruption) and name the regions of the world where they tend to occur.

## Hurricane wreaks havoc... SB p. 77

### Comprehension

1. Ferocious winds, torrential rain and flooding (ll. 2/3).
2. Kirk Fordice contacted President Clinton to ask him to declare a state of emergency in Mississippi. By doing so, federal aid (money) would be made available to rebuild the areas destroyed by the hurricane.
3. The National Guardsmen were called in to rescue people from flooded housing estates in Alabama and Florida.
4. Thousands of people sought shelter from the hurricane, ten thousand of them in the superdome of the New Orleans Saints (Col. 4, ll. 3–8). However, New Orleans managed to avoid the worst of the hurricane (Col. 3, ll. 19–21). A man was killed in a fire which had started as a result of candles being lit during a power cut (Col. 2, ll. 5–10).
5. People's lives were disrupted by heavy rain, power cuts, the closing of airports and highways and the imposition of curfews. Thousands of people were made homeless and there were also many fatalities in the Carribbean and Florida Keys.

### Vocabulary

Wind: hurricane (Col. 1, l. 1); ferocious winds (Col. 1, l. 2); gusts (Col. 1, l. 6); wind (Col. 1, l. 19) • Rain: torrential rain (Col. 1, l. 3); rain (Col. 3, l. 1); downpour (Col. 3, l. 7); relentless rain (Col. 3, ll. 21/22); Floods: flooding (Col. 1, l. 3) • Storms: eye of the storm (Col. 1, l. 10); storm surge (Col.3, l. 22) • Verbs: to unleash (Col. 1, l. 2); to blow (Col. 1, l. 19); to dump (rain) (Col. 3, l. 1); to batter (Col. 3, l. 6); to lash (Col. 3, l. 11)

→ Collect more words related to the weather and group them under the sub-headings you have chosen.

→ Write a newspaper report about a natural disaster that has occurred in Germany or that you have experienced.

### Grammar (participles) and translation

1. a) ...which border • ... who was killed ... which was started
b) Col. 1, ll. 13–18: "Kirk Fordice said he had asked President Clinton to declare an emergency, clearing the way for ...": ... to declare an emergency, which would clear the way ... • Col. 2, ll. 5/6: "... one storm-related death": ... one death which was related to a storm. • Col. 3, l. 21– Col. 4, l. 3: "Relentless rain and a storm surge could have submerged the low-lying city, protected only by levees.": ... low lying city, which is protected only by levees.
2. Während Tausende von Menschen evakuiert wurden, löste Orkan George in den an den Golf von Mexiko angrenzenden Bundesstaaten heftige Windböen, sintflutartige Regenfälle und Überflutungen aus. • Bislang hat der Sturm in den Südstaaten nur ein Todesopfer gefordert: ein Mann kam in New Orleans in einem durch Kerzen verursachten Feuer um, nachdem der Orkan die Stromversorgung unterbrochen hatte.

## Population SB p. 78–79

### Population trends by region... SB p. 78

### Analysing statistics

1. Highest population: the South • Lowest population: the Northeast
2. The South is the fastest growing region.
3. West: Alaska, Hawaii, Washington, Idaho, Montana, Oregon, Wyoming, California, Nevada, Utah, Colorado, Arizona, New Mexico
Midwest: North Dakota, South Dakota, Nebraska, Kansas, Minnesota, Iowa, Missouri, Wisconsin, Illinois, Michigan, Indiana, Ohio
Northeast: Pennsylvania, New York, Philadelphia, Connecticut, Massachussetts, New Hampshire, Rhode Island, Maine
South: Texas, Oklahoma, Arkansas, Louisiana, Mississippi, Tennessee, Alabama, Georgia, South Carolina, North Carolina, Kentucky, West Virginia, Virginia, Maryland, Delaware, New Jersey
4. Possible reasons for faster growth in the South: Booming economy attracting jobs; immigration from south of the border; climate; more room to spread out.
Possible reason for slower growth in the North: Traditional heavy industries in Northeast are in decline or undergoing automation, so fewer new jobs are being created and many existing jobs are disappearing. Climate may also be a factor.
5. a) California has by far the highest percentage of foreign-born citizens (24.9%), followed by New York (19.6%) and Hawaii (18.1%). Tennessee and Kentucky have the lowest (1.2%), followed closely by Alabama (1.3%).
b) California is on the Pacific coast and borders Mexico, which makes it attractive for Asian and Mexican immigrants. New York is also a traditional entry point for immigrants. Although population growth in the South is high, the percentage of foreign-born citizens in some southern states is relatively low. Despite the growth of cities like Atlanta, the South still tends to be predominantly rural. Foreign-born citizens tend to live in the more urban areas where there are big cities with lots of job opportunities.
6. The foreign-born population is concentrated in certain areas of the country. Old immigrant centres continue to have the highest percentages of citizens born in other countries. The statistics show that people have not been spreading out geographically as much as you might expect.

### West, South are building ... SB p. 79

### Comprehension

1. a) Col. 1, ll. 3–7: "If these trends continue through 2000, nine congressional seats would be picked up by seven fast-growing Western and Southern states ..."; Col. 1, ll. 12–17: "Population counts are crucial to states because they decided how many seats each will get in Congress. The more representatives a states has, the more influence it has when issues affecting the state come up for a vote."
b) If the population in the seven Western and Southern states continues to rise at the current rate, they will gain nine new seats in Congress. This will give the states greater influence when voting on issues that affect them in Congress because the number of seats a state has in Congress depends on the population of the state.
2. a) See table on p. 85.

| Name of state | Gainer/Loser | Reason for gain/loss | Political effect |
|---|---|---|---|
| Arizona | Gainer | Less congested; new jobs attract workers from North east and Midwest – especially to Georgia where the economy is booming | Two new seats |
| California | Gainer | | Two new seats |
| Nevada | Gainer | | One new seat |
| Florida | Gainer | | One new seat |
| Texas | Gainer | | One new seat |
| Montana | Gainer | | One new seat |
| Georgia | Gainer | | One new seat |
| New York | Loser | Population drain from older industrial states ("domestic outmigration") | Two seats lost |
| Pennsylvania | Loser | | Two seats lost |
| West Virginia | Loser | Death rate exceeding birth rate; demise of coal mining | No information |
| Kansas | Gainer | Meatpacking industry attracts foreign and domestic workers. | No information |

b) – (See 'Skills files: Essay writing', SB, p. 124 and 'Writing a summary', SB, p. 125.)

### Further activities

● – (See 'Skills file: Giving a presentation', SB, p. 129. Websites are given in the SB. This task should be treated as a mini-project and can be carried out by students individually or in pairs or small groups.)

## Focus on the South    SB p. 80–83

### Getting started

● –

[i] **Gone with the Wind** (1936): Best-selling novel by Margaret Mitchell set during the American Civil War. It was made into a successful film in 1939.
**Spirituals** (Negro spiritual): religious song of the kind sung in Baptist and Pentecostal churches in the southern US. They derive from a combination of the hymns of early white settlers with traditional African elements such as the pentatonic (five-note) scale.
**Martin Luther King** (1929–68): Black American Baptist minister and civil-rights leader. King opposed discrimination against blacks by organizing non-violent resistance and peaceful mass demonstrations, including a year-long black boycott of the local bus company in Montgomery, Alabama, in 1955. He also organized a march on Washington involving 200,000 demonstrators in 1963 and gave a famous speech beginning "I have a dream …". He was awarded the Nobel Peace Prize in 1964, and was assassinated in Memphis in 1968.
**Civil Rights Movement:** The National Association for the Advancement of Colored Peoples (NAACP) and the National Urban League were the main organizations involved in the campaign to fight for the equality of black Americans as guaranteed by the Constitution. Their methods included boycotts and court action, followed by sit-ins, marches and demonstrations. These efforts culminated in the Civil Rights Act of 1964, which banned discrimination based on race, religion or sex in employment and in programmes that received federal funds. The failure of this to bring immediate improvement, and the assassination in 1968 of Martin Luther King, led to the development of black power organizations such as the Black Panthers, who rejected the policy of non-violence in favour of more militant tactics.
**Confederate States of America:** The eleven southern states (Alabama, Arkansas, Florida, Georgia, Louisiana, Mississippi, North Carolina, South Carolina, Tennessee, Texas, Virginia,) which seceded (= withdrew) from the United States in 1860/1 and formed a confederacy of their own. It was this act that sparked off the American Civil War. The Confederate states were defeated in 1865, after which they rejoined the US.

### Collecting information in a mind-map

*Note: Encourage students to add their own ideas. Get them to describe their mind maps once they have completed them. Alternatively, they could produce and present a more detailed mind map in groups once they have finished covering the topic. (See 'Skills file', SB, p. 121.)*

### The southernisation of America    SB p. 81

*This is the second long text which students encounter in this chapter. Remind them of techniques for gist-reading and understanding texts without using a dictionary (see 'Skills file', SB, p. 134). The 'While you read' task will focus their attention on the most important aspects while reading.*

### While you read

● *Possible paragraph summaries:*
*ll. 1–8: The South is special and different to other states because inhabitants are strongly rooted to their region and there is relatively little immigration from other places.*
*ll. 9–16: The South is more rural than elsewhere in the USA and traditions are strongest in rural areas.*
*ll. 17–24: Typically Southern attitudes, e.g. conservatism, love of church and family, have been mocked by Americans but they make the South special.*
*ll. 25–34: Technology (air-conditioning) and commerce are making the South more like the rest of America.*
*ll. 35–42: The workforce is also changing and becoming more like the rest of America.*
*ll. 43–47: However, the South is still unique.*
*ll. 48–54: America is being 'southernized', i.e. Southern attitudes are beginning to prevail over liberal ones.*
*ll. 55–63: Some people are not happy about America becoming more like the South, but on the whole, the South is having a positive effect.*
*ll. 64–67: People fear that the 'American Dream' is over.*
*ll. 68–76: The economy in the South is strong, Southerners are less worried about the future than Northerners.*
*ll. 77–87: The South still has problems but so does all of America. The South may take the lead in dealing with them.*

# 5 Welcome to America

### Collecting information from the text  SB p. 83

*Note to teacher: This task requires intensive reading. You may prefer to start with the comprehension tasks. Alternatively, the comprehension tasks can be omitted if students produce detailed enough outlines.*

<u>Economic changes</u>
*Spread of retailing has homogenizing influence, making South look more like rest of USA.*
*Shift to service jobs (as elsewhere in the USA)*
*Booming economy (despite continued rural poverty)*
<u>Political changes</u>
*Conservative southern values are taking hold elsewhere in the USA (as confirmed by the 1994 mid-term elections). 'Harsher tone' to American life. Co-operation between southern businessmen and state governments. Southern Republicans confident of success.*
<u>Climate and geography</u>
*South used to be isolated (distance from big cities in the North, hostile climate). However, technological developments such as air conditioning and jet aircraft have made the South less forbidding and more accessible to outsiders.*
<u>Changes in attitudes</u>
*Little change. In fact, Southern conservatism has spread to other parts of America. The liberals are in the minority. There is a general mood of optimism.*

### Comprehension

*1. In the past the South used to be characterised by "poverty, racism, peculiar politics" (ll 1/2).*
*2. The jet aircraft made the South easily accessible and air conditioner made the climate bearable.*
*3. The US has started to adopt traditionally Southern political attitudes, the tone of life in America as a whole is harsher (l. 55) and more people throughout the US support the religious right (l. 56).*
*4. The American Dream is still alive in the South because their economy is booming. The poverty they are used to experiencing is disappearing. Southeners are confident that this trend will continue.*
*5. Southern problems that are relevant to the US as a whole: racial prejudice, rural poverty, education, crime. All of these are also international problems.*

### Vocabulary: definitions & word families

*1. rural: in or of the countryside or farming • urban: relating to towns or cities • suburbs: residential areas on the outskirts of a town or city • majority: most, or the main part • service jobs: employment in the tertiary (non-manufacturing) sector, e.g. in insurance, banking, retailing, health, transport • southernisation: influencing with southern values and characteristics; making the rest of America more like the South • traditionalists: people who believe in keeping things the way they are, or who would like to go back to how things used to be*
*2. (noun/verb/adjective):*
*life/to live/living; live*
*attachment/attach/attached*
*inhabitants/inhabit/inhabited/inhabitable*
*population/populate/populated/populous*
*accusation/accuse/accused*
*significance/signify/significant*
*isolation/isolate/isolated*
*distinction/distinguish/distinctive; distinguishable*
*economy/economise; economize/economic; economical*

*NB: economical = opposite of 'wasteful' (sparsam). Compare: An economic boom (= a boom in the economy) • Energy-saving lightbulbs are economical. (= They help to save energy and money.)*

### Grammar: relative clauses

*1. a) There has always been a special feel about southern life, which is not only marked by poverty and racism.*
*b) Southern states still have remarkably few inhabitants who are born outside the region.*
*c) The attachment to family and place, which is strong in the South, is especially strong in rural areas.*
*d) You can still see young men who look like extras from a 50s television show, with crew-cuts and driving their pick-ups.*
*e) Attitudes like conservatism and love of church and family, which are famous southern attitudes, give it a special character and set it apart from other regions.*
*f) Yet, a state like North Carolina, which is the most industrialised state in the country, has a high population of the workforce in manufacturing.*
*2. a) Armadillos, egrets and alligators are types of wildlife which can be found in Florida.*
*b) Liberals are people who believe in tolerance.*
*c) Fast food joints are restaurants which/that serve cheap food quickly.*
*d) A minority is a group which/that forms a small percentage of a whole.*
*e) Southerners are people who live in the South or who were born there.*
*f) A retail outlet is a shop or group of shops which sells goods to the final consumers.*

## Southern rock  SB p. 84–85

**CC:2/5 CD2:19  Sweet Home Alabama**  SB p. 84–85

*The students will undoubtedly know this song which is still frequently played by cover bands in Europe and the US. The South is, of course, famous for other types of music: notably jazz, blues and spirituals. This song was chosen because students will find it easier to identify with. (See also 'Further activities'.)*

### *i* Interpretation

Verse 1: The singer is returning home to his family and friends in the South (his "kin"), who he has missed. "And I think it's a sin" refers to the next verse: the songwriter thinks that the way Neil Young speaks about the South is a sin.
Verse 2: Neil Young's songs Alabama and Southern Man are quoted ("A Southern Man don't need him around,"). Neil Young had recorded pop songs criticizing the South in general and Alabama in particular, which offended many Southerners. Skynyrd's verse was received by many fans as a much needed re-assertion of Southern pride, following a difficult period in which the South had been much criticized. "Sweet Home Alabama", written after the extreme racial turbulence of the 1960s, re-asserted the South's regional pride and suggested that Neil Young viewed the South too negatively: The South itself is not bad, but good. There are bad individuals in the South, but the region as a whole cannot be talked about in this manner. This is especially brought out in the next verse.
Verse 3: The governor referred to in the first line ("In Birmingham they love the guv'ner") is George Wallace, a notorious racist and

Welcome to America 5

opponent of the Civil Rights Movement during the 1960s. Birmingham had a large black community which had been subject to appalling violence in the 1960s, and at that time Wallace was much hated there. However, by 1974, Wallace had passed through a 'dark night of suffering' (which left him wheelchair-bound and in constant pain), undergone a spiritual transformation, and found redemption, promoting racial reconciliation and harmony. In 1974 the all-black Alabama State University conferred an honorary doctorate on Wallace in recognition of his repentance and work for racial harmony, which included an emotional visit to the Montgomery church where Dr. Martin Luther King had started the Civil Rights Movement. The second line ("Now, we all did what we could do") refers to the work that Southerners did to promote change. The "we" in this verse can be taken to refer to both black and white Southerners or to white Southerners in particular. If the latter, the line takes on an additional meaning, i.e. there were a lot of Southern whites who wanted the situation in the South to change and they worked in whatever way they could to help things improve. The third line ("Now, Watergate does not bother me") refers to the 'Watergate Affair'. This famous political scandal began on June 17th 1972. A security guard at Washington's Watergate hotel and apartment complex alerted police when he noticed a stairwell door lock had been taped in the open position. Five intruders were caught inside the headquarters of the Democratic National Committee. The burglars were there, it turned out, to adjust bugging equipment they had installed during a May break-in and to photograph the Democrats' documents. The investigation of the June 17, 1972 break-in led directly to the re-election campaign of Richard M. Nixon and unravelled a web of political spying and sabotage, bribery and the illegal use of campaign funds. The disclosure of these activities, and the administration's cover-up, resulted in the indictments of some 40 government officials and the resignation of the president. The fourth and fifth lines ("Does your conscience bother you?/Tell the truth") suggest that if critics of the South don't feel responsible for the Watergate affair, they cannot accuse Southerners of being responsible for what happened in the 1960s. The juxtaposition of President Nixon (who resigned in 1974) and Governor Wallace (who received his doctorate from a black university in 1974) is profound: Just as the nation seemed to be falling apart, the South had got its act together.
Verse 4: Though Muscle Shoals is a town in Alabama, the reference here is to Muscle Shoals Sound Studios in Sheffield, Alabama, the studio where the band did its early recording work. "The Swampers" was the band's nickname for the studio crew at Muscle Shoals.
Verse 5 is essentially a re-working of the chorus and includes an additional reference to the now-repentant Governor Wallace (who was re-elected in 1974) and the state capitol, Montgomery. The reference to the governor being "true" probably means that Wallace is now a good, honest governor. "Montgomery's got the answer" suggests that the rest of America should take a look at and learn from the South.

### Working with the song

1. Assuming the title is meant seriously, the songwriter feels affectionate towards his home town, Alabama ("Sweet Home Alabama", "I miss Alabamy once again") and is looking forward to returning.
2. –
3. a)/b) The following expressions could be given to students to choose from:

Describing a melody: tuneful; catchy; sad; plaintive; lively; cheerful; monotonous
Describing a singer's voice: deep; high; hoarse; clear; sweet; versatile; whiny; sexy; a good range
Describing the text: lyrical; banal; easy to understand; difficult to understand; meaningful; meaningless
4. 'Her' probably refers to Alabama or 'the Southland'.
NB: Some people use 'she' and 'her' to countries, although 'it' is more common in modern English.
5. a) Verse 2: The singer's name was Neil Young. The song is 'Southern Man'.
b) Verse 3: The political scandal was Watergate. This happened after a failed attempt to bug the national headquarters of the Democratic Party (in the Watergate building in Washington, D.C.) during the US election campaign of 1972. The scandal led to the resignation of President Nixon in 1974.
c) Verse 4: The recording studio is Muscle Shoals. The recording team is called the Swampers. Muscle Shoals is also a town in Alabama, but the studio is actually located in Sheffield (see   ).
d) Verse 1: The singer is driving (or being driven) and singing songs about the South. He misses Alabama.

→ Work in groups, each group dealing with one of the following topics. Find out as much as you can about the topic and prepare a group presentation.
Neil Young • Birmingham, Alabama and Martin Luther King, Jr. • Montgomery, Alabama and Rosa Parks • George Wallace • Watergate • Southern music: blues, jazz and spirituals • Southern food

### Tandem Crossword

*Copymaster 4: TRB, p.92 & 93/CD-ROM.*
*Solutions: TRB, p. 138.*

These tandem crosswords include important vocabulary covered in this chapter.

## Project: Planning a trip to the US     SB p. 85

*For further information on project work see TRB, pp. 5–7 and 'Skills files', SB, pp. 121 & 139.*

Further suggestions:
→ Write a letter thanking the travel agency for their donations and outlining the trip you have planned.

→ You realise that the donation you have been given will not be enough to cover your expenses. Write a letter to a potential sponsor, such as a manufacturer of sportswear, in which you try to persuade them to finance your trip. Think of reasons why it would be in their interest to sponsor you (for example, you will wear their products to promote the brand name, they will be doing a service to the community, etc.).
(See 'Skills file: Letter writing', SB, p. 137.)

## Test: Notes from a big country

*Copymaster 5: TRB, p. 94/CD-ROM (exercises/questions)*
*Solutions: TRB, p. 139, vocabulary: TRB, p. 142*

# Listening comprehension

**Welcome to America 5**

## A conference call

First listen to the recording without taking notes. Then listen again and complete the details below:

### Call 1

1. Franco's cell phone number: _____
2. Why Traci is calling: _____
3. What Traci will do now: _____
4. What Traci wants Franco to do: _____

### Call 2

5. Company where Franco is now: _____
6. Franco's surname: _____
7. Traci's conference number: _____
8. Time in New York when Traci calls: _____
9. Latest time Franco can call back: _____

### Call 3

10. Time when Traci calls Sally: _____
11. Problem that prompted Traci's call: _____
12. Traci's request: _____
13. How much time does Sally have to do this? _____
14. How Sally feels about this: _____

### Call 4

15. Why Franco did not respond to Traci's message earlier: _____
16. Why Franco wants the call to be short: _____
17. Time when Traci calls Sally: _____
18. Details of Franco's next meeting in London:

    Name of company: _____

    Day of meeting: _____

    Time: _____

    Day of arrival in London: _____

    How he will get home from the airport: _____

19. What Franco has to tell Dee: _____

**Further activity**

Work in groups of three. Imagine how the conference call between Traci, Franco and Sally might continue and practise it.

# Conference call

**Welcome to America 5**

## Call 1
FRANCO *(on mail box)*: Hi. You've called Franco Scicchitano of International Advertising. I'm afraid I'm not available on this number right now. You can call me on my cell phone on 7182218131. Or if you leave your name and number after the beep I'll ring you back as soon as possible. Thanks for calling. *(Bleep)*

TRACI: Hi Franco! This is Traci Grey. I need to speak to you urgently. I'll try contacting you at Alpha. But if I haven't spoken to you before you get this message can you call me right away please? Thanks. Bye.

## Call 2
RECEPTIONIST: Alpha Sponsoring. Good evening, Can I help you?

TRACI: Hi. My name's Traci Grey of International Advertising. I'm trying to contact my colleague Franco Scicchitano. He's at a presentation with you this evening, I think.

RECEPTIONIST: Just a second I'll check our visitor's list – err– Scicchitano, could you spell that for me, please?

TRACI: Oh God, how does he spell it – emm I think it's S-C-I-C-C-H-I-T-A-N-O.

RECEPTIONIST: OK. Franco Scicchitano, I found him. Yes, he should be at our reception in PR by now. I can put out a call for him. It might take a few minutes though. Would you like to call back?

TRACI: Yeh, good idea. Or tell you what: Could you get him to call me back right away at my conference number. That's 2456789234.

RECEPTIONIST: 2456789234 – and you are?

TRACI: Traci Grey. Tell him it's really urgent. He should call me by … what's the time there in New york now?

RECEPTIONIST: Five after seven.

TRACI: OK – then by seven thirty.

RECEPTIONIST: Will do Ms Grey. Thanks for calling and have a nice evening.

TRACI: Yeh, thanks a lot. Bye.

RECEPTIONIST: Bye now.

## Call 3
SALLY: Hallo

TRACI: Hallo there, Sally? Is that you? Traci Grey here! How are you? How's Frankfurt?

SALLY: Traci? Traci Grey?

TRACI: Traci Grey, Los Angeles office!

SALLY: Oh, hi Traci! Do you know what time it is here?

TRACI: We-ll, I guess it must be pretty late …

SALLY: More like pretty early: it's gone one in the morning. This better be important, Trace, I've got a busy day tomorrow with our clients at ABF in Frankfurt.

TRACI: Sorry, Sally, but it is important. Listen: the Promotions manager of the Opus Corporation just called up. Bad news: The directors liked the film material we sent but they didn't like our slogan. And they want a new one fast – or we stand to lose the contract.

SALLY: In the middle of the night, Traci?

TRACI: The campaign is scheduled to start on the networks next week. We have to have the new slogan by this evening so we can get it into production and ready for broadcast. So listen: you've got twenty minutes to get your head clear and I'll call you back then. Franco's calling me from the Alpha presentation in New York so we can get down to some serious brainstorming together, OK?

SALLY: Well, don't expect much creativity out of me. I've got a stinking headache and I'm more than half asleep.

TRACI: It shouldn't take long. Look – I've got to get off the line in case Franco calls. Speak to you again in twenty minutes, OK?

SALLY: Do I have any choice? Speak to you then!

TRACI: Thanks Sal. Bye.

## Call 4
TRACI: Traci Grey, International Advertising. Good afternoon.

FRANCO: Hi Traci. Franco here. Sorry I'm a bit late calling. Couldn't call in before: We were in the middle of the presentation, when I got your message. So what's the problem?

TRACI: Hi Franco. Yeh, Sorry to have to bother you – but it sounds like the serious stuff is over now – judging by the background noise!

FRANCO: Too right. And the sooner I get back the better. As you know, all the real deals get done when the official part is over.

TRACI: OK, OK, I get the picture. I won't keep you long I hope. Look, I've got to get Sally on the other line – she's going to be really pleased: you know what time it is in Frankfurt, don't you?

FRANCO: Well, I'd say around 2 am.

TRACI: Right. … By the way, before I forget. Dee called in for you from London and said that the meeting with Robertson's is set for Friday at 9 am – that's local time. If you let her know what flight you're on she'll pick you up at the airport Thursday evening. And, of course, she's looking forward to seeing you then.

FRANCO: Great, thanks. Looking forward to seeing her, too. But what's the problem now. Why'd you call me?

SALLY *(sleepily)*: Hallo?

TRACI: Hi Sally, it's me again. Franco's on the line now too.

FRANCO: Hi there Sal. How are ya? Bit sleepy?

SALLY: Very funny. So – can we get on with this, so I can get a couple of hours sleep.

TRACI: OK. Just so you both know what's going on: The PR manager of the Opus Corporation called this afternoon and …

# Tricky situations (1/2)

**Welcome to America** 5

---

### At a hotel
**Hotel guest A**
Hotel guest B
Hotel Manager

**Situation:** At a hotel

**Role:** Hotel guest A

**Time:** 8 pm

You arrive at the only hotel in a small town half an hour before guest B.
You want to book a single room with WC, shower and TV for one night.
You haven't made a reservation.
You accept the room offered to you, pay and go to your room.

---

### At a hotel
Hotel guest A
**Hotel guest B**
Hotel Manager

**Situation:** At a hotel

**Role:** Hotel guest B

**Time:** 8.30 pm

You arrive at the only hotel in a small town half an hour after guest A.
You have booked a single room with WC, shower and TV for one night. However when making the reservation you told the hotel manager you would arrive by 6 pm.
You are annoyed when you find out what has happened and demand to speak to guest A to "sort things out"!

---

### At a hotel
Hotel guest A
Hotel guest B
**Hotel Manager**

**Situation:** At a hotel

**Role:** Hotel manager

**Time:** 8 pm

Guest A arrives at your hotel.
Your hotel is fully booked but one guest (guest B) who had booked a room with shower, WC and TV was supposed to arrive by 6 pm and hasn't turned up. You decide to give the room to guest A.

**Time:** 8.30 pm

Guest B arrives! The only room you could possibly offer is one of the staff rooms on the third floor (no lift!) which has neither WC, shower nor TV!
Try to solve the dilemma without upsetting your guests!

---

### At a Restaurant
**Guest 1**
Guest 2
Waiter/Waitress

**Situation:** At a restaurant

**Role:** Guest 1

It is your friend's birthday. After going to the movies together you invite him/her to a meal in a steakhouse.
You order salad to start with and steak and chips for the main course.
You find an insect in your salad and complain to the waiter/waitress.
You accept the soup he/she offers, but when it arrives it is cold.
Then the waiter/waitress tells you there is no steak left.
You are hungry and it is too late to go anywhere else.

# Tricky situations (2/2)　　　　　　　　　　　　　Welcome to America 5

---

### At a Restaurant
**Guest 1**
**Guest 2**
**Waiter/Waitress**

**Situation:** At a restaurant

**Role:** Guest 2

It is your birthday. After going to the movies together your friend invites you to a meal in a steakhouse.
You order salad to start with and steak and chips for the main course.
Your salad has too much dressing on it so you complain to the waiter/waitress.
You accept the soup he/she offers, but when it arrives it is too salty.
Then the waiter/waitress tells you there is no steak left.
You are hungry and it is too late to go anywhere else.

---

### At a Restaurant
**Guest 1**
**Guest 2**
**Waiter/Waitress**

**Situation:** At a restaurant

**Role:** Waiter/Waitress

It has been a busy night and you are the only person left serving. Two guests arrive twenty minutes before the kitchen closes.
You find them a table and take their order.
When they complain about their salads apologize and offer them tomato soup instead.
When they complain about the soup offer them a free drink.
The kitchen then informs you that there is no steak left. You offer fried chicken wings or barbecued spare ribs instead.
Try to keep calm and solve the situation without other guests hearing what is going on!

---

### In a supermarket car park
**Driver 1**
**Driver 2**

**Situation:** In a supermarket car park

**Role:** Driver 1

You are driving slowly around a very busy car park looking for a space.
There is an angry-looking driver in the car behind you who keeps blowing his/her horn.
You see a child who you think is about to run out from behind a parked car in front of your car so you stop suddenly.
The car behind you crashes into the back of your car!

---

### In a supermarket car park
**Driver 1**
**Driver 2**

**Situation:** In a supermarket car park

**Role:** Driver 2

You are on your lunch break from work and have only half an hour to do your shopping and get back to the office.
You are trying to find a parking space, the car park is very busy and the driver in front of you is driving very slowly. You get very angry!
Suddenly the car in front of you stops and you crash into it!

# Tandem crossword (1/2)

**Welcome to America 5**

You and your partner have got different halves of the same crossword. Your partner has got the words you need, and you have got the words your partner needs. Help each other to complete the crossword. Give each other clues, but don't say the words. This crossword is for role A.

**Example:**

> **Role A:** Can you give me a clue for three down, please?

> **Role B:** (Yes.) It's an adjective that describes the weather in the American South.

| | | | | | | | | | | | | | | | |
|---|---|---|---|---|---|---|---|---|---|---|---|---|---|---|---|
| ¹M | ²T | | ³ | | | | | | | | | ⁴J | | ⁵ | |
| I | ¹E | | ⁶T | A | X | E | ⁷S | | ⁸ | ⁹R | | E | | | |
| ¹⁰N | E | A | R | | | | | | | U | | T | | | |
| O | | | ¹¹A | L | L | I | G | A | T | O | R | | | | |
| ¹²R | ¹³C | | | | | ¹⁵R | E | T | A | ¹⁶I | L/ | ¹⁷O | U | T | L | E | T | S |
| ¹⁸T | I | T | L | E | ¹⁹E | | ²⁰S | | | | N | | | | ¹⁴S |
| I | Y | | | | | | U | | | ²¹H | | | | | A |
| E | | ²² | | | | | B | | | A | | | | | T |
| S | | | | | U | | | | | B | ²³G | | | ²⁴ | ²⁵E |
| | ²⁶S | | ²⁷A | I | R | – | C | O | N | D | I | T | I | O | N | E | R | X |
| | ²⁸L | | | B | | | | | T | | S | | | ²⁹A | R | T |
| ³⁰R | A | | | | | | | ³¹A | | T/ | ³² | | | | R |
| E | ³³V | | ³⁴ | ³⁵C | | | | N | | | | | | | A |
| D | E | | | R | | ³⁶ | | T | | | | | | | |
| N | R | | | I | | ³⁷ | | S | | | | | | | |
| E | Y | | ³⁸D | R | E | A | M | | | | | | | | |
| C | | | E | | E | | | ³⁹H | U | R | R | I | C | A | N | E | ⁴⁰S |
| K | | | E | | | | | O | | | | | | | |
| ⁴¹S | | | P | | ⁴²C | O | A | S | T | | ⁴³ | | | | |

# Tandem crossword (2/2)

**Welcome to America 5**

You and your partner have got different halves of the same crossword. Your partner has got the words you need, and you have got the words your partner needs. Help each other to complete the crossword. Give each other clues, but don't say the words. This crossword is for Role B.

**Example:**

**Role B:** Can you give me a clue for eleven across, please?

**Role A:** (Yes.) It's a dangerous animal that lives in the Everglades.

## Notes from a big country

A remarkable thing about America, if you have been living for a long time in a snug little place like the UK, is how very big and empty so much of it is. Consider this: Montana, Wyoming and North and South Dakota have an area twice
5 the size of France but a population less than that of south London. Alaska is bigger still and has even fewer people. Even my own adopted state of New Hampshire, in the relatively crowded Northeast, is 85 per cent forest, and most of the rest is lakes. You can drive for very long periods in New
10 Hampshire and never see anything but trees and mountains – not a house or a hamlet or even, quite often, another car. [...]

The curious thing is that nearly all Americans, as far as I can tell, don't see it that way. They think the country is way too crowded. Moves are constantly afoot to restrict access to
15 national parks and wilderness on the grounds that they are dangerously overrun. Parts of them *are* unquestionably crowded, but that is only because 98 per cent of visitors arrive by car, and 98 per cent of those venture no more than 400 yards from their metallic wombs. Elsewhere, however,
20 you can have whole mountains to yourself even in the most crowded parks on the busiest days. Yet I may soon find myself barred from hiking in many wilderness areas, unless I had the foresight to book a visit weeks beforehand, because of perceived overcrowding. [...]

The fact is America is already one of the least crowded
25 countries on earth with an average of just sixty-eight people per square mile, compared with 256 in France and over 600 in Britain. Altogether, only 2 per cent of the United States is classified as "built up".

Of course, Americans have always tended to see things in a
30 different way. Daniel Boone famously is supposed to have looked out of his cabin window one day, seen a wisp of smoke rising from a homesteader's dwelling on a distant mountain and announced his intention to move on, complaining bitterly that the neighbourhood was getting too
35 crowded.

(359 words)

From *Notes from a Big Country* by Bill Bryson,
London: Black Swan, 1998, pp. 55-58.

### Content
1. Compare Bill Bryson's perception of his country with that of his fellow Americans.
2. Summarize the two examples Bill Bryson uses to illustrate his point about Americans having a distorted perception of their country.
3. Explain what makes the National Parks seem more crowded than they actually are.

*(Your teacher will tell you which of the following tasks you should complete.)*

### Comment
1. If you felt (or feel) crowded where you live, would this be reason enough to make you want to move? Give reasons for your answer.
2. Explain what you think Bill Bryson means when he uses the expression "metallic womb" (l. 19) to describe how Americans feel about their cars.

### Form
1. Describe the tone of this text. What stylistic elements does the author use to achieve this tone?
2. Show how the author makes use of comparison and contrast and talk about what effect these devices have.

### Language
1. Find expressions in the first two paragraphs (ll. 1–24) that fit the following definitions.
    a) surprising
    b) warm and protected
    c) congested
    d) full of people
    e) to limit who can go in
    f) to risk going somewhere that might be dangerous
    g) ability to see what is likely to happen in the future
2. Explain the meanings of the underlined words in sentences.
    a) "Parts ... are unquestionably crowded." (ll. 16–17)
    b) "Yet I may soon find myself barred ... ." (ll. 21–24)
    c) "... Americans have always tended to see things ... ." (l. 30–31)
3. Give the noun forms of the following words.
    a) to consider (l. 3)
    b) curious (l. 12)
    c) to announce (l. 34)
    d) to complain (l. 35)

# The American political system XtraFile

## Didaktische Hinweise

In beiden XtraFiles handelt es sich um die Vermittlung eines faktischen Basiswissens, vor dessen Hintergrund dann in den Jahrgangsstufen 12 und 13 die Themen 'Politik im Vereinten Königreich' sowie die 'Politik in den USA' vertieft werden sollen. Die XtraFiles werden durch eine gewisse Reduzierung dem Stellenwert des entsprechenden Themenbereiches in der Klasse 11 gerecht und ermöglichen daher eine zielorientierte Wissensvermittlung in ausgewogener Gewichtung. Zur Lernzielkontrolle dienen die Kopiervorlagen des TRB/ der CD-ROM.

### CC:2/6 CD2:20 Checks and Balances  SB S. 86–87

Dieses Hörspiel wurde speziell für die Zielgruppe konzipiert und beinhaltet die wichtigsten Informationen zur Geschichte und Gegenwart des amerikanischen politischen Systems.

Kopiervorlage **1**: TRB, S. 97/CD-ROM.
Lösungen: TRB, S. 139.

Dies ist ein Fragebogen mit multiple-choice Fragen zu dem politischen System der Vereinigten Staaten. Der Fragebogen kann nach dem Hören/Lesen des Hörspiels eingesetzt werden, oder einmal vor der Bearbeitung des Hörspiels, um die Vorkenntnisse der S festzustellen, und danach ein zweites Mal als Lernzielkontrolle.

### Listening comprehension  SB S. 87

In den Vereinigten Staaten wird im Radio eine wöchentliche Ansprache vom Präsidenten gesendet. Dieser Hörverstehenstext ist die Rede von Bill Clinton vom 12. September 1998 und bezieht sich inhaltlich im wesentlichen auf junge Leute und deren Probleme und Bedürfnisse in der Gesellschaft. Weitere Radioansprachen befinden sich im Internet als Text- und Audio-Dateien: http://www.pub.whitehouse.gov

Kopiervorlage **2**: TRB, S. 98/CD-ROM
Lösungen: TRB, S. 139

→ Alternative/zusätzliche Aufgabe zu Aufgabe 2 auf der Kopiervorlage (words and definitions):
Listen to the speech again and complete the sentences using the words given below.
to assume responsibility • bipartisan • to combat • community • to curb • to empower • to ensure • exhausting • grant • to reverse • surplus • trend

a) It's been an _(exhausting)_ and difficult week
b) I want to tell you about the latest steps we're taking _(to combat)_ a truly alarming _(trend)_.
c) We can _(reverse)_ this terrible trend
d) by working together at the _(community)_ level
e) When we _(assume responsibility)_ for bringing down crime, something remarkable happens
f) We can have a similarly dramatic effect in _(curbing)_ the use of drugs among our young people.
g) (a) media campaign _(to ensure)_ that the message comes across
h) these _(grants)_ _(empower)_ communities to do more of what works
i) We are committed in a _(bipartisan)_ way to fight against drug use among our young people.
j) setting aside the _(surplus)_ – every penny of it

### CC:2/2 CD:45  Radio address to the nation (Transcript)

THE PRESIDENT: Good morning. It's been an exhausting and difficult week in the Capitol, not only for me, but for many others. But as I told my Cabinet on Thursday, we cannot lose sight of our primary mission, which is to work for the American people, and especially for the future of our children. The most important thing to do now is to stay focused on the issues the American people sent us here to deal with, from health care to the economy to terrorism.

Today that's exactly what we're doing. I want to tell you about the latest steps we're taking to combat a truly alarming trend, the growing use of drugs among our young people. The good news is that overall drug use has dropped by half since 1979. But among our children the problem is getting worse. In fact, if present trends continue, half of all high school seniors will have smoked marijuana by the time they graduate. That's a frightening development. When we know that drugs lead to crime, to failure in school, to the fraying of families and neighborhoods, we know we must do better.

We can reverse this terrible trend if we attack it in the way we did the crime problem, by working together at the community level, neighborhood by neighborhood, block by block, person by person.

Crime overall has dropped to a 25-year low now, because whole communities are taking responsibilities for their own streets and neighborhoods, and because here in Washington we're giving them the tools they need, such as support for community policing programs. When we assume responsibility for bringing down crime, something remarkable happens – crime does go down. We can have a similarly dramatic effect in curbing the use of drugs among our young people. But all of us have a responsibility to send our young people the same simple message: drugs are wrong, drugs are illegal, and drugs can kill you.

This summer my administration launched an unprecedented media campaign to ensure that the message comes across when young people watch television, listen to radio, or read the newspaper. But media is not enough. We also must enlist the efforts of parents, teachers, ministers and clergy, coaches, principals from the community of adults around them. That's why, with the support of both Democrats and Republicans in Congress, and under the direction of General Barry McCaffrey, we're extending new help to community-based groups all over our nation. Representatives of some of those groups are here with me in the Oval Office today. Already they are working to curb drug use by reclaiming drug houses, reaching out to at-risk foster kids, teaching parents to deliver the antidrug message.

Today I'm delighted to announce the first round of high-impact, low red-tape grants to 93 communities. Their dollar amounts are not large, but if these grants empower communities to do more of what works to keep young people away from the scourge of drugs, their effect will be enormous.

Now, we also need the support of Congress on other serious issues facing our country. We are committed in a bipartisan way to fight against drug use among our young people. We must similarly be committed in a bipartisan way to continue our economic growth by staying with our economic strategy that has made our country the envy of the world; by maintaining our fiscal discipline, setting aside the surplus – every penny of it – until we save Social Security first. We have to restore strength in growth to the world economy by investing our proportionate share in the International Monetary Fund.

All of you know that the world economy has been going up and down and changing quite a bit lately. Treasury Secretary

# XtraFile  The American political system

Rubin and I will go to New York on Monday, where I will discuss the current challenges of the global economy and the risks to our prosperity unless we act on the IMF request and take some other steps designed to make sure that America does not become a sea of prosperity in an ocean of distress.

We also have to continue to invest in the education of our people. We have to have smaller classes, more teachers, modernize schools, all the classrooms hooked up to the Internet, and higher standards. We need a real patients' bill of rights. We need to protect the environment. We need to protect our democracy by passing bipartisan campaign finance reform. All these items also are before Congress now.

It is truly encouraging to me how we have put aside partisan differences to save our children and their future from drugs. We have to do that on other issues critical to our future now – and even in the weeks before the election in November. We must stay focused on your business.

Thanks for listening.

Radio address by President Bill Clinton to the nation, 12 September 1998,<br>The Oval Office, The White House

## The US political system ...   SB S. 88–89

*Die stringenteste Bearbeitung ermöglicht das gemeinsame Lesen und die Zusammenfassung der Texte und des Diagrammes im Unterricht: nachdem der Wortschatz geklärt ist, können die wichtigsten Punkte des Inhalts in Stichpunkten an der Tafel aufgelistet werden. (S. auch KV 3.)*

*Es wäre ebenfalls denkbar, dass sich die S im Vorfeld Karteikärtchen besorgen. Für die einzelnen Kärtchen werden dann gemeinsam im Unterricht Überschriften gefunden, unter denen dann die wichtigsten Stichpunkte auftauchen.*

*Kopiervorlage **3**: TRB, S. 99/CD-ROM.*
*Lösungen: SB, S. 88.*

*Auf dieser Kopiervorlage befindet sich das Diagramm aus dem SB, S. 88, das S anhand der Angaben vervollständigen sollen.*

## Klassenarbeit

*Kopiervorlage **4**: TRB, S. 100*
*Lösungen: TRB, S. 139.*

*Da die Thematik der politischen Systeme in erster Linie Vermittlung von Fachwissen ist, wurde hier die Herübersetzung als Form der Klassenarbeit ausgewählt.*

*Auf der CD-ROM befindet sich zusätzlich ein themenunabhängiger Übungstext, der allgemeine Schwierigkeiten bei Übersetzungen aufweist.*

# Checks and balances quiz

**The American political system** XtraFile 1

Many students in America have to pass an American government examination in order to graduate (SB, pp. 86–87). These are the kind of questions students have to answer. Find out how much you know!

1. **What was another name for the group of delegates who agreed upon the Constitution?**
   - a) the colonialists
   - b) the founders
   - c) the constitutionalists
   - d) the framers

2. **What was added to the Constitution in 1791?**
   - a) the Bill of Rights
   - b) a Bill of Law
   - c) a writ of 'habeas corpus'
   - d) a clause stating that the Constitution would be rewritten every 10 years

3. **Why is the US political system known as the system of 'checks and balances'?**
   - a) because one branch checks to see that everyone has the same amount of work
   - b) because one branch checks the others to make sure that it remains the most powerful
   - c) because the main job of all the branches is to check that they all have a balanced budget by the end of the fiscal year
   - d) because all of the branches check each other to see that no one gets too much power, and so there is a balance of power between all of them

4. **How many branches of government are there, and what are they called?**
   - a) 3, the legislative, executive, and judicial branches
   - b) 4, the senatorial, representative, executive and judicial branches
   - c) 3, the Democrat, the Republican, and the judicial branches
   - d) 3, the Washingtonian, Jeffersonian, and judicial branches

5. **The House of Representatives contains how many members?**
   - a) 100
   - b) 435
   - c) 345
   - d) 200

6. **How often are Senators elected?**
   - a) every 2 years
   - b) every year
   - c) every 6 years
   - d) every six months

7. **What branch of government does the President belong to?**
   - a) the Democratic branch
   - b) the legislative branch
   - c) the judicial branch
   - d) the executive branch

8. **How long is a President's term? How many terms can the President serve?**
   - a) 2 years, 2 terms
   - b) 4 years, an unlimited number of terms
   - c) 3 years, 2 terms
   - d) 4 years, 2 terms

9. **Is it correct to say that the President is directly elected by the people? Why / Why not?**
   - a) correct, this is an important part of the democratic process
   - b) only in even-numbered election years. State electors, who are chosen by the people, cast their votes for presidential candidates in odd-numbered years
   - c) incorrect, state electors, who have been elected by the people, do the casting of the votes for President
   - d) incorrect, members of the most powerful political party cast their votes for the presidential candidate

10. **What is the judicial branch made up of?**
    - a) just the Supreme Court
    - b) the Supreme Court and the federal courts
    - c) the Supreme Court, the federal courts, and a lawyers' association
    - d) the federal courts and the prison system

11. **What is a bill?**
    - a) a Senator who is re-elected
    - b) a proposal by a representative to call a meeting
    - c) a proposal to balance the budget
    - d) a proposal for a new law

12. **When can the Supreme Court become involved in the law-making process?**
    - a) when it rules that a law does not follow the principles of the Constitution
    - b) when it rules that a law is too constitutional
    - c) when legislators can't make up their minds and they need others' opinions
    - d) whenever the judges have some extra time on their hands

# Listening comprehension

**The American political system** XtraFile 2

## Radio address to the nation by President Bill Clinton

**to fray** [freɪ] to come apart
**policing programs** *here:* where citizens keep watch over their neighbourhoods
**minister** ['---] *Pfarrer*
**principal** ['prɪnsəpl] *(AE)* for headmaster
**at-risk** in danger
**foster kids** ['fɒstə] *Pflegekinder*

**high-impact** ['ɪmpækt] having great effect
**low red-tape** uncomplicated
**fiscal** ['fɪskl] financial
**Social Security** *amerikanische Sozialversicherung*
**International Monetary Fund (IMF)** *Internationaler Währungsfonds*
**distress** the state of needing help [-'-]

1. Listen to President Clinton and then mark the statements true (T) or false (F).

| Statement | T/F |
|---|---|
| 1. The President had a busy but easy week. | |
| 2. The Cabinet's job is to work for the future of the American people, and especially for children. | |
| 3. There's good news concerning drug use in general. | |
| 4. Among children and young people, the drug problem is getting worse. | |
| 5. People must fight this drug problem alone. | |
| 6. Adults' major responsibility is to have young people put into jail if they take drugs. | |
| 7. Mass media support the fight against drugs with their advertising campaigns. | |
| 8. Parents and other community leaders must also join in the fight against drugs. | |
| 9. The government is going to give money to help communities fight the war against drugs. | |
| 10. Other nations are envious of the US because of its economic growth and prosperity. | |
| 11. The President warns that although America is a wealthy country, it is at risk of becoming less rich. | |
| 12. The President believes that many aspects of the educational system must be improved. | |
| 13. Another serious issue that the President mentions is poverty in America. | |
| 14. The President is disappointed that the parties won't forget their differences and fight the drug problem together. | |

2. The words on the left below were used by Bill Clinton in his radio address. Match them with their definitions.

   1. exhausting
   2. to combat
   3. trend
   4. to reverse
   5. community
   6. to assume (responsibility)
   7. to curb
   8. to ensure
   9. grant
   10. to empower
   11. bipartisan
   12. surplus

   a) statistical tendency
   b) to give s.o. or s.th. the means to achieve a goal
   c) very tiring
   d) to make sure that s.th. happens
   e) involving two political groups or parties
   f) to limit
   g) to take on (responsibility)
   h) to cause to go in the opposite direction
   i) s.th. of which there is extra
   j) to fight against or try to stop s.th.
   k) money given by a government or organization
   l) the people who live in a certain place or area

3. Write a short 'political speech' (max. 10 sentences) about a political event or issue of your choice. Use at least four of the words from task 2 in your speech. You can talk about an issue in the news or at your school or make up an event if you wish.

# Checks and balances

**The American political system** XtraFile 3

## The US political system: 'Checks and balances'

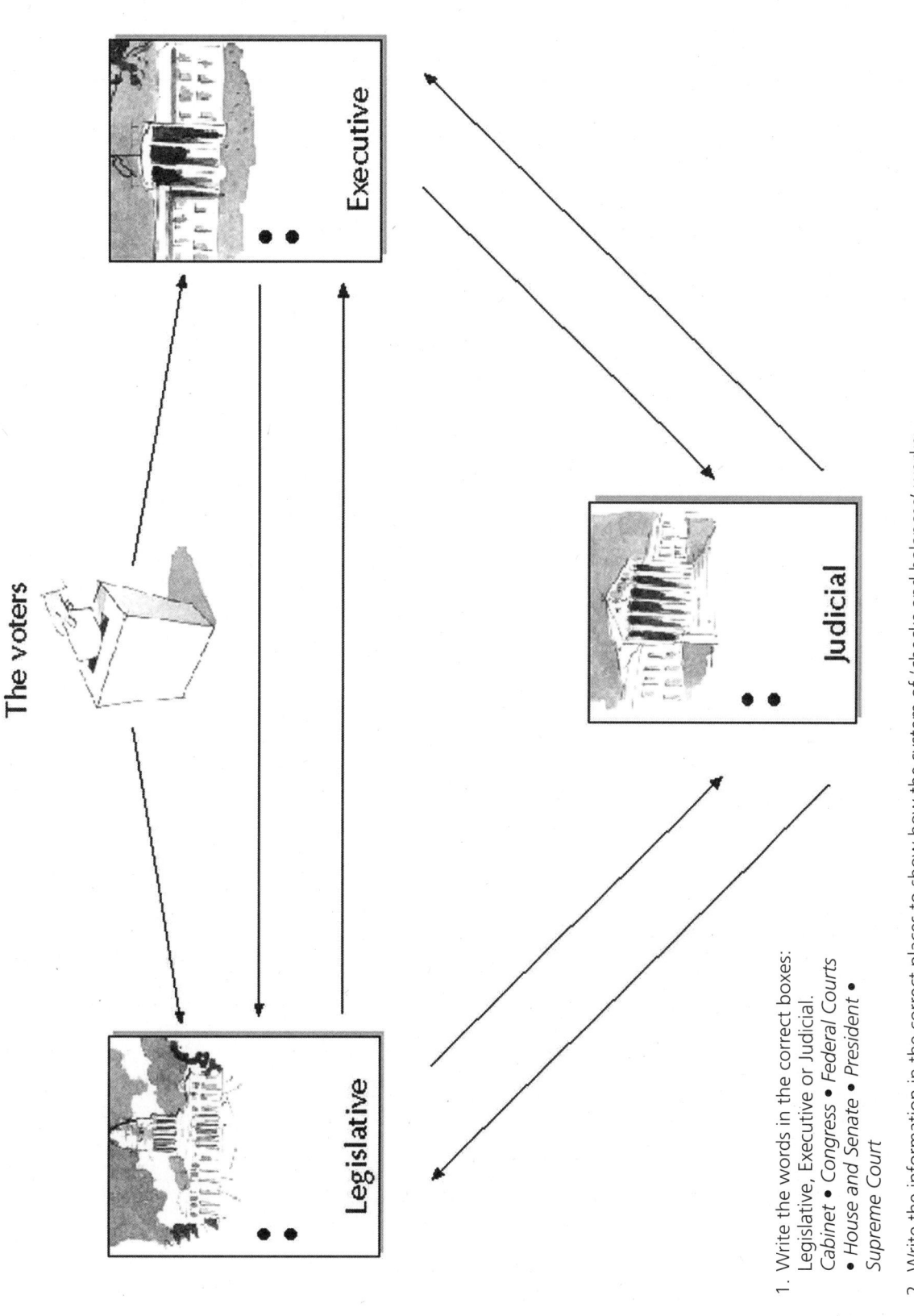

[Diagram showing three boxes labeled **Legislative**, **Executive**, and **Judicial**, connected by arrows, with "The voters" and a ballot box shown above.]

1. Write the words in the correct boxes:
Legislative, Executive or Judicial.
Cabinet • Congress • Federal Courts
• House and Senate • President •
Supreme Court

2. Write the information in the correct places to show how the system of 'checks and balances' works:
The President suggests legislation and can veto laws passed by Congress. • Congress can pass laws over the President's veto by a two thirds majority. • The court can declare laws unconstitutional. • The President appoints federal judges. • The Senate must confirm the President's judicial appointments. • Congress ratifies treaties and declares war. • The court can declare presidential acts unconstitutional. • direct vote • indirect vote (via state elections)

99

## Government and politics

It is practically impossible for an American citizen to escape the impact of government and the political process. From the variety of taxes paid, to environmental and consumer regulations, voting and elections, or interest rates paid on a credit, the citizen confronts the diverse effects of political decision-making by an elected or appointed public official at the local, state, or federal government level. On the other hand, a citizen can also influence his or her political world by exercising the constitutional freedoms included in the Constitution.

The American constitutional system goes back to the dramatic events of the 1787 convention in Philadelphia. The fifty-five delegates possessed certain political ideals and a desire to create a stronger nation. The compromises they agreed to and the document they produced have clearly stood the test of time. (137 words)

4 **interest rates** charge for the use of credit or borrowed money
12 **convention** meeting, congress

*From* Introduction to Government *by Larry Elowitz,*
*New York: HarperCollins Inc., 1992, p. 1.*

# Life in the city: Atlanta 6

## Didaktisches Inhaltsverzeichnis

| Title | Text type / Topic | Skills & Tasks | 💿📄 |
|---|---|---|---|
| **Facts and figures** (SB S. 90) | • photos and statistics | • Speaking: talking about pictures and statistics | |
| **Atlanta timeline** (SB S. 91) | • timeline | • Grammar: relative clauses/the present and past tenses/ the passive voice | |
| **Introducing Atlanta** (SB S. 92) | • travel guide article (606 words) | • Reading: for detail<br>• Grammar/Vocabulary: adjectives, their definitions and synonyms<br>• Writing: texts to promote one's area | |
| **Talking about Atlanta** (SB S. 93) | • interview with a public relations manager | • Listening comprehension | 1 TRB, S. 112<br>2 TRB, S. 113 |
| **Atlanta flying high, via world's No. 1 airport** (SB S. 94) | • newspaper article (469 words) | • Reading: for detail<br>• Grammar: if clauses and the conditional<br>• Vocabulary: travel terms and symbols<br>• Translation<br>• Writing: essay/dialogue/story | |
| **What's on the minds of Atlantans?** (SB S. 96) | • magazine article (604 words)<br>• Atlantans' opinions on city problems | • Reading: for detail<br>• Vocabulary: categorizing terms beneath headings/ mind maps/definitions<br>• Grammar: participles and subordinate clauses<br>• Writing: summaries and statements | |
| **Congestion, urban sprawl and quality of life** (SB S. 98) | • magazine article (407 words) | • Reading: for detail<br>• Grammar: adverbs<br>• Writing: headings/summarizing statements | |
| **Reasons for increases in traffic today** (SB S. 99) | • pie chart<br>• statistics showing reasons for traffic increase | • Speaking: radio interview | |
| **A sense of community** (SB S. 100) | • magazine article (310 words) | • Reading: for detail<br>• Speaking: giving one's opinion<br>• Vocabulary: explaining words in context/using adjectives to describe city and community life | 3 TRB, S. 114<br>4 TRB, S. 115 |
| **Atlanta's new main street: Buford Highway** (SB S. 101) | • newspaper article (526 words) | • Reading: for detail<br>• Vocabulary: countries and nationalities/explaining words in context<br>• Writing: creating a visitor's guide for your area | |
| **From Terminus to Atlanta** (SB S. 103) | • novel excerpt from 'Gone with the Wind' (854 words) | • Reading: for detail<br>• Grammar: relative clauses<br>• Writing: analysing styles<br>• Translation | |
| **Project: A talk on improving your town** (SB S. 105) | | | |
| **Test: America's cities: they can yet be resurrected** | • newspaper article (343 words) | | 5 TRB, S. 116 |

# 6 Life in the city: Atlanta

## Einleitung

Ziel dieses Kapitels ist es, einen Blick in das amerikanische Stadtleben zu vermitteln. Am Beispiel Atlanta, Georgia, lernen die S vieles über die Infrastruktur dieser Stadt sowie über die Herausforderungen (z. B. Verkehrsprobleme, Kriminalität, 'urban sprawl'), mit denen nicht nur Atlanta, sondern Großstädte im Allgemeinen konfrontiert werden. Es werden wichtige Einzelheiten Atlantas vorgestellt, anhand derer die S die Entwicklung dieser Stadt vom Dorf zur „Hauptstadt des 'New South'" nachvollziehen können.

## Facts and figures                SB 90–91

Für dieses Kapitel bietet sich als Einstieg die vereinfachte Moderationsmethode an. Der hier ausgearbeitete Vorschlag beinhaltet die im Buch aufgeführten Einstiegsaufgaben, die bei Zeitmangel auch ohne die Moderationsmethode anhand des SB bearbeitet werden können.

Moderationsmaterialien:
- das Bild von Atlanta und die dazugehörigen Fakten auf S. 90 im SB
- die US-Karte im SB
- verschiedenfarbige Moderationskärtchen und dicke Filzschreiber
- 3–6 Moderationswände mit folgenden Themenbereichen:
First impressions of Atlanta • Atlanta's location • Adjectives describing this city • Description of these buildings and their function • Surprising facts • *(evtl.)* Comparison of facts

→ *Einstieg in die Moderation:*
*Ausgangsfrage:* Imagine that you were in a plane landing at the William B. Hartsfield Airport and you got this first glimpse of the city. What are your first impressions of Atlanta?

Alle S erhalten gleichfarbige Moderationskärtchen, auf denen sie kurz ihre Eindrücke festhalten sollen. Diese werden unter der Überschrift First impressions of Atlanta an der ersten Moderationswand angeheftet (und eventuell vom Moderator – der Lehrperson oder einem Mitglied der Schülergruppe – nach Themen geordnet). Zeitaufwand: ca. 15 Minuten (abhängig davon, wie geübt die Klasse in der Moderationsmethode ist).

### Getting started

Als Erstes sollen die S Gruppen von 3–4 Mitgliedern bilden.
1. **Atlanta's location:** Die S suchen Atlanta, Georgia, auf der Landkarte und beschreiben die Lage der Stadt. Alle Gruppen erhalten Moderationskärtchen (für jede Gruppe eine andere Farbe), auf denen die Gruppenmitglieder zusammen ihre Stichwörter festhalten sollen. Diese werden von einem Mitglied jeder Gruppe unter der Überschrift 'Atlanta's location' an der zweiten Moderationswand angeheftet. Einzuführende bzw. zu wiederholende Vokabeln sind z. B. next to • north/south/east/west of • nearby • situated in • in the vicinity of
2. a) **Adjectives:** Diese Aufgabe kann in Kleingruppen bearbeitet werden. Die Gruppen erhalten einsprachige Wörterbücher, um Schreibfehler zu vermeiden. Außerdem bekommt jede Gruppe Moderationskärtchen (für jede Gruppe eine andere Farbe), auf denen sie Adjektive notieren.
Die S sollen als Gruppe die von ihnen gefundenen Adjektive zuordnen und an der dritten Moderationswand ('Adjectives describing this city') anheften. Diese Moderationswand wird in zwei Kategorien unterteilt: 'positive aspects', und 'negative aspects'. Anschließend wird der Eindruck und dessen Wertung in einem gemeinsamen Kurzvortrag begründet. Diese Übung zeigt, dass manche Adjektive sowohl positiv als auch negativ gebraucht werden können, während andere eine eindeutige Wertung beinhalten.
Z. B: *"We think Atlanta looks huge, and that's a negative aspect because you can get lost easily."*
oder: *"… that's a positive aspect because you can see a lot of interesting things there."*
Weitere mögliche Nennungen: *big, built-up, new, confusing, busy, bustling, business orientated/oriented, impressive, modern, shining, crowded, empty, hostile, wealthy*
Zeitaufwand: Kurzvorträge der Gruppen: variiert je nach Klassengröße zwischen 10 und 15 Minuten. Für eine einzelne Einführungsstunde sollte an dieser Stelle zum Buch übergegangen werden. Steht eine Doppelstunde zur Verfügung, so kann die nächste Fragestellung wieder in Gruppen nach der Moderationsmethode bearbeitet werden:
2. b) **Description of buildings and their function:** Die vierte Moderationswand wird in die Kategorien 'The buildings' und 'Their functions' unterteilt:
Die Schülergruppen können hier entweder ein bestimmtes Gebäude herausgreifen oder sich allgemein auf die Skyline beziehen. Antworten werden an der Wand angeheftet.
Mögliche Antworten:
*Buildings: skyscrapers, many floors, glittering, business-orientated, high-tech, high-rise, modern, official, urban*
*Functions: office buildings, law firms, news agencies/bureaus, companies, administration/government buildings, high rise hotels or apartment buildings*
3. **Surprising facts/Comparison of facts:** Nach dem Lesen der facts sollte geklärt werden, dass Null Grad Celsius 32 Grad Fahrenheit entspricht; die Durchschnittstemperatur also bei 5,5 ° C im Januar und bei 25,8 ° C im Juli liegt.
Antworten werden an der fünften und sechsten Wand angeheftet.
Mögliche Antworten: *young average age • large metropolitan population as compared to the city population • lots of churches*
Der Vergleich der Fakten sollte besser als HA bearbeitet werden, um den S zu ermöglichen, im Internet, in der Bibliothek und in anderen Zeitschriften, Almanachen, usw. nach Informationen zu suchen.
4. **Writing a paragraph:** Diese Aufgabe kann entweder sofort nach dem ersten Teil der Aufgabe 3 'Surprising facts' oder in der nächsten Klassenstunde nach 'Comparison of Facts' durchgeführt werden.

### Language & grammar

1. The Coca-Cola Company, which was established in 1892 by Asa Candler, is shown in photograph a). • Dr Martin Luther King, Jr., who was awarded the Nobel Peace Prize in 1964, is shown in photograph b). • In photograph c) you can see Jimmy Carter, who was governor of Georgia and who was also elected the 39th president of the United States. • Photograph d) is a brochure about MARTA's Rapid Rail System, which began operation in 1979.• Photograph e) is of the Cable News Network (CNN), which was established in 1980 and was the first television station to broadcast 24-hour news around the world. • Atlanta, which after the Civil

War underwent a period of reconstruction starting in 1865, is shown in photograph f).
2. –
3. a) 1843: is renamed • 1885: is founded • 1892: is established • 1936: is published • 1964: is awarded • 1976: is elected • 1980: is established • 1994: is held
b) Active to passive:
1868: The first daily morning newspaper, the "Atlanta Constitution" is published.
1974: Babe Ruth's lifetime home run record is broken by Hank Aaron of the Atlanta Braves.
1996: The biggest sports event in its history, the Summer Olympics, is hosted by Atlanta.
1999: The latest innovations in the world of communications are presented by SUPERCOMM.
Passive to active:
1892: Asa Candler establishes the Coca-Cola Company in Atlanta.
1976: The United States citizens elect Jimmy Carter, governor of Georgia, to be the 39th president.
1980: Cable News Network establishes itself in Atlanta as the first television station to broadcast 24-hour news around the world.

→ *Die S schreiben in GA einen kurzen geschichtlichen Abriss der Entwicklung ihrer Heimatstadt nach dem Muster der Atlanta Timeline. Nun werden die Jahreszahlen der Ereignisse vertauscht und als Quiz für die anderen Gruppen auf Folie geschrieben.*

## CC:2/7 CD2:25 Introducing Atlanta SB S. 92–93

### Before you read

*Informationsquellen: library (city or university) • Deutsch-amerikanisches Institut/Amerika-Häuser • Internet: http://www.ci.atlanta.ga.us/ oder http://www.acvb.com/html/*

→ *Die S können der Frage, welche Informationen über Atlanta sie am meisten interessieren, aktiv nachgehen, indem sie in GA einen Artikel auf der Homepage von Atlanta (Internetadresse s.o.) auswählen und dessen Inhalt der Klasse präsentieren. Zeitaufwand (bei 4–5 Gruppen mit ca. 5 S): Suche und Auswahl: 1 Schulstunde; Ausarbeitung der Präsentation: 1 Doppelstunde/2 Schulstunden; Präsentation der Ergebnisse: 1 Schulstunde*

### While you read

*Alternative names:*
Big A, Capital of the New South, International Gateway City: Atlanta is an international meeting place, business center and a city of superlatives (world's largest airport). Atlanta is a very modern city that exhibits urban sophistication.
Dogwood City: This name describes the spirit of the Old South that is also to be found in this city. Lots of flowers in spring create a romantic atmosphere of southern hospitality and gentility.

### Comprehension

1. Architecture: innovative (l. 4) • glittering glass skyscrapers (ll. 4/5) • ancient winery (replica of 16th century French chateau) (l. 51) • colonnaded mansions (Antibellum homes) (l. 17)
Infrastructure: world's largest airport (l. 7) • clean and safe mass transportation system (l. 45) • three interstate highways (l. 14) • major shopping facilities (ll. 12/13) • 29 universities and colleges (l. 13)
Business: home to hundreds of businesses (l. 8) • well-equipped business city (Convention center, home for many business headquarters, e.g. CNN, Coca-Cola, Delta Airlines) (ll. 7–11)
Sport: Summer Olympics in 1996 (l. 12) • Super Bowl in 1994 (ll. 11/12) • big-league sports (l. 40)
Culture: theatres (l. 38) • art and science museums (ll. 38/39) • symphony, opera, ballet (ll. 39/40) • presidential library (l. 50) • botanical garden (l. 50) • parks (e.g. Stone Mountain park) (l. 52)
History: founded as a railway crossroads (junction) (ll. 55/56) • home of Margaret Mitchell, author of the novel Gone With the Wind (ll. 23–25) • Civil War history (ll. 25–27) • where Martin Luther King Jr. was born and died (l. 47) • the past is honored (l. 59)
People and lifestyle: hospitable and gracious people (ll. 27–31) • people who like culture and eating (as is shown by the broad culinary variety) and celebrations (e.g. picnics, cookoffs, etc.) (ll. 21–23, ll. 41/42) • nice temperature most of the year (ll. 43/44) • dynamic yet also leisurely pace (l. 28) • urban sophistication (ll. 35/36)
2. The style of this text is sophisticated due to sentences which are sometimes quite long (e.g. ll. 35–42 or ll. 45–53) and an advanced level of language (e.g. verdant (l. 20), culinary spectrum (l. 41)). Many adjectives and adverbs are used to describe Atlanta in a very positive (sometimes almost exaggeratedly positive) way. Adverb/adjective and hyphenated adjective compounds are often used. e.g. architecturally innovative downtown area (l.4), small-town exuberance (l. 21), delightfully temperate climate (ll. 43/44), clean and safe state-of-the-art urban mass-transportation system (l. 45), forward-looking city (l. 58).
Target groups: This text is aimed at people of all types, ages, and interests, from youth in search of fun and action (sports ll. 11/12; nightlife l. 43) to students looking for a place to study (l. 13), from young ambitious adults wishing to pursue careers and start businesses (ll. 1–10), to history fans in search of the Old South (ll. 23–27), or to people of all ages interested in culture (ll. 35–44).
3. –

### Language: adjectives

1.

| Word | Definition | Synonym |
| --- | --- | --- |
| ever-expanding | getting bigger all the time | constantly growing |
| innovative | s.th. that is done in a completely new way | new, original |
| glittering | s.th. that reflects light in all directions | glistening, shiny |
| bustling | full of activity and people | lively, busy |
| state-of-the-art | s.th. made to the most modern technological standards | modern, up-to-date |
| historic | s.th. from long ago | old |
| forward-looking | pointing towards the future | modern, future-oriented/orientated |

2. a)/b) –

# 6 Life in the city

## Over to you

*Bei dieser Aufgabe können die Internet-Seiten über Atlantas sister cities (AE)/twin towns (GB) (http://www.ci.atlanta.ga.us/) als Hilfe für den Aufbau genommen werden; besonders eignet sich der Artikel über Newcastle upon Tyne (GB).*

## Listening comprehension SB S. 93

Kopiervorlage **1**: TRB, S. 112/CD-ROM
Lösungen: TRB, S. 139

CC:2/3
CD:52  **Talking about Atlanta** (Transcript)

*In this interview, you will hear Karen McNealy (K), Public Relations Manager of the Public Relations Department at Atlanta Convention and Visitors Bureau, talk about the city of Atlanta. NcNealy, an enthusiastic resident, has been with the Convention and representing this city for 7 years. She is 32 years old.*

**How would you describe Atlanta to someone who has not been there before?**
K: I would describe it as a very exciting city. There are a lot of different things to see and do, depending on your interests. We've got major league sports teams, four of them, and there aren't very many American cities – I think maybe only twelve – who have all four sports teams: football, basketball, baseball, and we're about to get a national hockey league franchise team.

**Atlanta is a very historical city. I understand that there are a lot of sights to see.**
K: Mmm-hmm. For example, Atlanta is the birth place of Dr. Martin Luther King. Visitors to the city can visit his birth home. His gravesite is just a block away from that; there's an area called the Martin Luther King Historic District and there's also a museum and the church, Ebenezer Baptist Church, where he preached. So that's a very historic area. The Margaret Mitchell house is located here. Margaret Mitchell wrote a portion of *Gone With the Wind* in this apartment building, which has been restored and is open for visitors.

**Is history important in Atlanta everyday life? For example, are people aware that this city played a major part in the Civil War and that this was a place where important events went on during the Civil Rights Movement?**
K: I think most people are aware of this and I think even visitors to the city are as well. That's one of the reasons that they come. That's one of the things that they identify Atlanta with. And they're looking for glimpses of historical aspects as well as *Gone With the Wind*. They think they're going to come and see Tara, which doesn't exist, but at least now we have the Margaret Mitchell house that they can visit.

**Are there aspects about living in Atlanta that set it apart from living in any other American city?**
K: Well, Atlanta has a lot of unique neighborhoods that are nice and very different from one another, like Buckhead, which is kind of the upscale area, where you find a lot of the mansions as well as the nicer restaurants and upscale shopping. You've got Virginia Highlands, that's a smaller neighborhood where a lot of the young professionals live and it has some of the more 'one of a kind' shops and smaller restaurants. Little Fivepoints which is the kind of funkier area with sort of biker bars and tattoo parlours and things like that. It's a really neat neighborhood too. And then Midtown, which is the arts and financial area of town, which has a lot of neat restaurants and art galleries and museums.

**V: How are the different neighborhoods distinct? How would you know when you go from, say, Buckhead to Midtown?**
K: There's kind of a feel for each neighborhood, like Buckhead is really fast and glitzy and has a lot of the bigger restaurants and more active nightlife, I guess. Whereas Virginia Highlands has a little bit slower pace. And in the last couple of years, the downtown area has gone through a kind of renaissance. People are moving back into the inner city, and that's people of all ages, whether students, young professionals or retired people. And with that, we're getting new restaurants downtown, new shopping areas and things like that.

**I take this to mean that Atlanta has had a problem with suburban sprawl in the past, with people fleeing the downtown areas and moving out into the suburbs?**
K: The sprawl has happened over the years, but in the last couple of years we're beginning to see people move back in closer to their work.

**What makes them come back?**
K: I think they're primarily tired of fighting the traffic! People want to spend more time with their families instead of sitting in traffic. Also, of course, the quality of life has gotten better inside town.

**Would you say that Atlanta's population is multi-racial?**
K: It really is. People here are from all over the world, really. There's an area here that can be described as almost like a China town and there is a predominantly Hispanic area of town here. There are little ethnic pockets throughout the city, although people of these nationalities also live spread throughout the city. I think we'll continue to see people of a variety of nationalities moving here.

**I understand that you have a fine public transport system.**
K: Yes, it's called MARTA, Metropolitan Atlanta Rapid Transit Authority, and it is a series of trains and buses that can pretty much get you anywhere you want to go around the city. And it just costs a dollar fifty for each ride.

**I have read some articles talking about how Atlanta, like many other big cities, must deal with some typical city problems. What measures is Atlanta taking to deal with crime, for example?**
K: Well one interesting program that we started around the time of the Olympics is called the Atlanta Ambassador Program. This program is part of Central Atlanta Progress, which is an organisation that promotes industry and development in the downtown area. In the Ambassador Program, there are about fifty or sixty people who are uniformed but unarmed ambassadors who walk the streets downtown. They provide information and escort people to their cars and act as extra eyes and ears for the police. They're referred to as the Friendly Force. You can go ask them for directions or if, for example, you were working late one evening and wanted somebody to walk you to your car, you could just call them and they'd come and escort you. They walk around and make sure people aren't snooping around parking lots trying to break into cars and things. The program has been very successful and it is getting ready to expand into the Midtown area. It is funded through the downtown business owners, who have taxed themselves to finance this program. It has really had a major impact in reducing crime in the downtown area.

**What do you think makes Atlanta an attractive place to do business in, and what kind of businesses are attracted to Atlanta?**
K: A variety of businesses are attracted to Atlanta: financial institutions, we've seen a lot of technology orientated businesses come into the city. ... I think one thing that attracts businesses is the quality of life in Atlanta. It's an economical city to live and do business in compared to other major cities. We also have a very efficient airport, Hartsfield International Airport, which has been named the busiest airport in the world. ... Atlanta's the hub for Delta Airlines, so it's a gateway city for international travel.

We've also got over seventy-five thousand hotel rooms for people coming into the city on business travel, so this city is very accommodating. Atlanta is also a major convention center city. We've got the Georgia World Congress Center, which is one of the top five convention centers in the country. I think those things make this city very attractive.

**With so many businesses coming into Atlanta, there are probably lots of job opportunities for young people.**
K: Yes, yes definitely.

**I believe I've heard that Atlanta is a two-hour plane ride from just about every city in the United States, is that right?**
K: I think about eighty percent of the U.S. is within a two hour plane ride away from Atlanta. A lot of people come to Atlanta to get to other places and we get a lot of traffic through the airport that way too.

**What is there to do in one's free time in this city, especially for younger people?**
K: You can go to all sorts of sports events. Shopping is a popular thing, and we've got some great shopping malls. Some of the neighborhoods have unique shopping areas. The arts are pretty big in Atlanta, especially for the Southeast. We've got the High Museum of Art, which over the last couple of years has been hosting blockbuster exhibits. Right now we have an impressionism exhibit, earlier this year we had a pop-art exhibit, and last year we had a Picasso exhibit. Coming up in the fall, we'll have a Norman Rockwell exhibit that'll be hosted there. There is a lot of theater in Atlanta, from small theater up to major Broadway shows that are touring and stop here. Concerts are a big deal. The Fox Theater, which is an historic theater, hosts concerts, as does Chastain Park and Lakewood Amphitheatre, which are both outdoor venues. Dining out is a popular activity. We've got more than eight thousand restaurants in metropolitan Atlanta. Atlanta has kind of evolved into a dining destination and has become home to some great chefs and some really, really fine restaurants in the last couple of years.

Atlanta is also the home of CNN Broadcasting. There's a CNN studio tour that's very popular, and then there are family attractions for people to visit like the World of Coca-Cola, where you can learn about the history of Coca-Cola, which was founded here. You can visit Centennial Olympic Park, which people are very familiar with from the Olympic Games and which was the world's gathering place during the Olympics. Other attractions include Six Flags Over Georgia, which is an amusement park, and we have a great zoo – Zoo Atlanta …. So, there's really something for everybody.

**You mentioned the Olympics. What effects has the hosting of such major events as the Olympics and the Superbowl, for example, had on Atlanta?**
K: I think it's really put the world's eye on Atlanta. People who really didn't know a whole lot about Atlanta before these events have a better awareness of the city, and that's good for attracting new business as well as visitors and new residents to the city. In preparation for the Olympics, the city underwent more than two billion dollars worth of renovations and built new facilities that are now left for residents and visitors to enjoy, from improvements to the airport infrastructure, to our streets, new parks like Centennial Park, hotel renovations and the construction of new hotels and new facilities like Turner Field, which was the former Olympic stadium and now has been converted into a baseball field where the Atlanta Braves baseball team play.

**What are you most proud of about your city?**
K: I think it's a very friendly city. Many people think that the phrase "southern hospitality" is just a cliché, but you really find this here. You've got very friendly residents who welcome visitors to the city. It's a very attractive city also. In many major cities there's just a lot of buildings and concrete, but Atlanta has a lot of trees and flowers and things that make it a really pretty city.

**You just mentioned the phrase "southern hospitality". How would you define this for someone who has never been to the South?**
K: Southern hospitality means very friendly, very gracious. In some cities when you walk down the street people do not say hello to each other. In Atlanta if you pass someone on the street, whether you know them or not, you would at least acknowledge the fact that they're there. Men still hold doors open for women, things like that, just courtesy, graciousness.

**What's going to happen in your city in the next ten years?**
K: I think we'll continue to see an influx of people coming back into the city; new housing, new restaurants. I think on the business side, we'll continue to try to attract major industry to the city, I think a lot of these industries are going to be focused on technology.

**It sounds like Atlanta is a positive example of a city that has taken problems that may exist and is working with these problems and overcoming them.**
K: I agree. Yes, exactly.

**Is there anything else you would like to say that hasn't been touched upon?**
K: Oh, just invite everyone to come and visit!

*Interview with Karen McNeely, Public Relations Manager, Atlanta Convention and Visitors Bureau*

---

*Im Anschluss an das Interview können die S nun versuchen, selbst einen Fragebogen zu erstellen:*

→ Try to think of interesting questions about your town or city. Create a questionnaire in English and interview a friend. Some aspects to talk about are: information about the person interviewed • environment, family • freetime activities (i.e. cultural opportunities) • crime rate in the neighborhood • historical aspects • public transport/commuting possibilities • job opportunities • plans for the future
Present the results in class and discuss them.

*Je nach der zur Verfügung stehenden Zeit kann bereits die Stichwortliste in der Klassengemeinschaft erarbeitet werden, was erfahrungsgemäß zu interessanten Ergebnissen führt. (Bei Zeitproblemen stehen mit Kopiervorlage 4, TRB, S. 115/CD-ROM bereits vorbereitete Fragen für ein Interview bereit.)*
*Bei der Präsentation der Ergebnisse kann jeder S kurz die auffälligsten Punkte seines/ihres Interviews darlegen, oder es kann auch versucht werden, mehrere Bogen in GA (z. B. nach Alter, Geschlecht oder Beruf der befragten Informanden) auszuwerten und Trends zu formulieren. Es ist darauf hinzuweisen, dass zahlenmäßig derart begrenzte Umfragen statistisch nicht aussagekräftig sind!*

→ *Anhand des 'Questionnaire' (Kopiervorlage 2) können die S den S in Atlanta/the metro area auch direkt Fragen über Atlanta stellen.*

*Kopiervorlage 2: TRB, S. 113/CD-ROM*

*Im Voraus soll L Kontakt mit einigen High Schools in Atlanta/the metro area aufnehmen, um eine entsprechende Klasse zu finden. Adressen für public und private High schools finden Sie unter http://www.surfatlanta.com/schools.htm.*

# 6 Life in the city

S schicken dann möglichst per E-Mail den Fragebogen an eine oder mehrere Schulen in Atlanta und werten dann die Rückmeldungen aus. Daraus sollte/könnte ein E-Mail-Austausch zwischen den amerikanischen und den deutschen S entstehen.

→ Weiteres Projekt:
Falls entsprechend Zeit zur Verfügung steht, kann hier eine größere Anzahl von Personen interviewt und fächerübergreifend gearbeitet werden. Z. B:
- Berechnung des Korrelationskoeffizienten im Mathematikunterricht
- Erstellen eines Auswertungsprogramms/einer Statistik der Ergebnisse im DV-Unterricht
- Zusammenfassung der Ergebnisse in einem Artikel für die Lokalpresse im Deutschunterricht

## World's Busiest Airport  SB S. 94–95

### Before you read

● Advantages of an international airport:
An international airport gives a city international status because it connects the city more closely to the world. • Companies can more easily transport their raw materials all over the world. • Companies can sell their products worldwide with a minimum of transport expense and time • International meetings and conferences can be held, which makes the city even more popular for businesses and companies. • These advantages attract firms to this city, so lots of jobs are created. • With more jobs in the area, more people move to the region, which secures more taxes for the community/city • High profile cultural, political and sports events can be easily organized in a city with a well-developed transportation system. • This also attracts tourists to the city.

## Atlanta flying high, ...  SB S. 94–95

### Comprehension

1. He was mayor of Atlanta for six terms and had guessed 75 years ago that air traffic would become the most important way to travel and to transport goods.
2. a) It is open 24 hours. (l. 16)
b) It covers 3,800 acres (approx. 1,537.8 Hektar). (ll. 17–18)
c) Hartsfield Airport employs 42,300 people. (Col. 3, l. 24)
d) It has got four runways. (Col. 3, ll. 28/29)
e) You can fly to 195 cities and to 20 foreign countries. (Col 3, ll. 30–32)
f) The most important airline in Atlanta is Delta Airlines. (Col. 3, ll. 32/34)
3. a) "World's Busiest Airport":
open 24 hours • more than 2.8 billion passengers went though this airport in 1998 (2.9% increase from 1997) • four runways that take passengers to 195 cities and 20 foreign countries • could already claim the title in the 1960s but received title officially from the Airports Council International in 1998
New York to Miami airmail service:
the federal government wanted to start airmail service in 1920 • either Atlanta or Birmingham were to be the intermediate stop • Atlanta won the competition because they treated a visiting postal official so well. • The city developed rapidly as a result of winning the competition.
Olympic Games:
According to Mayor Campbell, the airport was the major factor that brought the Olympics to Atlanta.

Economy and employment:
The airport is an "engine that drives the economic train". (Col. 3, ll. 8–11) • brings in approx. 15 billion to Ga. economy • employs 42,300 people • population is increasing because of the airport
b) Wichtig ist hier die Gliederung, da die Stichworte sinnvollerweise in eine chronologische/kausale Abfolge gebracht werden müssen. (S. auch 'Skills File: Connectives', SB S. 125.)

### Grammar: Conditional sentences

1. a) If William Hartford <u>hadn't realised that air traffic would soon be more important than rail travel</u>, he <u>would not have had the racetrack turned into an airfield</u>.
b) If a top postal official <u>hadn't been treated like a VIP in Atlanta</u>, then Atlanta <u>would not have won the postal service route from New York to Miami</u>.
c) The Olympic games <u>wouldn't have come to Atlanta</u> if Atlanta airport <u>hadn't been so good</u>.
2. a) What you did:
• I remembered my mum's birthday today (,) so mum was not upset with me. / I will remember my mum's birthday today (,) so mum will not be upset with me.
• I arrived at the cinema early last night (,) so I didn't have a problem getting a good seat.
• I went to Josie's party last Saturday (,) so I met Toby and Simon.
What would have happened otherwise:
• If I hadn't remembered my mum's birthday today, mum would have been upset with me.
• If I hadn't arrived early at the cinema last night, I would have had a problem getting a good seat.
• If I hadn't gone to Josie's party last Saturday, I wouldn't have met Toby and Simon.
b) Als Anregung können Satzanfänge dienen, die sich auf historische Ereignisse beziehen: If Christopher Columbus hadn't discovered America, ... etc.

→ Ein Satz wird vorgegeben, z. B. "If I hadn't come to this school, I wouldn't be learning English now." Ein S nimmt den Satz auf und formuliert ihn um: "If I weren't learning English now, I couldn't travel to countries where English is spoken in my summer holidays." Der Nächste fährt fort: "If I couldn't travel to countries where English is spoken in my summer holidays, I would have to visit my aunt." usw. Die Regeln werden vorher festgelegt, zum Beispiel ob Sätze im Conditional I oder Conditional II gebildet werden müssen.

### Vocabulary

1. airport (Col. 1, l. 6) • air traffic (Col. 1, l. 8) • airfield (Col. 1, l. 13) • passengers (Col. 1, l. 20) • airport traffic (Col. 1, ll. 22/23) • airmail service (Col. 2, l. 17) • intermediate stop (Col. 2, l. 21/22) • runways (Col. 3, ll. 28/29) • carrier (Col. 3, l. 29) • destination (Col. 3, l. 31) • airline (Col. 3, l. 38)
2. a) departures • arrivals • taxi • telephone
b) Z. B.: The symbol for lift or elevator is an arrow which points up or downwards or a stick figure standing between two vertical lines • The symbol for a cash point is a rectangle with "ec" in it • The symbol for a post office is a horn.
c) Mögliche Antworten:
a male and a female figure (restroom signs) • an "i" (information stand/office) • running stick figure (emergency exit) • credit card stickers (indicates where one can pay with a credit card)

# Life in the city 6

## Translation

*Schwierige Stellen:* Geneva-based *(Col. 1, l. 31)* • AIC, *(Col. 1, l. 33)* • New South *(Col. 1, l. 34)* • In as much as *(Col. 1, l. 38)* • it has done so *(Col. 1, l. 39 – Col. 2, l. 1)* • there wasn't that much difference *(Col. 2, ll. 12/13)*

*Übersetzungsvorschlag:*
Der Titel „Meistgenutzter Flugplatz der Welt", der vom internationalen Flughafenrat (AIC) in Genf verliehen wurde, ist ein Coup für diese 'New South' Hauptstadt mit ihren historischen Ambitionen, eine internationale Stadt zu werden.
In welchem Maße Atlanta diese Träume verwirklicht hat, ist hauptsächlich seinem Flughafen zu verdanken. Die Geschichte des Flughafens ist die Geschichte des modernen Atlanta.
"Um zu verstehen, was der Flughafen für Atlanta bedeutet, muss man die Uhr auf die Mitte der 20er Jahre zurückdrehen," sagt der Politikwissenschaftler Charles Bullock von der Universität Georgia. "Zu diesem Zeitpunkt gab es keinen so großen Unterschied zwischen Atlanta und Birmingham (Alabama)."

→ Aus dem Internet werden Informationen über Birmingham vorgegeben (http://www.birminghamnet.com). *Die S suchen Vergleichspunkte zwischen* Birmingham *und* Atlanta *und schreiben sie in einer Liste anhand der Tipps in den* Skills Files *('Adjectives' und 'Adverbs' auf S. 149 im SB).*
*If clauses:* If Birmingham had won the postal service route from New York to Miami instead of Atlanta, … .
*Comparisons:* Atlanta's population is … than Birmingham's.

## Creative writing

*"World's …est town"* und *"International Airport":* Um diese Themen vorzubereiten, kann wieder nach dem Moderationsprinzip in Gruppen mit Schlagwortkärtchen vorgearbeitet werden, so dass dann eine Sammelliste der Vor- und Nachteile/Begründungen des '…est' Wortes auf der Moderationswand entsteht.
Airport story/dialogue: Zur Unterstützung der Kreativität können die S Bilder von Leuten aus Zeitschriften aussuchen und diese Leute als Figuren in ihre Flughafengeschichten/Dialoge einbauen.

## What's on the minds of Atlantans   SB S. 96–97

### Before you read

● Problems in your area/city: e.g. pollution, traffic jams, crowded areas, not enough parks/stores/schools, etc., crime, unemployment
● Problems in the world: e.g. crime, unemployment, pollution, global warming, poverty, hunger, overcrowding

### Comprehension

1.

| Problems | Effect on city life | Possible solution |
|---|---|---|
| Traffic/commuting problems | • Skilled/educated work force won't want to move here • Inhabitants' quality of life suffers | • Put fewer cars on the road • Raise parking prices • Promote public transportation |
| Poor public educational system | • Skilled/educated work force won't want to move here • shortages of people with skills/knowledge to fill existing technological jobs | • Improve the schools |
| Inner-city crime | • Entertainment establishments, etc., flee to the suburbs | Promote the family and church |
| School busing | • Deterioration of neighbourhoods | |
| Mismanagement of natural resources | • Deterioration of the quality of life • Destruction of the environment | • Put fewer cars on the road rather than simply building more roads • Manage and conserve resources (e.g. air, water, land, etc. better |
| Little contact between business leaders and young people | | • Leaders should encourage awareness in their organizations about these problems |
| Only dealing with problems when there is media attention | | • Deal with these problems full time |

2. a) James Soutouras: top executive in a firm that recruits executives ('headhunter' firm) • Chris Coleman: head of what is probably a high-tech firm • Neal Reynolds: head of a business • Chuck Martin: Mayor of the City of Alpharetta
b) James S. and Chris C. want the traffic and education problems solved so that the area will attract qualified candidates for executive and technological positions. Neal R. wants traffic, crime and busing problems solved so that the area will attract more people, and in turn more people will come to his shop. Mayor Chuck M. wants environmental, educational and communication problems dealt with on a full-time basis in his constituency.

### Working with words

1. education: private schools (l. 13); semi-literate (l. 23); semi-skilled (ll. 23/24); educational system (l. 25); school busing (l. 32), schoolchildren (l. 36)
environment: felling trees (l. 27); laying asphalt (l. 28); rapid transit (l. 28); cars (l. 29); road (l. 29); natural resources (l. 46); air, water, land (ll. 46/47)
work: executive search firm (l. 3); recruit (l. 3); client companies (l. 3); candidates (l. 4); company (l. 5); positions (l. 6); skilled/educated (l. 9); work force (l. 9); out-of-town executives (l. 12); technology-related industry (l. 22); national domestic product (ll. 22/23)

# 6 Life in the city: Atlanta

*transport & travel:* traffic (l. 2); traffic problem (l. 7); metro area (l. 13); commuting (l. 16); traffic mess (ll. 19/20); rapid transit (l. 28); laying asphalt (l. 28); cars (l. 29); road (l. 29); parking prices (l. 39); public transportation (l. 40)
*crime:* inner-city crime (l. 31); entertainment establishments flee to the suburbs (ll. 34/35); deterioration of neighborhoods (l. 37); killing (l. 41)
2. to deal with = to do s.th. about (hier: bewältigen) • to have a long way to go = to still have a lot of work to do before a problem can be solved (Wir haben noch einen langen Weg vor uns.) • to promote = to encourage (fördern) • to put more emphasis on = to take s.th. more seriously (mehr Bedeutung beimessen) • to be concerned that = to worry that (um etwas Sorgen machen/besorgt sein) • to address an issue = to talk about problems (Probleme ansprechen)
3. (S. 'Skills File: Writing a summary', SB S. 125.)
Alle in Aufgabe 1 genannten Hauptprobleme sollten angesprochen werden.

**Grammar: participles & subordinate clauses**

1. a) When we recruit out-of-town executives with children for a move to the Atlanta metro area, they almost always ask about private schools.
b) The three biggest problems that the metro is facing are traffic, inner city crime and school busing.
c) The businessman who was killed while getting off at the Lenox MARTA Station several weeks ago sure doesn't help.
2. a) One of the first questions always asked by candidates: ...
b) ... when recruiting people for positions in the Atlanta area.

**Over to you**

💬 Die Ergebnisse können von den S auf eine gemeinsame Diskette übertragen werden, so dass eine Art ‚Regionalzeitung' zum Thema entsteht, die durch ergänzende Bilder und entsprechendes Layout ansprechend gestaltet wird.

## Congestion, urban sprawl ... SB S. 98–99

**Before you read**

💬 Es empfiehlt sich, diese Aufgabe zuerst als Brainstorming-Aktivität durchzuführen: In GA können die S die drei vorgegebenen Stichwörter aufschreiben und entsprechende Definitionen und weitere Stichwörter darunter auflisten. Nachdem die S ihre Listen und mögliche Verbindungen zwischen den Themen diskutiert haben, können sie ihre eigenen Texte schreiben. S. 'Comprehension'-Aufgabe 5. für einen Textvorschlag.

**Comprehension**

1. Atlanta has spread quickly to include a very large metro area, as opposed to other cities, which have spread more slowly but are more densely populated. Thus, many Atlantans live in areas very far away from where they work, which also makes their commute very long.
2. According to Williams, people waste time and also money on gas when they are caught in a traffic jam. This also negatively affects their physical and mental health.
3. Many neighborhoods created in the past spread out into increasingly larger areas further away from where people worked.
This has contributed to the increased commuting times for suburban residents. Also, some of these neighborhoods were not built up in ways that encourage community interaction. Williams tries to create mixed-use-neighborhoods that encourage this sense of community and where people can live nearer to the place where they work.
4. a) He already had experience important for this job because he had worked as a developer in urban as well as suburban counties. He was vice chairman of the Cobb County Chamber twice and also chairman of the Regional Business Coalition.
b) He has strong positive feelings about the city where he grew up and where he wants to stay for the rest of his life. Although he didn't actively try to get this stressful job, he is proud to help improve the city he loves.
5. Die S sollen merken, dass das Wort 'sprawl' nicht Synonym für 'growth' ist, weil 'sprawl' in diesem Zusammenhang einen negativen Sinn hat (Wachstum, das sehr schnell stattfindet und deswegen nicht ausreichend vorgeplant ist), während 'growth' einen neutralen oder positiven Sinn hat.
*Suggested answer:* Congestion led to people moving outside city limits to less crowded areas. As a result, metropolitan areas have "sprawled" into increasingly wider areas around the cities. Many new building developments have been built quickly, and they are more like "bedroom" communities, where people only come home from work and sleep, rather than real neighborhoods where people actually live and interact. People spend considerable time commuting to their work places, many of which are still downtown. These people's quality of life suffers, as they have to spend more time sitting in traffic and less time doing what they want to do.

**Grammar: adverbs**

1. fundamentally – basically (l. 3) • a <u>quite</u> large amount of – fairly (l. 3); very (l. 12) • as a result – consequently (l. 5) • clearly – obviously (l. 12) • some time ago – previously (l. 25) • a viewpoint which <u>almost</u> no-one else has – roughly (l. 30)
2. Mögliche Antworten:
<u>Above</u> <u>all</u> we wanted to live in a city with a low crime rate. • This is <u>basically</u> the situation in our home town. • Mugging, <u>for example</u>, is not as common here as in other big cities. • <u>Similarly</u>, there seems to be fewer burglaries here. • <u>However</u>, there is no such thing as a town without any crime. • <u>In fact</u>, there are some really dangerous places in this town where one shouldn't go at night. • <u>Consequently</u> we try to avoid them after dark. • But <u>recently</u> there has been a lot of improvement in those areas. • <u>Fortunately</u> the new mayor has started a program to reduce crime. • <u>Of course</u> it will take time for the results of this program to become evident. • The mayor will <u>probably</u> have to convince his political opponents to remain patient and give the program a fair chance. • These opponents <u>usually</u> challenge whatever actions and measures the mayor tries to put through. • <u>Generally</u> these opponents try to convince voters that their plans are better than those of the mayor's.

**A step further**

1. Possible headings: living in-town • unlimited city growth • advantages of growth
2. in-town living costs and conditions: lack of city schools that are up to standard • high rents that are increasing because of more people wanting to move in-town
positive aspects of urban sprawl: growth that has increased Atlanta's prosperity • increased profits for real estate business and related businesses that also benefit from more people moving to the area

Atlanta's unique geographical position: Atlanta's growth has no natural boundaries that limit its expansion, and hence it can continue to grow. • Without such a boundary, houses don't have to be cramped together. • Prices don't rise because of limited space. • A person's freedom to choose where they want to live: Because of Atlanta's lack of growth boundaries people can live where they want.

### Role play: an interview

💬 Bei dieser Aufgabe ist eine gemeinsame Gesamtaufnahme als simulierte Radiosendung denkbar, indem die S mögliche Gründe für diese Zahlen und mögliche Folgen diskutieren. Ein 'Sprecher' übernimmt jeweils die kurze Überleitung zwischen den einzelnen ausgearbeiteten Beiträgen. (S. 'Skills Files: Talking about statistics' und 'Useful phrases for discussions', SB S. 131 & 132.)

## The Best Place to Live?  SB S. 100–101

### Before you read

💬 Diese Aufgaben können im Voraus in EA erarbeitet werden. Schließlich erzählen die S, welches Kriterium am wichtigsten für sie ist (entweder von der vorgegeben Liste oder ihr eigenes Kriterium) und warum. Die Ergebnisse werden an der Tafel oder am OHP festgehalten und verglichen.

→ Diese Aufgabenstellung kann auch als spontanes Rollenspiel einer Straßenumfrage durchgeführt werden.

💿 Kopiervorlage 3: TRB, S. 114/CD-ROM
   Kopiervorlage 4: TRB, S. 115/CD-ROM

Dazu werden Rollenkärtchen mit Persönlichkeitsprofilen ausgeteilt (Kopiervorlage 3). Die Klasse bewegt sich frei im Raum und die S versuchen, sich ihrem Rollenkärtchen gemäß zu verhalten und zu bewegen. Einige 'Reporter' übernehmen es, nacheinander an beliebige Mitschüler und Mitschülerinnen Fragen zum Thema Stadtleben zu stellen und nach den Gründen für die gegebenen Antworten zu fragen. (Fragebogen Kopiervorlage 4).
Natürlich kann der Fragebogen auch im Klassenverband erarbeitet werden. In einer leistungsstarken Klasse ist es ebenfalls möglich, auf Rollenkärtchen zu verzichten und es den S zu überlassen, spontan möglichst interessante Persönlichkeitsprofile zu entwickeln.

### A sense of community  SB S. 100–101

### Talking about the photo: –

### Vocabulary

1. a commute – the distance one travels to work every day • cost of living – the money you need for everyday expenses • in-town ambience – the pleasant atmosphere of the city center • urban lifestyle – the way people live in big cities • public transportation – transport network e.g. public busses, trains, subways, streetcars • common feature – something several people or things have in common • sense of community – feeling of belonging together or having something in common with a group of people, e.g. shared interests
2. town centre – downtown (l. 9) • block of flats – condo (l. 10) • flat – apartment (l. 12)

### Comprehension

1. a) The Hills chose to live in Suwaree as they wanted a house relatively near to work, but where the air is clean, and where it is fairly cheap to live.
On the other hand, John Burrison prefers to live in downtown Atlanta since he likes the atmosphere there. He walks to work and uses public transportation as he does not own a car. At night he also enjoys looking out his apartment window at the neo-gothic buildings highlighted against the rest of the Atlanta skyline.
b) Auch hier lassen sich bei mangelnder Schülerbeteiligung die Rollenkärtchen der Kopiervorlage 3 einsetzen, da sich dann Begründungen aus den jeweiligen Lebensumständen der Personen ableiten lassen.
Die Aufgabe eignet sich auch als Thema für einen 'Comment', der evtl. als HA angefertigt werden kann.
2. There are several different types of neighborhoods in Atlanta: one with historical houses in a funky area, a town that is 137 years old, new developments, a planned community, a neighborhood built in the countryside, or downtown neighborhoods receiving city and/or other sources of funding for renovation and development.

### Language

1. a) big city: huge, frightening (l. 20-21)
community: comforting, reassuring (l. 24)
b) Zu erwartende Nennungen:
big city: exciting, anonymous, busy, bustling, noisy, unhealthy, expensive, stressful, colourful, interesting, varied, multicultural
small community: boring, predictable, quiet, personal, traditional, safe, healthy, pleasant
2. (S. 'Grammar File: Adjectives', SB S. 149.)

### Over to you

💬 Für diese Aufgabe können wieder nach dem Moderationsprinzip Vorarbeiten geleistet werden, indem die Kleingruppen versuchen, die Vor- und Nachteile des Stadtlebens stichwortartig zu nennen. Aus einer solchen tabellarischen Aufstellung können dann individuelle Stellungnahmen entstehen. Wie Aufgabe 1. b) ist auch diese Fragestellung ein ergiebiges Thema für einen 'Comment'.

## Changing communities …  SB S. 101–103

### Before you read

💬 Mögliche Nennungen:
Positive changes in your community: improved public transport • more entertainment • integration of foreigners • new schools, cinemas, pubs etc. • pedestrian zone • more parking space downtown • more restaurants, shops and businesses • playground grounds for children • more parks and trees
Negative changes in your community: more crime • no sense of neighborhood • racism • prejudiced people • pollution • smog • congestion • higher rents
💬 Mögliche Nennungen:
Positive aspects: place where members of many races, colours and religions live together • people can benefit from learning about each other's different ideas and beliefs • people living together learn to be tolerant • prejudices are broken down • ethnic diversity

# 6 Life in the city: Atlanta

*Negative aspects:* tensions (i.e. racial) because people with many different ideas and beliefs are living close together • fights between groups with different interests • lack of common interests, ideas and beliefs • misunderstandings between various groups

## Atlanta's new main street ...  SB S. 101–103

### Comprehension

1. Buford Highway can be called multi-cultural because people of many different races, religions, cultures and traditions live there. These people live together peacefully and run successful businesses, and no single group seems to dominate.
2.

| Name | Country of origin | Reasons for coming to Atlanta | Current employment |
|---|---|---|---|
| Eddy Suantio | Indonesia | | vendor |
| Kim Phuong | Vietnam | refugee | owner of two bridal shops |
| Lily Lee | China | | business woman |
| Jesus Brito | Mexico | poverty | owner of shopping center/ grocery |
| Paige Perkins | American (USA) | | development director |

→ Gruppen mit fünf Leuten sollten gebildet werden. Die Teilnehmer spielen die im Artikel genannten Personen. Zusammen schreiben sie ein Rollenspiel über die Vorteile und Nachteile der Einwanderersituation Atlantas. Schließlich können die Gruppen ihre Rollenspiele vor der Klasse spielen.

3. a) "The old Americans" were residents who had lived in this area before the current immigrant influx. They moved out because they decided that the area wasn't good enough for them anymore and because they thought they could be more successful elsewhere.
b) What they have in common is first of all the fact that they are immigrants or refugees. Many of them have borrowed money from their relatives and work very hard to succeed in establishing their own businesses. They are very industrious and ambitious.
4. The area would have become a ghost town with nothing and nobody there. It would have become really run down and an area where nobody would want to live.
5. a) The change of population along Buford Highway is clearly viewed positively. In this text there are only examples of success stories along Buford Highway; there is no mention of any problems that may have occurred as a result of this change.
b) –
6. Zum Beispiel:
Buford Highway is <u>typical</u> of multi-cultural communities because in most big cities there are many different ethnic groups living together and doing business with each other. • Buford Highway is <u>not typical</u> of multi-cultural communities because in most big cities there are often no multi-cultural areas but rather ghettos where members of one ethnic group live together without much contact with other groups.

### Working with words

1. a)

| Country | Nationality |
|---|---|
| Thailand | Thai |
| Mexico | Mexican |
| Africa | African |
| Jamaica | Jamaican |
| Asia | Asian |
| Korea | Korean |
| China | Chinese |
| America | American |
| Russia | Russian |
| Poland | Polish |
| Vietnam | Vietnamese |

b) –
2. to talk in the language of the country of your birth = speaking in one's native tongue (l. 10) • to have a quick look around = to take a glance around (l. 13) • a choice a person makes for himself/herself = decision (l. 19) • time when you are not at work = time off (l. 20) • a person who has left their country e.g. for political reasons = refugee (l. 22) • for example = for instance (l. 42) • people who live in a particular area or building = residents (l. 42)

### Over to you

Die S können zusätzliche Informationen über ihre Stadt entweder in der Stadtbibliothek oder bei der Redaktion der Stadtzeitung bekommen. Auch die Stadtverwaltung und/oder das Stadtarchiv bieten oft nützliche Informationen an.

## CC:2/8 CD2:32 From Terminus ...  SB S. 103–105

### Comprehension

1. Scarlett was particularly interested in Atlanta because her father had told her that Atlanta was just as old as she was.
2. a) Both belong to the same generation. They are young, lively and stubborn and are inclined to change at a moment's notice. Scarlett sees herself as unpredictable and modern and that's how Atlanta was generally seen at the beginning as well.
b) In the beginning there was only a tiny settlement in north Georgia, and there were no railroad tracks here. This village came to be known as Terminus, as it was here that the southern end of the railroad line going from the South and into the new western territory was located. After a few years the town became Marthasville and nine years after its foundation it became Atlanta. Eventually, four railroad lines met here, and therefore this city developed quickly in terms of importance, size and population.
c) Atlanta's first settlers were adventurous and energetic (and pushy, according to those who lived in the older cities) and didn't want to live in the sedate and slow-paced atmosphere of the older towns. These people were proud of the fact that they were creating a new and exciting city, and with their efforts Atlanta grew quickly.
3. Einige Beispiele, die zeigen, dass der alte Charakter dem neuen sehr ähnlich ist:

# Life in the city: Atlanta 6

| Historic Atlanta | Modern Atlanta |
|---|---|
| • "… grow so fast?" (l. 48) | • urban sprawl |
| • "Atlanta was of her own generation …" (l. 14–16) | • young city (median age of population: 31.5) |
| • "Born of a railroad …" (l. 39) | • Atlanta airport, MARTA |
| • "Restless, energetic people from older sections …" (ll. 51–53) | • people from other countries are settling here |
| • "They built … (ll. 53–58) | • newcomers develop the businesses, infrastructure of Atlanta |
| • "They were proud … " (ll. 57–58) | • interviews show how people today love their city (e.g. John A. Williams, Karen McNealy etc.) |

## Looking at style

1. ll. 11–14: "Savannah and Charleston had the dignity of their years, one being well along in its second century and the other entering its third, and in her young eyes they had always seemed like aged grandmothers fanning themselves placidly in the sun."
ll. 14–16: "But Atlanta was of her own generation, crude with the crudities of youth and as headstrong and impetuous as herself."
ll. 27–28: "Atlanta, born Terminus, …"
ll. 45–47: "The older, quieter cities were wont to look upon the bustling new town with the sensations of a hen which had hatched a duckling."
ll. 41–42: "It had become the crossroads … and the little village leaped to life."
l. 59: "Atlanta did not care."
2. ll. 21– 41: "When Gerald first moved … with the North and East."
3. Mögliche Antwort:
Margaret Mitchell had very strong positive feelings for her home town and wanted to present it in a favourable way in comparison to other southern cities. She used a factual style in order to clearly present the historical facts of Atlanta's birth and growth, but she also used personification to present a clear picture of Atlanta and its people. Also as a result of this personification, the story is more lively and the readers do not become bored by the facts.

## Grammar: relative clauses

Savanna, which was well along in its second century, and Charleston, which was entering its third, had the dignity of their years and in her young eyes they had always seemed like aged grandmothers who fanned themselves placidly in the sun.

## Translation

Aus der Eisenbahn geboren, ist Atlanta mit der Eisenbahn gleichzeitig aufgewachsen. Mit der Vollendung der vier Linien wurde Atlanta jetzt mit dem Westen, dem Süden, der Küste und durch Augusta mit dem Norden und Osten verbunden. Er wurde zur Kreuzung des Reiseverkehrs nach Norden, Süden, Osten und Westen, und das kleine Dorf wurde auf einmal lebendig.
Innerhalb eines Zeitraums von kaum länger als Scarletts 17 Jahren wuchs Atlanta von einem einzelnen in den Boden gehämmerten Pfahl zu einer prächtigen Kleinstadt mit 10.000 Einwohnern heran, die den Mittelpunkt des gesamten Staates bildete. Die älteren, ruhigeren Städte neigten dazu, diese neue belebte Stadt mit den Augen eines Huhns zu betrachten, das ein Entenküken ausgebrütet hat. Warum unterschied sich dieser Ort so sehr von jenen anderer Städte in Georgia? Warum ist er so schnell gewachsen? Schließlich, dachten sie, hat diese Stadt nichts, was für sie spricht – nur seine Eisenbahnen und eine Menge sehr aggressiver Leute.

## Project: A talk on improving … SB S. 105

Zusätzliche Hinweise zur Projektarbeit: TRB, S. 5–7 und 'Skills files', SB, S. 139.
Zusätzlich kann eine Internetseite der Heimatstadt oder ein Werbeplakat für den Heimatort entworfen werden.

## Test: America's cities: they can yet be …

*Kopiervorlage 5*: TRB, S. 116/CD-ROM
Lösungen: TRB, S. 140, Vokabeln: TRB, S. 142

**Listening comprehension**                                    Life in the city: Atlanta  6

## Talking about Atlanta

**franchise team** ['fræntʃaɪz] professional sports team
**upscale** ['--] wealthy
**mansion** ['mænʃn] large and fancy home
**glitzy** ['glɪtsɪ] glamorous
**to sprawl** [sprɔːl] to spread out over a wide area

**predominantly** [-'----] mostly
**unarmed** not carrying a weapon
**to snoop** to secretly look around a place
**to break into** *einbrechen*
**accomodating** [-'----] s.th. or s.o. that suits o.'s wishes and needs
**blockbuster** *(informal)* successful

**a big deal** *here:* very important
**hospitality** welcoming behaviour towards guests and strangers
**courtesy** ['kɜːtəsɪ] *Höflichkeit*
**graciousness** ['greɪʃəsnəs] *Liebenswürdigkeit*
**to touch upon** to mention

1. Listed below are topics that are discussed in the interview with Karen McNeely. As you listen to the interview, number the topics in the order in which they are talked about.
2. Work with a partner. One of you chooses the topics on the left and the other the topics on the right. Listen to the interview again and take notes about your topics. Then together write a summary of Karen McNeely's description of Atlanta.

| Unique neighborhoods: | Historic city: |
|---|---|
| Dealing with crime: | Urban sprawl: |
| Successful business center: | Different cultures and races: |
| Effects of the Olympics: | Freetime activities: |
| Perspectives for the future: | Southern hospitality: |

**Questionnaire: About Atlanta**                                    Life in the city: Atlanta 6

Try to get first hand information about Atlanta by sending the questionnaire below in an e-mail (or fax) to a school or schools in the Atlanta area. Your teacher should be able to give you suitable e-mail addresses. Include the questionnaire as part of the e-mail or as an attachment (enclosure (Enc.) = *Anlage*).

---

**To:** [E-mail address of school in Atlanta]
**Re:** Can you help us?
**Enc:** Questionnaire: About Atlanta

---

Hi!
We're a group of students at [name of your college], which is a high school in [name of your town/area] in Germany.
We've been learning about Atlanta in our English class and we'd like to find out what young people think about living in Atlanta.
We'd really appreciate it if you would take the time to answer the questions below and e-mail (fax) us your answers by [latest date you want to receive any answers].
Thanks in advance for your help! We look forward to hearing from you!
[your name + surname]
[school name]
[school (or home) address]
**Tel.:**   [school (or home) phone number]
**e-mail:** [school (or home) e-mail address]

---

**Questionnaire**

1. How old are you?
2. Are you male or female?
3. How would you describe Atlanta to someone who has never been there before?
4. Are there aspects about living in Atlanta that make it different from any other American city?
5. Do you live in the center of the city or in a suburb? (If in a suburb, please tell us its name!)
6. Please describe the place in which you live (i.e. house, apartment, townhouse, etc.).
7. When you go to school, to stores, or to participate in freetime activities how do you most often get there? (e.g. on foot, by car, by public transportation, etc.)?
8. We've read that in the past a lot of people left the city center and moved to the suburbs. Is this still so? Please explain.
9. Are there any other freetime activities that you would like to be able to do that aren't available in the Atlanta area?
10. What kinds of businesses are attracted to Atlanta, and why?
11. Do you feel safe where you live? Why or why not?
12. What does Atlanta do to combat big city problems such as crime?
13. What are you most proud of about your city?
14. What would you most like to change about your city?
15. Please describe what you think will change in your city in the next 10 years.
16. Is there anything else that you would like us to know about your city?

# Role play cards

**Life in the city: Atlanta**

### Person A
**16 years old**

- you are wearing a New York Mets baseball cap and a Leeds football jersey
- you speak German with an American accent
- you are riding a mountain bike

### Person B
**20 years old**

- you are wearing a blue ski jacket and black leather boots
- you are on your way to work and are already late
- you are listening to a hip-hop CD at top volume

### Person C
**17 years old**

- you are wearing a black leather jacket and have spiked orange hair
- you are carrying a large cloth bag with books in it
- you no longer go to school

### Person D
**16 years old**

- you are wearing jeans and a T-shirt with the words 'I love Paris' on it
- you work for the local tourist office
- you are carying a map of the area in your back pocket

### Person E
**19 years old**

- you are dressed in a suit and a tie and red leather shoes
- you have a picture of your partner in your wallet and you like to show it
- you play the electric guitar in a band

### Person F
**19 years old**

- you are carrying a one-year-old child and a heavy shopping bag
- you are on your way to university
- your favourite hobby is bungee jumping

### Person G
**25 years old**

- you are wearing trainers underneath your designer business suit
- you are the vice president of an Internet start-up company
- you work 60 hours a week

### Person H
**25 years old**

- you are wearing big dark glasses and a pink hat
- you want to be a movie director but you haven't found a job yet
- you like to videotape people walking by

### Interviewer
**20 years old**

- you are doing an internship with a youth magazine
- you really hope to be taken on permanently after your internship

### Interviewer
**20 years old**

- you are doing an internship with a rock magazine
- you need to impress your boss

### Interviewer
**25 years old**

- you worked at a serious newspaper for two years but now you are writing for a tabloid
- you write sensational stories

### Interviewer
**25 years old**

- you write for a financial newspaper but you hate your job
- you are really interested in finding out if you can start an internet business in this area

**Survey sheet**  Life in the city: Atlanta

1. How old are you?
2. Do you live in a city, a suburb, or in the country?
3. Do you prefer life in a big or a small community? Why?
4. What is your occupation?
5. Is it important for you to live within walking distance of your place of work / your school? Why / why not?
6. Does your community offer public transportation? If so what kind, and how often do you use this?
7. Which stores and services do you most often need?
8. Do you do any sports? If so, which ones?
9. Does your community provide enough shopping, entertainment and sports facilities, or is anything missing?
10. Is it important for you to live near a lot of parks and green areas? Or do you prefer a more urban environment? Please give reasons.
11. Do you feel safe in your community?
12. What most needs improvement in your community?
13. Are you happy living here, or would you rather move away? Why?

# Test

## Life in the city: Atlanta

## America's cities: They can yet be resurrected

The immaculate homes of Bethesda, in Maryland, almost caricature the American dream. Two cars stand in the driveway; a manicured front lawn stretches to a gleaming sidewalk; overfed white children throw footballs across the
5 smoothly surfaced road. Less than ten miles (16 km) away, in the heart of Washington, DC, is the American nightmare. Unemployed blacks sit on the grimy front-steps of crumbling houses that were once grand; old cars skirt the roads. The contrast between outer suburbs and inner cities is bleak.
10 Yet America also has its urban optimists. They point out that the picture is better than it was. Unemployment in the 50 biggest cities has fallen by a third over the past four years, to around 6%. Rates for serious crime have declined to their lowest in a generation. Cities such as New York – which 20
15 years ago nearly went bankrupt – and Los Angeles, victim of race riots and earthquake within the past six years, are growing in both population and confidence. Even Detroit, a metaphor for urban decline, finally presents promising figures for new investment. [...]

Lately in America a growing economy has helped cities and suburbs alike; but cities are probably the more vulnerable to the next downturn, when it comes. By the standards of Europe and Japan, they still suffer terrible crime, [...] social disparities and remarkable deficits in education. [...]

The mostly white middle classes began to move to the suburbs after the second world war, but most cities remained vigorous enough until the 1960s, when court-mandated desegregation of the schools turned the white exodus into a full-scale stampede. Jobs, business and services left, too; the tax base narrowed; taxes rose, pushing still more employers out, as well as the black middle class. What remained was a huddle of people without means or motivation to leave, most of them black, most of them unemployed, and all of them a prey to rising crime and rapidly deteriorating schools.

(324 words)

*From the article in* The Economist, *January 10, 1998.*

### Content
1. Describe the two different faces of American cities in your own words.
2. Are the urban optimists positive about America? Give evidence for your answer.
3. Summarize what happened to American cities after the Second World War.

*(Your teacher will tell you which of the following tasks you should complete.)*

### Comment
1. Imagine that you are the mayor of a city who is to hold a speech in which you talk about city improvements. Describe three measures you would take to improve your city and say why these measures are important.
2. If you had the chance to move to America, would you move to a city or a suburb? Give reasons for your answer.

### Form
1. There are no direct quotations in this excerpt. Would you find this text more informative or convincing with quotations? Why or why not?
2. This informative text begins as if it were a play and the scene is being set. Do you think that this is an effective opening? Why or why not?

### Language
1. Provide the noun forms of the following words.
   a) caricature (l. 2)   b) surfaced (l. 5)   c) declined (l. 13)   d) deteriorating (l. 34)
2. Provide the adjective forms of the following words.
   a) contrast (l. 9)   b) optimists (l. 10)   c) economy (l. 20)
3. Explain in a complete sentence (without using the underlined words.)
   a) "The contrast between outer suburbs and inner cities ... ." (ll. 8–9)
   b) "Rates for serious crime have declined ... ." (l. 13)
   c) "... turned the white exodus into a full-scale stampede." (ll. 28–29)
4. Put these sentences into the passive or active.
   a) The experts warn us that too many people moving to the suburbs can harm city centres.
   b) The inner cities have been deserted by the mostly white middle classes.
5. Provide opposites for the following words.
   a) unemployed (l. 7)   b) optimist (l. 10)   c) fallen (l. 12)
6. Use the underlined words below to make a sentence with two relative clauses. Start your sentence "Blacks ...".
   a/b) "Unemployed blacks sit on the grimy front steps." (l. 7)
7. Complete the sentence using the verbs in the correct tenses. Give at least two correct versions.
   a/b) If an economic downturn (to come), cities (to be) probably more vulnerable than suburbs.

# Glued to the tube – TV in the USA   7

## Didaktisches Inhaltsverzeichnis

| | Title | Text type / Topic | Skills & Tasks | |
|---|---|---|---|---|
| | **Are you glued to the tube?** (SB S. 106) | • multiple-choice questionnaire (283 words) | • Reading/writing: a self-assessment questionnaire<br>• Vocabulary: core vocabulary | |
| | **Growing up on television** (SB S. 106) | • quotation (120 words)<br>• cartoon | • Speaking: finding arguments<br>• Reading/writing: interpreting cartoons/writing titles | |
| | **Did you know? American viewing habits** (SB S. 107) | • facts & statistics (220 words) | • Speaking: giving and responding to information; small talk<br>• Writing: a comment | |
| | **What's on? TV Guide** (SB S. 108/109) | • programme schedule<br>• cartoon | • Speaking/writing: carrying out a survey; studying and comparing schedules; organizing a new TV channel | |
| | **The price is right** (SB S. 110) | • game show description (250 words) | • Speaking: dialogue/small talk<br>• Writing: creative writing<br>• Grammar: adjectives/adverbs | |
| | **All my children** (SB p. 111) | • soap opera synopsis (145 words) | • Writing: writing a comment<br>• Grammar: connectives | **1** TRB, S. 127 |
| | **Ratings and guidelines** (SB S. 112) | • informative text (516 words)<br>• cartoon | • Speaking: giving opinions<br>• Writing: organizing information in a table<br>• Grammar: passive and active | **2** TRB, S. 128 |
| | **TV stations and networks in the USA** (SB S. 114) | • informative text (486 words) | • Vocabulary: semantic field 'television'<br>• Translation | |
| | **Media research** (SB S. 115) | • table | • Speaking: asking and answering questions<br>• Writing: completing/reorganizing a table; writing an analysis<br>• Speaking/writing: doing a survey | **3** TRB, S. 129 |
| | **Talking TV** (SB S. 116) | • comic strip<br>• TV and art of conversation | • Speaking: continuing a dialogue; discussing | |
| 🎧 | **The shock of recognition** (SB S. 116) | • satirical short story (520 words)<br>• TV and family life | • Listening comprehension | **4** TRB, S. 130 |
| | **Blame the couch potatoes …** (SB S. 117) | • novel excerpt concerning viewers' responsibility (775 words) | • Vocabulary: semantic field 'television'; synonyms, opposites<br>• Speaking: organizing and carrying out a panel discussion | **5** TRB, S. 131/132 |
| | **Project: A panel discussion** (SB S. 119) | | | |
| | **Test: TV and Me** | • magazine article (425 words) | | **6** TRB, S. 133 |

# 7 Glued to the tube – TV in the USA

## Einleitung

*Thema dieses Kapitels ist Fernsehen in den USA. Die Darstellung soll Unterschiede und Gemeinsamkeiten bewusst machen, um zu einem kritischen Nachdenken über den eigenen Umgang mit dem Medium Fernsehen anzuregen. Zuerst wird der Einfluss des Mediums auf Gesellschaft und Familie betrachtet. Es folgt eine nähere Betrachtung des Fernsehangebotes. Insbesondere werden die 'gameshow' und die 'soap opera' unter die Lupe genommen.*

*Die Klassifizierung von Programmen nach Inhalt, die Bedeutung von 'ratings' und Unterschiede zwischen stations und networks werden dann erläutert. Abschließend wird das Thema Verantwortung im Umgang mit dem Medium von Seiten der Zuschauer und der Fernsehenindustrie anhand eines fiktionalen Textes behandelt. Im Kapitel befinden sich zahlreiche Cartoons, die bei Bedarf zum zusätzlichen Behandlungsschwerpunkt gemacht werden können.*

## The influence of television    SB S. 106–107

### Are you glued to the tube?    SB S. 106

*S beantworten den Fragebogen einzeln und ermitteln ihre Punktezahl. Anschließend können sie ihren Typ ermitteln (vgl. Auflösung SB S. 119) und können ihre Ergebnisse mit dem Nachbarn vergleichen. Falls das Ergebnis nicht mit ihrer Selbsteinschätzung übereinstimmt, belegen und begründen sie eventuelle Unterschiede.*

→ *Der L gibt anstelle der fertigen Beschreibung der einzelnen Typen nur deren Bezeichnungen an. Die S erarbeiten sodann Beschreibungen.*

→ *Zusätzlich können S den Fragebogen um eigene Fragen erweitern.*

### Growing up on television    SB S. 106

**Finding arguments**

1. (Mögliche Antwort): TV dominates children's lives – their daily schedule is planned around it. It allows them little time for interacting with family and friends, and for other more beneficial activities.
2. Counter arguments: TV can widen children's experience and stimulate their imagination, just as reading can. Visual images and spoken language are not necessarily inferior to written words – it depends on the content of the TV programmes.
*S begründen ihre Antwort mit persönlichen Erfahrungen, Gelesenem oder Gehörtem, z. B. Verhalten im Freundeskreis.*
3. –

**Looking at the cartoon**

1. A child will imitate behaviour seen on TV, because it seems that this behaviour is desirable. As this rather young child cannot be capable of critical thinking, he/she has to think that everything presented is positive. The child is too young to understand and cannot cope with the confusing content. Parents should evaluate information and decide on what their children should watch.
2. a) Modern research reveals that even very young children are capable of quite complex thought, and could easily draw the conclusions shown in the cartoon. Language is not necessary for such reasoning. That the toddler is able to put his/her thoughts into words is the (slight) element of exaggeration involved.
b) Children of that age are not mature enough to process the information they are getting from TV, let alone put their conclusions into words.
c) Very difficult to justify!
3. Possible titles: TV education/Educational TV • The new parent? • Learning by viewing?

## Did you know? American viewing habits    SB S. 107

### Small talk

*S führen die Aufgabe als 'ping-pong game' mit ihrem Nachbarn durch: Wie beim Tischtennis wandert dabei der Gesprächsimpuls zwischen den Sprechern hin und her. Wichtig ist, dass beide Beteiligte das Gespräch gleichberechtigt steuern und dafür sorgen, dass der Gesprächsfaden nicht abreißt.*
*Sinn der Übung ist es, die Techniken des small talk in der englischen Sprache einzuüben.*
*Bei stärkeren Klassen lässt sich die Übung erweitern, indem der jeweilige Sprecher zu jeder Erwiderung eine neue Information hinzufügt. Das Spiel funktioniert dann nach dem Schema: ask – answer – add (AAA). Ziel hierbei ist es, zusätzliche Gesprächsimpulse zu schaffen.*

**ⓘ German viewing habits**
According to a report in *Wirtschaft und Unterricht* (25 November 1999, no. 10) the amount of time spent watching TV is still increasing in Germany. In 1999 viewers spent an average of 201 minutes a day in front of the TV compared to 145 in 1985, a rise of approx. 39%. Interestingly the viewing time for children under 13 only rose by 20% in the same period rising to an average of 99 minutes per day. See also the following website:
http://www.iwkoeln.de/WuU/

### Writing a comment–    SB S. 107

*S verwenden Angaben und Lösungen zu den Aufgaben auf S. 106–107 als Grundlage für den 'Comment'. (S. auch 'Skills file', SB, S. 124.)*

## What's on? TV Guide    SB S. 108–109

### Quick survey    SB S. 108

1. a)–f) *Aus Zeitgründen empfiehlt sich die Bereitstellung der folgenden Tabelle als OHP oder Arbeitsblatt, um sie dann als Grundlage für eine Strichliste zu benutzen.*
*Vorab sollte L kurz die genaue Fragebildung mit S üben: z. B. a): "How many different channels have you got on your TV at home?" Dieser Teil der Umfrage kann sowohl als Unterrichtsgespräch als auch als GA bearbeitet werden. (Klasse in 4 Gruppen Teilen (A, B, C, D). A und B befragen sich gegenseitig so wie C und D. Die Ergebnisse werden dann als Tafelbild/OHP zusammengetragen.) Von Vorteil ist es jedoch, wenn die Beantwortung der Frage 1. c) und d) auf Gruppen verteilt wird, die dann die Informationen sammeln und in Form einer Tabelle oder eines Balken- oder Tortendiagramms der Klasse präsentieren.*

118

# Glued to the tube – TV in the USA 7

| Channels | TV type | time per day |
|---|---|---|
| 1–3 Channels | terrestrial | 1 hour or less |
| 4–20 Channels | satellite | 2–4 hours |
| more than 20 channels | cable | more than 4 hours |

*2. Hier können die Ergebnisse in Listenform wie auf S. 107 des SBs präsentiert werden. Möglich ist jedoch auch eine Darstellung in Form einer Wandzeichnung mit einzelnen Diagrammen.*

**Finding & comparing information**

*Ziel der Aufgaben: Wortschatzerweiterung (programme categories); Zusammensetzung von TV-Programmen zu bestimmten Tageszeiten, um bestimmte Zuschauerquoten zu erzielen; Vergleich US und D TV-Programmgestaltung.)*
*1. a) This Morning: (local) news • The Price is Right: game show • All my Children: serial / soap opera • D.C. Cab: comedy.*
*b) cartoon • drama • fantasy • interview • documentary • thriller • adventure • discussion • religion • basketball • children • speculation • puppets • crime drama • profile • fitness • magazine • horror • interview • talk show • political • weather report • feature film • etc.*
*c) A sitcom (= situation+comedy) is a comedy series based on a particular situation and constellation of characters. A drama is any serious piece of fiction: it can be a single TV play or a series.*
*d) Als HA mit mündlicher Überprüfung in der folgenden Stunde oder mündliche Bearbeitung in Klasse mit Festhalten der Lösungen auf OHP (von S!).*
*2. a)/b) Beide Aufgabenteile lassen sich gut in Tabellenform darstellen (s. unten). S sollten erkennen, dass ein Zusammenhang zwischen dem jeweils dargebotenen Fernsehprogramm und den Zuschauern (Zielgruppe) besteht. S können auch neue Kategorien erfinden, z. B. lifestyle, internet news, usw.*

| time of day | dominant categories | target audience |
|---|---|---|
| early morning (7 am) | • news<br>• cartoons | • adults getting ready for work<br>• children before school |
| mid morning (11 am) and lunch time (1 pm) | • talk shows<br>• fitness<br>• comedy and drama series<br>• educational programmes | • housewives<br>• people on lunch break or who do not go to work<br>• children who are not yet in school all day |
| evening (8 pm) | • comedy<br>• movies (thriller, fantasy) | • adults who want to relax |

*3. a) Die folgenden Sendungen aus dem Programmheft sind oder waren auch im deutschen Fernsehen zu sehen:*
*Tiny Toon Adventures; Bugs Bunny; Dr. Quinn (Dr. Quinn – Ärztin aus Leidenschaft, SRTL); Jerry Springer; Quincy; Spenser; Walker Texas Ranger; Dallas; Candid Camera (Versteckte Kamera)*
*b) L sollte US Programmheft in den Unterricht mitbringen (evtl. aus dem Internet!). S bringen Programmzeitschrift ihrer Wahl mit und erarbeiten die verschiedenen Merkmale. Folgende Unterschiede dürften allgemein erkennbar sein:*
*In American TV guides programmes are sorted by starting time, in German TV guides programmes are sorted by channel. A possible explanation for this is the variety of different channels in the USA. In American TV guides there is a parental guidance scheme, in Germany there isn't.*

**Looking at the cartoon**  SB S. 108

The host in the cartoon and in the English programme is Cilla Black, who became famous as a pop singer in the early sixties. She has a northern accent (hence "luverly") and is famous for calling people "Chuck", a northern term of endearment.

1. The German title is 'Herzblatt' (ARD).
2. A blind date is when two people who have never met each other arrange to go out with each other (hence 'blind'). In this sense the English name is perhaps more appropriate as a title for the programme, as the couple see each other for the first time only when the screen slides back.
3. The aim of the game is for one contestant to choose a partner for a date from three people who he/she has never seen before by asking them three questions. The setting is a stage with a sliding screen in the middle, which the participants cannot see over. (The audience sitting in front can see the people on both sides of the screen.) The questioner sits on one side of the screen. Three people of the opposite sex sit on the other side. After asking the three questions and hearing each person's reply, the questioner chooses the person whose answers he or she likes best. They stand face to face on either side of the screen, the screen slides back and they see each other for the first time. They then go away on a short trip together – accompanied by the TV film crew! When they return they are interviewed about the trip and what they thought of their partner and are invited back on to the next programme to talk about it. In the cartoon the girl chooses number one but actually gets number three! (S. auch 'Skills file: Talking about cartoons', SB S. 130.)

→ Act a scene based on the Series 'Blind Date' with one questioner, one presenter and three candidates. As an element of fun, girls can pretend to ask/answer as boys and vice versa. As in the TV programme, the presenter should start the 'show' by interviewing the candidates and questioner to give them a chance to say something about themselves.

**TV programme websites:**
Spenser: For Hire:
http://www.tnt-tv.com/series/spenser/
NBC Dateline:
http://www.msnbc.com/news/DATELINE_front.asp
Allegra's Window:
http://teachers.nick.com/supplies/shows/ed_shows_allegras.html
Magic School Bus:
http://place.scholastic.com/magicschoolbus/index.htm

# 7 Glued to the tube – TV in the USA

**Over to you**

1. –
2. a)/b) Bei der Begründung ihrer Auswahl sollen S auf Inhalt der Sendungen (insbesondere Sex oder Gewalt), erzieherischen Gehalt, (das Alter der) Zielgruppe, etc. achten.

## Typical TV: … SB S. 110–111

**Before you read**

● Popular German game shows: Most of these originated in GB or the USA (apart from 'Wetten dass!'): *Der Preis ist heiß* ● *Glücksrad* ● *Wetten, dass …!* ● *Wer wird Millionär?*

● Possible reasons for popularity: the chance to participate and win prizes ● the chance to participate (as part of the studio audience) and share in the excitement ● the pleasure of seeing other people making fools of themselves.

## The longest running daytime … SB S. 110–111

**Comprehension**

1. Scene description: There are lots of bright and colourful lights. The audience is very excited. It's like being at a circus.
2. People behave so excitedly because they want to attract attention. This increases the possibility that they might be chosen to join the game.
3. Bob Parker is the MC (Master of ceremonies) or host. He leads the contestants through the show.
L sollte die S darauf hinweisen, dass die im Deutschen üblichen Begriffe 'Showmaster' und 'Talkshowmaster' in der englischen Sprache nicht existieren. Sie sind rein deutsche Erfindungen, die ein Muttersprachler nie benutzen würde. (Weitere Beispiele: *Handy* = mobile/cell phone, *Pullunder* = sleeveless top/tank top, *Smoking* = dinner jacket, *Stores* = curtains (S. auch 'Skills file', SB, S.122, 'False friends')

**Grammar: adjectives & adverbs**

1. Adjectives: frantic (l. 1) ● bright (l. 1) ● flashing (l. 1) ● entire (l. 2) ● spastic (l. 2) ● lively (l. 4) ● unspoken (l. 5) ● excited (l. 5) ● active (l. 5) ● better (l. 6) ● first (l. 7) ● ever-present (l. 8) ● past (l. 9) ● twenty-five (l. 9) ● last (l. 9) ● remaining (l. 9) ● running (l. 9) ● closest (l. 12) ● suggested (l. 12) ● quick (l. 14) ● frozen (l. 16)
Adverbs: finally (l. 8) ● longest (l. 9) ● identically (l. 13) ● even (l. 14)
L sollen darauf hinweisen, dass auch Substantive andere Substantive modifizieren können. Z. B. daytime game show (l. 10) ● retail price (l. 12) ● manufacturer's logo (l. 15) ● cleaning products (l. 16) ● sports cars (16)
2. a) 1. = adverb ● 2. adjective ● 3. adverb ● 4. adverb ● 5. adverb ● 6. adverb ● 7. adjective ● 8. adverb ● 9. adjective ● 10. adjective
b) Für stärkere S kann die Übung variiert werden, indem bestimmte Gruppen von Adverbien (z. B. Adverbien auf -ly) nicht verwendet werden dürfen.
Yesterday as I was driving <u>slowly</u> along Main Street I saw a <u>well-dressed</u> woman waving <u>wildly/franatically/with all her might</u> for me to stop. I stopped <u>at once</u> and <u>immediately/cautiously</u> opened the window. "Thank goodness," the woman said <u>breathlessly</u>. "Can you take me to the <u>new</u> TV studios? I have to be on stage in 15 minutes."
"On stage?" I repeated <u>incredulously</u>. Then I took a <u>good/long</u> look at her. "You're Annabel Chance, aren't you? You host that <u>ridiculous/great</u> game show."
c) –
Nachdem S ihre Fortsetzung geschrieben haben, können sie die erweiterte Szene als Rollenspiel spielen.

**Over to you**

S sollen insbesondere auf die Verwendung von Adjektiven und Adverbien achten, um ihre Beschreibung lebhafter und interessanter zu gestalten.

**Dialogue (small talk)**

1. Q: What kind of show is 'The Price is Right'?
A: It's a game show.
Q: So why is it called 'The Price is Right'?
A: Because the aim of the show is to guess how much things cost in the shops: in other words to get the price right.
Q: And who takes part in the game?
A: Well, there's the host, Bob Barker, and the contestants (the players) who are chosen from the audience.
Q: I see. And what exactly do the contestants have to do?
A: It's quite simple. All kinds of things are brought on stage and the contestants guess what the retail price of the thing is.
Q: Just a second. What kind of things are they?
A: All kinds of things: from washing powder and window cleaning liquid to sailing boats and cars!
Q: Wow, that's incredible. Why don't we go along and try and win a new TV set?
A: Funny you should mention it, because I just happen to have two tickets for the show next week!

→ Find examples in the dialogue of 'fillers' which are often used in casual conversation.
(= So … ● Well, … ● I see … ● Just a second … ● Wow! … ● Funny you mention that …)

2. a)/b) –
(S. auch 'Skills file', SB, S. 128.) Nach dieser Übung könnten S zur Vertiefung den Dialog abwandeln und über eine Show ihrer Wahl sprechen. Hierbei würden sich die Antworten ändern.

## All My Children … SB S. 111

[i] The soap opera has its roots in the serial radio plays that were so popular in the United States of the early 1930s. They came to be known as soap operas, because most of their major sponsors were manufacturers of soap and detergents. Soap operas originally dealt with topics relating to family fate and crisis, sin and violence. The original length of these soap opera radio programmes was about 30 minutes (including commercial breaks).
Soap operas found their way to the television screen almost as soon as television became accessible to a wider audience in the 1950s. Although many soap opera programmes still deal with traditional topics, since the 1970s the scope of topics has expanded in order to deal with topics that are of interest to viewers today, e.g. drug abuse, abortion and AIDS. Today some of the programmes last up to 60 minutes, and some are even aired during prime time evening viewing hours.

# Glued to the tube – TV in the USA 7

**Useful websites:**
http://abc.go.com/soaps/allmychildren/index.html
http://www.4chatroom.com/
http://soaps.about.com/entertainment/soaps/gi/chat/parachat/parachat.htm

## Comprehension

1. There are at least three different storylines:
- Woman in the woods / man unconscious in hospital;
- Parents preparing the birthday party;
- Woman and young girl in the coffee shop.

2. Typical elements of soap operas:
Basic elements: A permanent cast of actors, a continuing story and an emphasis on dialogue instead of action. The story is broken up into short glimpses of the characters' lives. They are treated in a consistently sentimental or melodramatic way.
Programmes deal with some every day events that viewers can identify with. Each episode ends with an open question (a "cliffhanger") to make viewers want to watch the next episode.

3. S benutzen Formen des simple past und des past continuous. Bei Bedarf sollten diese mit Hilfe des grammar file im SB wiederholt werden.
In the last episode, Dixie lay dying in the woods, and Tad – the only one who knew where she was – was unconscious in hospital. While the recently divorced Kerry and Darrell were preparing a birthday party for their daughter, Kerry complained that she had spent too little time with her daughter and argued with Darrell. He then revealed a secret from his past, namely that his mother had died on one of his childhood birthdays and so he had never been able to enjoy birthday parties since.
In a coffee bar, Kit met a strange woman and told her the way to a small hut in the woods which she used to play in when she was young. Later the woman went to the cabin and Kit's brother followed her. The woman turned out to be their long lost mother!

## Your view

Vor allem die erste Aussage ist nicht ganz leicht zu verstehen. Vorab sollte man deshalb folgende Wörter erklären (lassen):
<u>reference point:</u> a point which you can relate to *(Bezugspunkt)* (s. auch Zusatzaufgabe) • <u>to share an experience:</u> to do the same thing as s.o. else • <u>to compare notes:</u> to talk about / discuss s.th. with s.o. else and find out if they have the same opinion as you • <u>to interact:</u> to communicate or work with others
Die Übersetzung bzw. Erklärung der Aussagen erfolgt am Besten mündlich in KA. Danach sollten S in EA eigene weitere Gründe schriftlich erarbeiten. Diese werden dann von L (oder S) als OHP zusammengetragen. Der letzte Teil der Aufgabe soll dann wieder schriftlich in EA erfolgen (evtl. als HA).
• Translation "Soap operas offer …": Seifenopern bieten einen Bezugspunkt für gemeinsame Erfahrungen mit anderen: Man kann mit Personen, die auch zuschauen, darüber diskutieren, sich unterhalten und sich auseinandersetzen.
"The viewer's …": Das persönliche Leben des Zuschauers wird wahrscheinlich nie das der Charakter widerspiegeln, die er/sie zuschaut, aber durch den "soap" kann der Zuschauer dieses Leben leben, und wenn sie an einem Tag ihr Lieblingssoap verpassen ist es für viele Zuschauer wie wenn sie einen ganzen Tag im eigenen Leben verschlafen haben.
• Why soap operas are great (examples):
– Because you can talk about them with your friends. You can talk about: which characters you like best or least • what you think about each episode and about what will happen next • how a character has reacted in a certain situation.
– Because they deal with all kinds of real-life problems and you can learn how to solve your own problems through them.
– Because although the life of characters in a soap opera may not be exactly like your own life, the characters represent 'ordinary people', so you can identify with them.
– Because they give you something to look forward to every day and take your mind off other problems.
– Because if you don't like what is going on you can simply switch off!

⇒ Look up 'reference' and 'refer' in a dictionary and draw up a table showing the different meanings of both and giving examples of use.

⇒ **The Truman Show**
*Kopiervorlage 1:* TRB, S. 127 / CD-ROM
*Lösungen:* TRB, S. 140
An dieser Stelle könnte man den Film 'The Truman Show' zeigen. Zum Film: Truman Burbank ist ein berühmter Fernsehstar – er weiß es nur nicht. Rund um die Uhr wird sein Leben weltweit als Seifenoper übertragen. Alle seine Kontaktpersonen – einschließlich Ehefrau – sind Schauspieler.
Script zum Kultfilm: erhältlich von Klett: 3-12-577460-8
Videofilm erhältlich von Lingua-Video.com (www.lingua-video.com) E 102

## Ratings and guidelines     SB S. 112–113

### Before you read

● S evtl. auf Kategorien für Kinofilme als Ausgangspunkt verweisen. Aufgabe in GA oder PA erarbeiten lassen mit einem Zeitlimit von max. 20 Minuten.
Further example:
http://www.gospelcom.net/preview/Pages/ratingsanddefs.html

[i] The parental guidance scheme (PGS) was introduced after a serious national debate over the decline in television standards. In 1996 a research study analyzed shows that were aired between 7 and 8 pm. Although this time slot was originally designed for family viewing, results indicated that a lot of the shows contained obscene language or sexually explicit material.
See also FCC homepage: http://www.fcc.gov/

### Comprehension

(Schriftliche Erarbeitung in EA oder PA)
1.

| FCC | Children's Television Act (1990) | Telecommunications Act (1996) | Parental Guidance Scheme |
|---|---|---|---|
| gives licences to TV stations; acts as a control ensuring competition among stations | makes it illegal to broadcast indecent material between 6 am and 10 pm | rules V-Chip to be installed in every TV set | gives parents advice on the content of a programme (not compulsory for TV stations) |

121

# 7 Glued to the tube – TV in the USA

2. *V-Chip:* 'V' is the abbreviation for 'violent'. The V-Chip is a technical device installed in the TV-set that blocks programmes with violent content. The chip receives a signal sent by the TV stations. When a signal is detected the TV screen turns black. The viewer has to enter a code to override the signal.
3. The PGS is most concerned about sex, bad language and violence.
4. NBC sees this as a form of censorship which is against the principles of the First Amendment which states that:
"Congress shall make no law respecting an establishment of religion, or prohibiting the free exercise thereof; or abridging the freedom of speech, or of the press; or the right of the people peaceably to assemble, and to petition the Government for a redress of grievances."
5. a)/b) Sinn der Übung ist es, das 'PGS' anzuwenden. S sollen vorrangig mit Hilfe der von den Sendern zur Verfügung gestellten Hinweise entscheiden, welche Sendungen das Kind sehen darf. S werden feststellen, dass nicht alle Sendungen eine Bewertung haben, und müssen dann selber entscheiden, ob sie diese Sendungen für geeignet halten. Die Nützlichkeit (oder nicht) des Systems wird hiermit verdeutlicht. Mögliche Verbesserungen wären: das System obligatorisch für alle Sender zu machen; die Klassifizierung durch eine unabhängige Organisation machen zu lassen.

## Grammar: passive and active

1. Use of passive voice in the text:
Col. 1, l. 2: "All TV stations ... must be licensed ..." (simple present with modal auxiliary). Active: The FCC licenses all TV stations in the US.
Col. 1, l. 4: "Licenses are given ..." (simple present). Active: The FCC gives licences ...
Col. 1, l. 7: "... licenses can be taken away." (simple present with modal auxiliary). Active: The FCC can take licenses away
Col. 2, l. 2: "With a rating system designed by ..." (simple past). Active: With a rating system that the networks themselves designed ...
Col. 2, l. 6: "... parental guidance system has been introduced ..." (present perfect). Most TV networks have introduced ...
Col. 2, l. 21 (etc.): "These programmes are designed to be ..." (simple present) Best not changed to active. Possible solution would be: The programme designer designed these programmes ...
Col. 3, l. 12: "Additional codes may be added ..." (simple present with modal auxiliary). Active: The TV station can add ...
Col. 3, l. 21: "Childen under 14 should not be allowed to watch ..." (conditional). Active: Parents should not allow their children to watch ...
Col. 3, l. 30: "These programmes are made specifically ..." (simple present). Active: The networks make these programmes ...
2. a) Foul language is often dubbed out by TV broadcast networks.
b) I was told that the FCC was established by the US government in 1934.
c) The first fifteen seconds of a show must be watched by parents in order to see the ratings icon.
d) The violence shown in the TV film was strongly objected to by pressure groups.
e) The show was only aired by the networks after it had been given a rating by a team of editors.
f) All complaints against advertisements have to be dealt with by the Advertising Complaints Board.
g) If the TV stations want their licences to be renewed, the guidelines must be taken notice of.

## Your view

1. –
2. Possible advantages: informs parents of potentially questionable programme content/provides guidelines on programme content.
Possible disadvantages: only a few people make judgements about the programmes seen by many (censorship?); by limiting programme content, creativity may be restricted as well.
Possible conclusions may range from: "If exercised correctly, the parental guidance scheme protects children and is therefore a good thing." to: "TV stations can and do take responsibility for their own programming and should therefore not be policed by the parental guidance scheme."

[i] In Germany control in and over the television industry is exercised by a very complicated system of checks and balances. First there are the *Landesmedienanstalten* whose primary objective is to ensure fair competition between stations. They also pay special attention to the amount of advertising shown on TV. Secondly there are competitors and pressure groups, e.g. the *Verband Privater Rundfunk und Telekommunikation*, who watch out for violations of broadcasting laws (*Rundfunkgesetz*). Thirdly the TV stations themselves are very keen to avoid bad publicity. If a programme has a negative image it often leads to a drop in income from advertising. Serious discussions about the role of violence on TV resulted in the setting up of the *Freiwillige Selbstkontrolle Fernsehen (FSF)* in 1994 (cf. *Wirtschaft und Unterricht*, 1999).
Today some German shows (e.g. *Vera – Talk am Mittag*) 'bleep out' foul language after being advised to do so by the *Landesmedienanstalt*. An advantage of importing programmes from abroad is that as part of the dubbing process (e.g. from English into German) any bad language can be dubbed out and replaced by harmless or at least less offensive expressions.
For further information see: *Landesanstalt für Kommunikation* at: http://www.lfk.de/

## Looking at the cartoon

On the TV screen it says: "The following program may induce siezures in your children. Viewer discretion is advised."
*Seizure is spelt wrongly on the screen.*
(S. auch 'Skills file', SB, S. 130.)
1. Three children are sitting in front of the TV set. Their mother is washing the dishes. At the same time she is talking to a friend on the phone. She cannot see what the children are watching but it is 10 o'clock in the morning (there is a clock on the kitchen wall) and she clearly doesn't imagine there could be anything bad on TV. She tells her friend that the only time she can safely leave the children alone is when they are watching TV. Either the children can't read, so they don't know an unsuitable programme is coming up, or they are quite happy to be able to watch it!
2. The cartoonist is making fun of parents' belief that children are safe when they are sitting in front of the TV set. Perhaps the cartoonist is also implying that the very reason why children are badly behaved when they are not watching TV is that they are allowed to watch so many unsuitable programmes. Parents don't even realise there is a connection between TV and behaviour.
3. The V-chip would block out any material classified as unsuitable for children, and cause the screen to go blank. This would, however, destroy the TV's function as a babysitter!

→ **Discussing TV**
Kopiervorlage 2: TRB, S. 128
CD-ROM

# Glued to the tube – TV in the USA 7

*Auf der Kopiervorlage befinden sich drei Diskussionsthemen mit jeweils zwei Rollenkarten: einmal für und einmal gegen die aufgestellte These.*
*S in 4-er Gruppen aufteilen, die jeweils über ein Thema diskutieren und dementsprechend die zwei dazugehörenden Rollenkarten bekommen. Zwei Gruppenmitglieder argumentieren für und zwei gegen die These anhand der Ideen auf ihren Rollenkarten. S können/sollen weitere eigene Argumente ausdenken. S auffordern, während der Diskussion Notizen zu machen. Zum Schluss berichtet jede Gruppe über den Verlauf der Diskussion. (S. auch 'Skills File', SB, S. 131 & 132.)*

## TV stations and networks ...     SB S. 114–116

*Vorschlag zur Textbearbeitung: S bearbeiten Absätze in GA. Sie erstellen zu jedem Absatz ein oder zwei True/False-Aussagen, die sie dann (mündlich) der Klasse vortragen und um Bewertung und ggf. Berichtigung bitten. Alternativ: Auf OHP die unten stehenden True/False Aussagen präsentieren, die die S bewerten und ggf. korrigieren müssen.*

True or False? Correct the false statements.
- American viewers have to pay to receive all TV stations.
*(False: see ll. 6–8)*
- Commercial stations sell their programmes to networks.
*(False: see ll. 8–10)*
- CBS is one of the major networks.
*(True: It is one of the four biggest: see ll. 18–21)*
- BET stands for Better Entertainment on TV.
*(False: BET is a minority interest network and stands for Black Entertainment Television. See ll. 23–26)*
- PBS finances itself by selling advertising time to companies.
*(False: PBS relies on public funding. See ll. 26–32)*
- Over 56 million people are reached by cable.
*(True: see ll. 36–37)*
- The Playboy channel is the most widespread pay-TV channel.
*(False: See ll. 37–39)*
- The average American family watched TV for over 7 hours per day in 1998.
*(True: See ll. 41/42)*

### Vocabulary     SB, S. 115

*(S. auch 'Skills file', SB, S. 133.)*
1./2. <u>advertising</u>: information about products presented in such a way as to make people want to buy the product
<u>to broadcast</u>: to air programmes
<u>cable TV</u>: television service provided via cable, often for a fee
<u>commercial TV stations</u>: stations which buy their programmes from networks and are supported by advertising
<u>to compete</u>: to try to win
<u>independent stations</u>: stations which are not connected to a network
<u>cable networks</u>: programme providers for the cable TV system
<u>media research</u>: the study of trends and phenomena in the media
<u>networks</u>: commercial production companies which make and sell programmes to stations
<u>non-commercial TV stations</u>: stations which are supported by donations, grants and government funds rather than by advertising
<u>pay cable</u>: cable service where subscribers must pay a fee to view programmes
<u>programme</u>: a scheduled TV (or radio) show (NB Programme is a 'false friend': *Programm* = Channel or station. Programme (BE; AE = Program) = *Sendung*)

<u>to receive</u>: here: to get the television signals that allow programmes to be viewed
<u>subscriber</u>: person who pays a fee for a regular service

### Comprehension

The difference between ...
a) ... commercial and non-commercial stations is that commercial stations buy their programmes from the major networks, e.g. NBC, ABC, etc. and are financed through advertising. Non-commercial stations are financed by donations, grants, funds, etc. but not advertising.
b) ... TV stations and TV networks is that TV stations show programmes in their respective broadcasting areas. TV networks produce programmes and sell them to the stations nationwide. TV networks don't broadcast programmes.
c) ... PBS and NBC is that PBS is a non-commercial network which is financed through donations and grants. (PBS has produced such famous programmes as 'Sesame Street'.) NBC is a commercial network which is financed by companies, etc. who want their advertisements aired.
d) ... the time the TV set is on in an American household and the time Americans spend watching TV: In most US households the TV is on almost all day, but it is just a form of background noise, like a radio. So in fact the time Americans spend watching TV is far lower than the amount of time they have their TV sets on. (This is, of course a problem for advertisers and ratings!)

### Translation

*S sollen insbesondere die Übersetzung des Passivs, z. B. "was watched" einschießlich des infinitive passive "being watched" beachten. (S. auch 'Skills file', SB, S. 122.)*
*Angewurzelt vor der Glotze?*
*Der Nielsen Medienforschung zufolge wurde 1998 in einem durchschnittlichen amerikanischen Haushalt täglich 7 Stunden und 21 Minuten ferngesehen. Aber es gibt einen Unterschied zwischen der Einschaltzeit (Einschaltdauer) und des tatsächlichen Fernsehkonsums. Fernsehgeräte in Amerika werden wie Radiogeräte angeschaltet: als Hintergrundgeräusch bzw. -musik. Insbesondere Vormittags- und Nachmittagssendungen werden nur zwischendurch angesehen, während man gerade andere Dinge erledigt. Das Leben läuft neben dem Fernsehen weiter und es wird nur ferngesehen, wenn etwas Interessantes gerade passiert. Und selbstverständlich gibt es wahrscheinlich auch den "eigenartigen" Amerikaner, der überhaupt nicht fernsieht!*

### Media research     SB S. 115–116

#### Asking for information

*S daran erinnern, dass die 24-Stunden-Zählung im englischsprachigen Raum nicht gebräuchlich ist. Zeiten werden daher entweder mit dem Zusatz 'am/pm' oder 'o'clock' angegeben.*
*Die zwei Tabellen auf SB S. 115 & 116 können von L als Kopiervorlage vorab verteilt werden.*

*Kopiervorlage **3**: TRB, S. 129*
*Lösungen: TRB, S. 124*

**Websites to programmes:**
http://www.tnt-tv.com/series/er/
http://www.nbc.com/tvcentral/shows/friends/new_index.html
http://friends.warnerbros.com/

# 7 Glued to the tube – TV in the USA

http://www.nbc.com/NBCtvcentral/promo/promotional-shows.nbc?show=frasier/new_index

*1.12. Der Name der dritten Sendung (von oben) ist 'Frasier'. Dieser Name wurde weggelassen um zu kontrollieren, ob die S tatsächlich Fragen stellen und nicht einfach die Lücken mit Zahlen/Informationen füllen. Es bleibt dem/der L überlassen, den S im Voraus mitzuteilen, dass eine Antwort ganz fehlt. Diese Übung ermöglicht es auch, mit den S eine Variation der üblichen Frage-Anwort-Situation zu üben. Z. B.:*
- I don't have the name of the third program from the top on my list. Do you?
- No, I don't either. Are you sure that it isn't on your list?
- Yes, I'm sure it isn't! This answer must be missing.
- I guess you're right. Let's ask the teacher what the answer is.

| Rank | Program Name | Network | Day/Time | Audience |
|---|---|---|---|---|
| 1 | E.R. | NBC | Thurs, 10 pm | 9,998,000 |
| 2 | Friends | NBC | Thurs, 8 pm | 9,913,000 |
| 3 | Frasier | NBC | Thurs, 9 pm | 10,107,000 |
| 4 | 60 Minutes | CBS | Sun, 7 pm | 9,887,000 |
| 5 | 20/20-Wed | ABC | Wed, 10 pm | 9,846,000 |
| 6 | Will & Grace | NBC | Thurs, 9.30 pm | 9,727,000 |
| 7 | Touched by an Angel | CBS | Sun, 8 pm | 9,538,000 |
| 8 | Dateline NBC-Tue | NBC | Tue, 10 pm | 9,366,000 |
| 9 | Law and order | NBC | Wed, 10 pm | 9,174,000 |
| 10 | 20/20-Fri | ABC | Fri, 10 pm | 8,895,000 |

3. The ratings reveal the absolute number of people who have watched a programme.
Groups for whom the ratings system is important:
- advertising agencies and their clients (the companies advertising products): this information is used to decide when it is best to advertise which products in order to reach the widest target audience.
- TV networks and stations: the higher the rating, the higher the advertising fees can be. If a programme has low ratings the station can decide whether to change the time slot or take the show off the air.

4. *Wenn nicht bereits geschehen – zunächst anhand der TV Top Ten Tabelle allgemein über die verschiedenen Sendungen sprechen und Trends erkennen. S sollen dann aus dem statistischen Material eine zusammenhängende Analyse mit Hilfe von Konjunktionen erstellen. (S. auch 'Skills file', SB, S. 125, 'Connectives'.)*
Written analysis:
Over all, NBC has the most programs in the top listing followed by ABC and then CBS. For this particular week, audience numbers for NBC shows varied from 9,174,000 to 21,550 000. For NBC and CBS, however the numbers varied from 8,895,000 to 9,887,000. The programs aired by NBC were predominantly dramas and comedies (situation comedies, for example) whereas the programs from ABC and CBS were news magazine shows. The most popular viewing night was Thursday, and the most popular time was between 9–10 pm.

5. – *(Diese Aufgabe eignet sich gut als Referatsthema für individuelle S.)*

→ Discuss in class what you think the top ten programmes on German TV are and make a list. Then check the following websites to see what the top ten shows really are!

**German TV programme ratings:**
http://www.kress.de/tgl/frueh.html
http://www.quotentoto.de/

**Over to you**

● *In KA (mündlich) entscheiden S, welche Informationen (ggf. aus ihren 'TV Diaries' (s. unten) ) für die Umfrage benötigt werden, und wie diese am besten/schnellsten zusammengetragen werden können. (Festhaltung als OHP oder Tafelbild). (S. auch 'Skills file', SB, S. 140 & 141.)*

→ **A TV Diary**
Keep a 'TV Diary' for the next week. Keep a record of:
a) the names of the programmes you watch
b) which channels the programmes are on
c) when and how long you watch each programme
d) what you think of each programme, e.g. by giving a rating from 1 (very good) – 5 (terrible)
e) whether and how often you talked about programmes you watch with your friends.

## Talking TV! SB S. 116

*Im Cartoon, in den dazugehörigen Aufgaben und in der 'Over to you'-Aufgabe geht es darum, inwiefern Menschen weniger (oder mehr) miteinander kommunizieren, seitdem es Fernsehen gibt. Dies ist dann auch das Thema, das – fast 'ad absurdum' – in der Hörverstehensaufgabe aufgegriffen wird.*

**Looking at the cartoon**

1. – *(Als Variante den Cartoon als OHP/Arbeitsblatt bereitstellen, und die letzte Sprechblase zudecken bzw. ausblenden. S überlegen sich in PA die Fortsetzung des Cartoons und führen ihn als 'mini-play' vor der Klasse auf.)*
2. a) The cartoonist is either making the point that – contrary to the man's initial remark – TV hasn't destroyed the art of conversation because it provides us with things to talk about! (Rather unlikely!) Or the cartoonist is implying that TV has so reduced peoples' range of interests that they are unable to find anything else to talk about.
b) *Wenn S ein TV diary (s. oben) erstellt haben, können sie ihre Angaben zu Teil e) mit in die Diskussion einbeziehen. S könnten auch überlegen, inwiefern die Verbreitung von Kabel- und Satellitenfernsehen eine Rolle in dieser Frage spielt.*

**Over to you**

● *Diese Aufgabe sollte mündlich in GA erfolgen. S auf 'Skills files', SB, S. 128 ('Small talk') und S. 132 ('Useful phrases for discussions') verweisen.*

## Listening comprehension SB S. 116

Kopiervorlage **4**: TRB, S. 130/CD-ROM
Lösungen: TRB, S. 140

CC:2/4
CD:69 **'The Shock of Recognition'** (Transcript)

Recently, New York City had a blackout which caused all nine television stations in the area to go out for several hours. This created tremendous crises in families all over the New York area and proved that TV plays a much greater role in people's lives than anyone can imagine.
For example, when the TV set went off in the Bufkin's house in Forest Hills, panic set in. First, Bufkins thought it was his set in

the living room, so he rushed into his bedroom and turned on the set. Nothing.
The phone rang and Mrs. Bufkins heard her sister in Manhattan tell her that there was a blackout.
She hung up and said to her husband, "It isn't your set. Something happened to the top of the Empire State Building."
Bufkins stopped and said, "Who are you?"
"I'm your wife, Edith."
"Oh," Bufkins said. "Then I suppose those kids in there are mine."
"That's right," Mrs. Bufkins said. "If you ever got out of that armchair in front of the TV set, you'd know who we were."
"Boy, they're really grown," Bufkins said, looking at his son and his daughter. "How old are they now?"
"Thirteen and fourteen," Mrs. Bufkin replied.
"I'll be darned. Hi, kids."
"Who's he?" Bufkins' son, Henry asked.
"It's your father," Mrs. Bufkins said.
"I'm pleased to meetcha," Bufkins' daughter, Mary, said shyly.
There was an embarrassed silence all around.
"Look," said Bufkins finally. "I know I haven't been much of a father, but now that the TV's out, I'd like to make it up to you."
"How?" asked Henry.
"Well, let's just talk," Bufkins said. "That's the best way to get to know each other."
"What do you want to talk about?" Mary asked.
"Well, for starters, what school do you go to?"
"We go to Forest Hills High School," Henry said.
"What do you know?" Bufkins said. "You're both in high school."
There was dead silence.
"What do *you* do?" Mary asked.
"I'm an accountant," Bufkins said.
"I thought you were a car salesman," Mrs. Bufkins said in surprise.
"That was two years ago. Didn't I tell you I changed jobs?" Bufkins said in surprise.
"No, you didn't. You haven't told me anything for two years."
"Yup. I'm doing quite well too," Bufkins said.
"Then why am I working in a department store?" Mrs. Bufkins demanded.
"Oh, are you still working in a department store? If I had known that, I would have told you you could quit last year. You should have mentioned it," Bufkins said.
There was more dead silence.
Finally Henry said, "Hey, you want to hear me play the guitar?"
"I'll be darned. You know how to play the guitar? Say, didn't I have a daughter who played the guitar?"
"That was Susie," Mrs. Bufkins said.
"Where is she?"
"She got married a year ago, just about the time you were watching the World Series."
"How about that?" Bufkins said, very pleased. "You know, I hope they don't fix the antenna for another couple of hours. There's nothing like a blackout for a man to *really* get to know his family."

'The Shock of Recognition' from Down the Seine and up the Potomac by Art Buchwald, New York: Fawcett Crest, 1977, pp. 388–390.

## Blame the couch potatoes ... SB S. 117–119

[i] Ben Elton was born in Catford, South London in 1959. After studying drama at Manchester University he started his career as a stand-up comedian in 1980. In 1981 he joined the Comedy Store in London where he worked with Rik Mayall and Adrian Edmondson. Ben Elton soon built up a reputation as a writer with his sitcoms including *Blackadder* and *The Young Ones*. He also writes novels and plays. He currently lives in Notting Hill, West London. His other novels include: *Blast from the Past, Inconceivable, Gridlock*.
For more information see:
http://www.wesjen.simplenet.com/BritComElton/index.html

*Es ist unbedingt notwendig, vorab die Einleitung durchzulesen und zu verstehen. Folgende 'Who's who' könnte dabei behilflich sein bzw. könnten S anhand der Einleitung erstellen:*
Bruce: film director; makes sexist and violent films.
Wayne: psychopathic killer; fan of Bruce's films
Scout: Wayne's girlfriend and accomplice
Farrah: Bruce's ex-wife
Velvet: Bruce's daughter
Bill: cameraman
Karen: camerawoman

### Looking at the book cover  SB S. 117

Ben Elton probably chose the title 'Popcorn' because popcorn is associated with the cinema – especially in the USA – and can be considered a symbol of popular consumerist film culture.

### Looking at the cartoon  SB S. 118

1. *Falls S keine Ideen haben, könnte man folgende 'Captions' zur Auswahl stellen, und S danach auffordern eine eigene zu erstellen:*
Which of these captions do you think is best?
"Who called the fire brigade?" • "I don't understand what they're all screaming about. It's not everyday you get to be on prime time TV." • "Must remember to thank the fire brigade for bringing along their ladder." • "No smoke without fire."
2. –

### Considering the text  SB S. 118

1. Because the ratings are dropping so the TV company wants to stop the live broadcast. Wayne knows – or at least assumes – that his announcement will attract more viewers.
2. Farrah could have been saved if:
- viewers had turned off their TVs.
- the stations had refused to broadcast live.
- the camera team had refused to film.
- the SWAT team had stormed the building earlier.
3. Because on the one hand she thinks of/remembers the reporter's golden rule: "Never intervene", and she is scared of not doing what Wayne says, and on the other hand she feels a responsibility for Farrah's life.
4. –
5. a) <u>TV networks</u>: The TV producer asks Wayne not to kill Farrah, but keeping the ratings up is more important. Whilst the TV crew in the control truck do dicuss stopping the broadcast because some of them feel Wayne is "feeding off" the publicity and creating the news for them, it is never considered a real possibility that broadcasting will stop.
<u>The police</u>: Chief Cornell is "in agony", he knows that whatever decision he makes there will be bloodshed. He wishes someone else would take responsibility.
<u>Wayne & Scout</u> are remorseless, sadistic murderers, who are using the public for their own benefit.

# 7 Glued to the tube – TV in the USA

<u>Bruce</u> behaves quite calmly and tries to reason with Wayne until Farrah has been murdered, when he explodes.
<u>The public</u> is interested in action and drama. People switch off when Wayne and Bruce are having a discussion, but switch on when Wayne announces that Farrah is going to be shot.
b) Diese Aufgabe ist die Grundlage der folgenden 'Your view'-Aufgabe und sollte deshalb sorgfältig bearbeitet werden. Dies sollte idealerweise im Rahmen einer Diskussion geschehen. Es soll klar sein, dass es keine 'richtige' Antwort gibt!
*Responsiblity for Wayne and Scout's action, possible answers:*
*TV networks: responsible because the ratings are so important to them; because they broadcast Wayne live.*
*The police: not very responsible except in so far as they didn't manage to catch the killers earlier. They could have intervened as soon as Wayne announced his intention to kill Farrah.*
*Wayne & Scout: fully responsible for their behaviour, though influenced by Bruce's films in which this kind of gratuitous violence plays a major role.*
*Bruce: responsible for making such violent films which cause people like Wayne to behave the way they do.*
*The public: responsible for watching Wayne and Scout on TV and for wanting to see bloodshed.*

### Your view    SB S.118

*NB Sinnvoll wäre es, an dieser Stelle die 'Vocabulary & language'-Aufgaben (SB, S. 119, s. unten) zu machen und danach erst diese 'Your view'-Aufgabe, die schriftlich in EA gemacht werden soll. (S. auch 'Skills files', SB, S.124 & 125.)*

### Vocabulary & language

1. a) responsibility: to take responsibility: ll. 18, 32, 33; to be responsible: ll. 47, 50–52, 63, 70.
b) responsibility ≠ irresponsibility; responsible ≠ irresponsible
c) responsibility = duty (l. 11); to be responsible = to be up to s.o. ("It's up to you", l. 64); to be in s.o.'s hands ("the lives of us all are in your hands.", l. 65)
2. <u>people</u>: producer (l. 2), news-gatherer (l. 11), the media (l. 47), the public (l. 47); • <u>actions</u> (verbs): to drop (l. 3), to record (l. 4), to edit (l. 5), to tune in (l. 7), to climb (l. 21), to terminate the broadcast (l. 26), to turn off (l. 29), to censor (l. 30), to create news (l. 31), to switch to/on/off (ll. 49, 66), to keep rolling (l. 59), to watch (l. 66), to stay tuned in (l. 69); • <u>equipment</u>: monitor (l. 4), camera (l. 7), control truck (l. 25), computer screen (l. 20), ratings computer (l. 64)

### TV board game

*Kopiervorlage **5**: TRB, S. XX/CD-ROM*

S können in 4-er Gruppen spielen. Pro Gruppe braucht man ein Spielfeld und einen Satz Karten, die ausgeschnitten werden müssen. Zusätzlich braucht man pro Gruppe einen Würfel und pro Spieler eine Spielfigur. Die Seitenzahlen auf den fact cards verweisen auf die Seiten im SB, auf denen die Lösungen zu finden sind.
How to play:
• Place the fact and opinion cards face down on the spaces on the board.
• Throw a six to start.
• If you land on a fact space take a fact card and answer the question. The other players check your answer in the SB. If your answer is correct have another turn. If your answer is wrong, miss a turn.
• If you land on an opinion space take an opinion card and give your opinion. If the other players agree with you, have another turn, if they disagree with you, miss a turn.
• The first player to reach "The End" is the winner.

### Project: A panel discussion    SB S. 119

Als zusätzliche Vorbereitung wird jeder Gruppe die Rolle einer der Beteiligten zugewiesen. Die Gruppe bereitet dann den Standpunkt vor. Es wird ein Gruppenmitglied ausgewählt, das anschließend den Standpunkt vor der Klasse präsentiert bzw. vertritt.
Zusätzliche Hinweise zur Projektarbeit: TRB, S. 5–7 und 'Skills files', SB, S. 139.

### Test: TV and Me

*Kopiervorlage **6**: TRB, S. 133/CD-ROM (Aufgaben)*
*Lösungen: TRB, S. 141, Vokabeln: TRB, S. 142*

# The Truman Show — Glued to the tube 7

1. As you watch the first fifteen minutes of the the film, try to identify the main characters. Join the names and the correct descriptions.

2. Who says what? Watch the rest of the film and connect the speakers with these quotations.

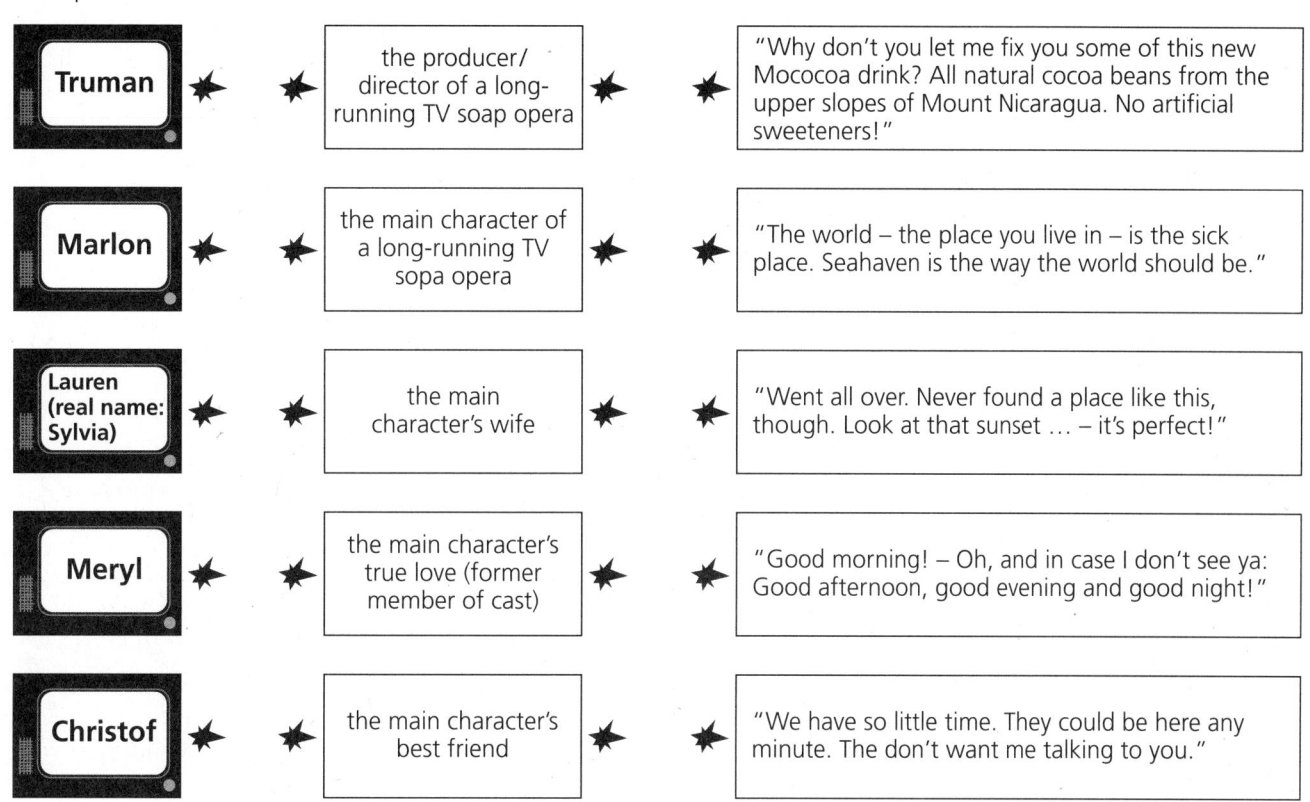

| Name | Description | Quotation |
|---|---|---|
| Truman | the producer/director of a long-running TV soap opera | "Why don't you let me fix you some of this new Mococoa drink? All natural cocoa beans from the upper slopes of Mount Nicaragua. No artificial sweeteners!" |
| Marlon | the main character of a long-running TV sopa opera | "The world – the place you live in – is the sick place. Seahaven is the way the world should be." |
| Lauren (real name: Sylvia) | the main character's wife | "Went all over. Never found a place like this, though. Look at that sunset … – it's perfect!" |
| Meryl | the main character's true love (former member of cast) | "Good morning! – Oh, and in case I don't see ya: Good afternoon, good evening and good night!" |
| Christof | the main character's best friend | "We have so little time. They could be here any minute. The don't want me talking to you." |

## Understanding content

Check how well you understood the film by completing these tasks:

1. Name one of the points where the main character gets suspicious.
   _____
2. Explain his obsession with going to Fiji.
   _____
3. There are no commercial breaks in 'The Truman Show', but products do get advertised. How?
   _____
4. What significance do you see in the central character's name?
   _____

## A Truman trivia quiz

Answer the following questions and see how closely you've watched the film!

1. How many cameras (approximately) are used on the set? _____
2. At the beginning of the film, how long has the show been running? _____
3. What is the name of the neighbour's dog? _____
4. How many different countries watched the Truman's first steps? _____
5. One character appears in the show in a second role – as what? _____

# Discussing TV

**Glued to the tube 7**

---

### "Young people watch too much TV."

Your view:

- TV isolates young people from each other.
- They spend so much time watching TV that they don't talk to each other.
- There are better things to do, e.g. meeting friends, doing sports, studying.
- Young people waste time worrying about fictional characters not real problems.

👎

---

### "Young people watch too much TV."

Your view:

- There's nothing wrong with watching TV.
- Young people watch more TV today because there are more channels and better programmes.
- They still have time for all their other hobbies, studying, etc.
- Fictional characters such as lawyers, doctors, etc., can be role models which make young people more ambitious.

👍

---

### "TV is an ideal babysitter."

Your view:

- Parents shouldn't use TV as a babysitter.
- They should talk to their children, play with them, make them use their imagination.
- Children should be encouraged to communicate and be active.
- Children watch unsuitable programmes if their parents aren't there to check.

👎

---

### "TV is an ideal babysitter."

Your view:

- It's OK to use the TV as a babysitter.
- There are lots of good programmes for children.
- TV stops children getting bored.
- Children are safe from harm while they are watching TV.

👍

---

### "There is too much violence on TV."

Your view:

- There's not as much violence on TV as critics say.
- Police dramas have to have some violence to be realistic.
- Violence doesn't have a negative effect on people.
- People can tell the difference between reality and fiction.
- People should have the right to choose what to watch for themselves without any government censorship.

👎

---

### "There is too much violence on TV."

Your view:

- There is far too much violence on TV and things are getting worse.
- People are confronted with violence in all programmes and at all times of the day.
- People are no longer bothered by violence: they start to accept it as normal.
- Watching violence causes people to behave violently themselves.
- The government should take action to restrict the amount of violence shown on TV.

👍

# Media research

**Glued to the tube** 7

A. Work with a partner. Look at the Nielsen Media research information below. Ask your partner questions and fill in the information missing in your table.

| Programme Name | Network | Day/Time | Audience |
|---|---|---|---|
| 20/20 – WED | ABC | Wed, 10 pm | 9,846,000 |
| WILL & GRACE | NBC | _____ | _____ |
| _____ | _____ | Thurs, 9 pm | 10,107,000 |
| DATELINE | NBC | Tue, 10 pm | 9,366,000 |
| LAW AND ORDER | _____ | Wed, 10 pm | _____ |
| _____ | NBC | Thurs, 10 pm | _____ |
| TOUCHED BY AN ANGEL | CBS | Sun, 8 pm | 9,538,000 |
| 60 MINUTES | _____ | _____ | _____ |
| 20/20 – FRI | ABC | Fri, 10 pm | 8,895,000 |
| FRIENDS | NBC | _____ | _____ |

**Possible questions**

What was on at (8 pm) on (Thursday)?
Which network was (Friends) broadcast on?
How many people watched (ER)?
What day/time was (ER) on?

*Source: Nielsen Media Research*

------------------------------------------------------------

B. Work with a partner. Look at the Nielsen Media research information below. Ask your partner questions and fill in the information missing in your table.

| Programme Name | Network | Day/Time | Audience |
|---|---|---|---|
| 20/20 – WED | ABC | _____ | _____ |
| WILL & GRACE | NBC | Thurs, 9.30 pm | 9,727,000 |
| _____ | NBC | _____ | _____ |
| DATELINE | NBC | Tue, 10 pm | 9,366,000 |
| _____ | NBC | Wed, 10 pm | _____ |
| E.R. | NBC | Thurs, 10 pm | 9,998,000 |
| TOUCHED BY AN ANGEL | _____ | _____ | _____ |
| 60 MINUTES | CBS | Sun, 7 pm | 9,887,000 |
| 20/20 – FRI | ABC | _____ | _____ |
| FRIENDS | NBC | Thurs, 8 pm | 9,913,000 |

**Possible questions**

What was on at (8 pm) on (Thursday)?
Which network was (Friends) broadcast on?
How many people watched (ER)?
What day/time was (ER) on?

*Source: Nielsen Media Research*

Klettbuch 510511 – *Challenge 21, Teacher's book*
© Ernst Klett Verlag GmbH, Stuttgart 2001.

**Listening comprehension**     Glued to the tube 7

## 'The Shock of Recognition' by Art Buchwald

**blackout** when all electrical power goes out
**meetcha** *(informal)* ['miːtʃə] short for 'meet you'
**for starters** to start with

**dead** *here:* absolute
**accountant** [əˈkaʊntənt] *Buchhalter(in)*

### 1. Listening comprehension

As you listen note down:

a) the names of the husband and wife: _____

b) the names of the kids who live at home: _____

c) the school they go to: _____

d) Mr. Bufkin's present job: _____

e) Mrs. Bufkin's job: _____

f) the instrument Henry plays: _____

g) the name of the daughter who has left home, and why she left: _____

h) the weaker word used for 'damned': _____

i) an important baseball championship series shown on TV: _____

### 2. Further activities

a) Which of the words/phrases in the box describe the story best in your opinion? Choose two and give reasons for your choice.

> *realistic • serious • makes fun of s.th • fantastic • funny*
> *satirical • ridiculous • interesting • makes a point*

_____
_____
_____

b) Comment on the point Art Buchwald is making in this story and give your own opinion. (120 words)

_____
_____
_____
_____
_____
_____
_____

(Continue on the back of the worksheet if necessary.)

### 3. Creative writing

You left school ten years ago and lost contact with your classmates. Now you are at your 10-year class reunion *(Klassentreffen)*. Everyone has changed so much that you hardly recognize them! Write about the meeting in the form of a play or a short story. (Write your answer on the back of the worksheet.)

# TV board game (1/2) — Glued to the tube 7

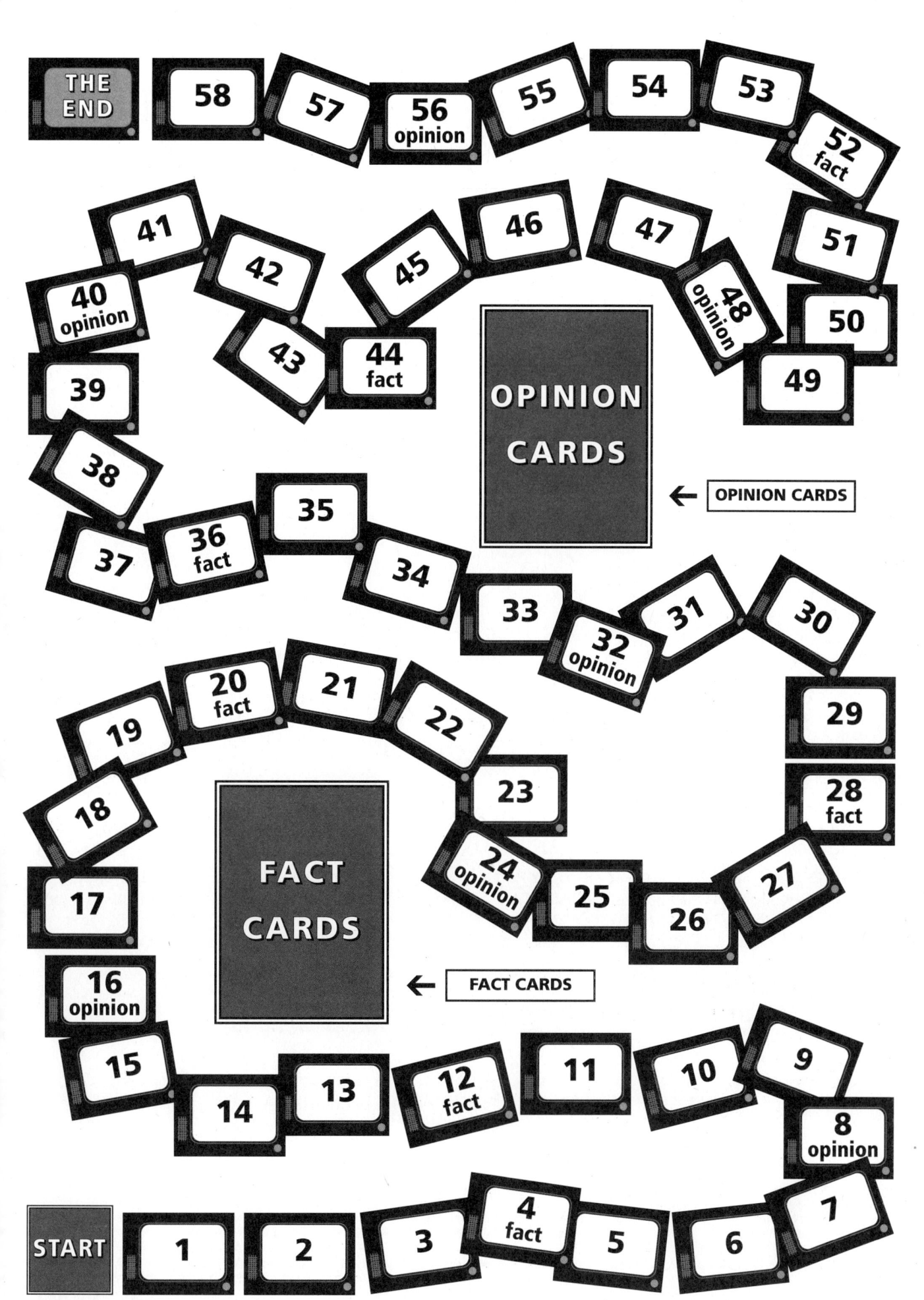

**START**

1, 2, 3, 4 fact, 5, 6, 7, 8 opinion, 9, 10, 11, 12 fact, 13, 14, 15, 16 opinion, 17, 18, 19, 20 fact, 21, 22, 23, 24 opinion, 25, 26, 27, 28 fact, 29, 30, 31, 32 opinion, 33, 34, 35, 36 fact, 37, 38, 39, 40 opinion, 41, 42, 43, 44 fact, 45, 46, 47, 48 opinion, 49, 50, 51, 52 fact, 53, 54, 55, 56 opinion, 57, 58

**THE END**

← OPINION CARDS

← FACT CARDS

# TV board game (2/2) — Glued to the tube 7

| OPINION | OPINION | OPINION | OPINION | OPINION |
|---|---|---|---|---|
| Who is your favourite TV host? Give a reason for your choice. | What is your favourite soap opera? Give a reason for your choice. | What types of TV programmes do you like best? Name two and say why. | What types of TV programmes do you like least? Name two and say why. | How do you usually decide what to watch on TV? Why do you use this method? |
| **OPINION** | **OPINION** | **OPINION** | **OPINION** | **OPINION** |
| Why are soap operas so popular with viewers? Give two reasons. | Are you in favour of or against a parental guidance system? Give two reasons for your answer. | How can TV affect children? Give two (good or bad) effects. | Does TV destroy the art of conversation? Give two reasons for your answer. | Would you like to take part in a game show? Give three reasons why/why not. |
| **OPINION** | **OPINION** | **FACT** | **FACT** | **FACT** |
| Can watching violent TV shows cause children to be more violent? Why/why not? | Do you think that watching TV is worthwhile? Give two reasons for your answer. | Which US TV network has the most viewers? (p. 114) | What is the difference between a station and a network? (p. 114) | What is a non-commercial station? (p. 114) |
| **FACT** | **FACT** | **FACT** | **FACT** | **FACT** |
| Give an example of what the Nielsen media ratings measure. (p. 115) | What is the FCC? Give an example of what it does. (p. 112) | Give two facts about American viewing habits. (p. 107, 114) | Explain two of the following categories: TV Y7, TV PG, V MA. (p. 112) | Name one right that is protected by the First Ammendment. (p. 112) |
| **FACT** | **FACT** | **FACT** | **FACT** | **FACT** |
| What is the Children's Television Act? (p. 112) | What is a V-chip? (p. 112) | What is a "couch potato"? (p. 117) | What is the name of the English equivalent of the programme Herzblatt? (p. 108) | Who wrote the novel Popcorn? (p. 117) |

# Test

# Glued to the tube 7

## TV and Me

Over the years the thing lost its grip. Possibly it began when we moved to an area with crummy reception. [...] Whatever, at some point I drifted out of TV orbit and never re-entered. I'll catch a Celtics game at a friend's house, or a presidential debate. But for weeks on end my only experience of TV will be through the window of a restaurant or bar. [...] I've never even owned one.

No doubt I'm out of it in some ways. For one thing, I'm a pop-culture illiterate [...]. From *Star Wars* to *Miami Vice* to *NYPD Blue*, it's all a big blank. But compared to the suffering in Bosnia and the rest, this seems a manageable burden. I think I'll survive.

I'm also free – of television at least. Program planners and sponsors don't set my schedule. In the evening, I do what I want: read a book, play basketball at the YMCA [...]. Nothing fancy. But at least I feel I've done something, instead of had something done to me. [...]

Also I think I've avoided that weird effect TV has on the sense of reality. I tend to see the world through my own experience, rather than through the ersatz and contrived version on the tube. The experience may be provincial, but at least it's mine.

This came home to me one night about a month ago, as I was getting off the G4 bus in Washington, near my house. A woman came rushing after me. "Excuse me," she said. "You've left your checkbook on the seat." It had slipped out of my back pocket. Without her intervention, my main financial record would have been lost.

At that moment, TV was telling millions of Americans that the OJ verdict had released a tide of racial animosity across the land. Yet this woman was black, and I am white – the only white person on that bus, in fact, and pretty much in the neighborhood, too. If racial tension existed the way TV said it did, I would have experienced it. But I didn't.

Was television merely reporting the supposed racial tension? Or was it also fomenting it? [...] Most Americans, white and black, live in racial ghettos, with little daily contact with one another. TV becomes the nation's racial reality – and so it turns us all into the version it portrays. This is true of a host of other problems as well.

What would happen, I wonder, if we all made a declaration of non-consent and insisted on experiencing these issues for ourselves?

(425 words)

*From* TV and Me *by Jonathan Rowe, TV-Turnoff Network*
*(http://www.tvturnoff.org)*

## Content

1. Has the author always been "free of television"? Give examples from the text to support your answer.
2. Why does the author think his way of spending his free time is better than watching TV?
3. What did the incident on the bus prove to the author?

*(Your teacher will tell you which of the following tasks you should complete.)*

## Comment

1. Do you think that being a "pop-culture illiterate" would be something to be proud of? Why or why not?
2. Can TV really affect one's sense of reality? Justify your opinion with examples of your own.
3. Try to answer the author's question in the last paragraph.

## Form

1. Find the other words and phrases used here for "television/TV". What attitudes do they express towards television?
2. What rhetorical device does the author use in ll. 10–12 *("But compared to the suffering ... I'll survive.")*?

## Language

1. Explain in a complete sentence (without using the underlined words).
   a) "... drifted out of TV orbit and never re-entered." (l. 3)
   b) "From Star Wars ... to NYPD Blue it's all a big blank." (ll. 9–10)
   c) "Program planners ... don't set my schedule." (ll. 13–14)
   d) "This came home to me one night about a month ago." (l. 23)
   e) "Without her intervention, my main financial record would have been lost." (ll. 27–28)
2. Find a synonym for the following words.
   a) crummy (l. 2)     b) weird (l. 18)     c) ersatz (l. 20)
3. Provide the correct verb forms (simple or progressive).
   a/b) I (watch) TV yesterday when suddenly the power (go) out again!
   c) The power (go) off two days before that already!
   d) I certainly hope that the power stays on today so that I (to be able to) watch my favourite TV show!
   e–g) I (look forward to) this all week, and I (go) crazy if I (have to) miss this week's episode!

# Lösungen zu den Kopiervorlagen

## 1 Who cares what I think?

### 3 Interview with an American teenager — S. 18

1. **F** Keith sees himself as "just an average kid."
2. **F** Keith thinks that he is a good basketball player, but not a hero because of his gambling.
3. **T**
4. **F** The American dream used to mean coming to America and starting a new and better life, but now for most people it means things like finding a good education, a good job, supporting your family and having a good life.
5. **F** Keith has a lot of ideas as to how he would like to make a difference in the world, like catching criminals or finding a cure for AIDS.
6. **T**
7. **F** The United States is his favourite country, but San Francisco is his favourite city.
8. **T**
9. **F** Keith hopes that all other nations will be like America in 50 years.
10. **T**
11. **T**
12. **F** Americans only care about themselves and not about their country, and they expect the government to do everything for them.
13. **T**
14. **F** Keith hasn't spoken Chinese as much over the years.
15. **F** Keith agrees with the stereotype that Asian pupils are smart.
16. **F** Keith says the major problem for kids who don't do well in school is that they don't have their parents' support and guidance.
17. **F** Keith's family observe only some of the Chinese holidays.

### 4 N'oubliez jamais — S. 19

**Missing words**
play • sing • something's • beat • anger • regrets • rebel • own • destiny • disagree • rules • dance • sing • something's • beat • heart • smile • own • searching • cure • sure

**Comprehension**
1. Mom, Dad, son = singer
2. reflective, a bit doubtful and sad (ll. 30–35)
3. "Same old songs" and "brand new songs" can be interpreted literally, but they also have symbolic meanings: this is the son's way of asking his parents why they haven't changed and/or don't continue to rebel against the rules and expectations of society. "Song" can also be interpreted as a particular person's or people's message to society.
4. A new generation is acting in its own way, testing the rules, and trying out new ideas and values.
5. Every generation a) is different, b) has its own songs, c) has a need to disobey/disagree and have conflicts with parents and other older people. Conclusion: it is normal and OK to rebel when one is young.
6. Themes and issues: different values of young and old, generation gap, finding one's identity, the need to be different
7. a) –
b) Every generation feels the need to develop its own characteristic features that make it different from the generation before; these features may be: social or political values, music and/or fashion trends, problems, etc.
c) –

### 6 Young give up condoms … — S. 22

**Research results**
**Findings:** Teens and young adults don't heed warnings about AIDS and are at greater risk of becoming infected./The number of teens and young adults having sex without using condoms is increasing./As opposed to 5 years ago, three times more 16 to 24-year-olds are having sex regularly (25% more have had 4 or more partners by age 24)./In this group nearly a third fewer people use condoms./Since 1995, the cases of gonorrhoea have gone up by nearly 30% for teens.

**Reasons for findings:** Young people settle down later and therefore have more partners before./Especially for women, the romantic notion behind relationships has faded, and both sexes are more willing to have casual relationships./In the last few years there have been fewer safe sex campaigns.

**Charlotte Davis**
**Previous attitude/reasons:** She was "terrified" of becoming infected and therefore insisted on using condoms./She was terrified by reports that everyone would know someone who was HIV positive.
**Current attitude/reasons:** The terrifying reports didn't turn out to be true, so she isn't as scared anymore./She no longer insists on using condoms.

**Anonymous person**
**Previous attitude/reasons:** He used to fear AIDS and always used a condom.
**Current attitude/reasons:** He has sex frequently and doesn't bother to use condoms because he's sure that there will be a cure for AIDS soon./He believes that this "reckless" attitude is typical of his generation.

### 7 Test: Children of 8 join … — S. 23

**Content**
1. The hospital reports are surprising because they show that across the country, the numbers of underage (child and teen) drinkers suffering from alcohol-related illnesses and accidents has never been higher./At Alder Hey children's hospital, ten times more children have been admitted for problems caused by alcohol over the last 10 years.
2. In modern society, children are forced to mature very fast, and many don't have sufficient parental guidance to help them./Alcohol is glamorised by pop stars and advertising and is therefore more attractive to children.
3. Children get alcohol by paying older youths to buy it for them or buying or making their own homemade variety.

**Comment**
1. Provide children and teens with more information about the effects and dangers of alcohol./Ban ads that glorify alcohol./Parents should pay more attention to their children./There should be tougher restrictions where alcohol is sold so that children and teens can't get hold of it./The penalties for youth who buy alcohol for minors should be increased.
2. Advantages for today's youth: more wealth for middle and upper class youth/more technological advances and new devices to help them pursue their goals and make their lives easier and more enjoyable/more opportunities to travel and to work abroad
Disadvantages for today's youth: more pressure (e.g. to achieve goals, to grow up faster, peer pressure)/lack of proper guidance to help them set priorities and form their morals and ideas

**Form**
1. The use of direct quotations and statistics brings across important points more clearly and convincingly to the reader.
2. This is a persuasive text: A lot of direct quotes are used which cause the reader not only to understand what is going on but also to "feel" the emotions of the speakers about the subject (indirect quotes tend to be more impersonal and impartial)./Statistics make the impact of certain facts and events more tangible for the reader./There is no attempt to remain impartial by presenting both sides of the issue. The standpoint of the author is clear.

**Language**
1. a) suffering; b) suggestion; c) estimation, estimate; d) contribution;
2. a) When something *teaches you a lesson*, you change your behaviour/attitude because you know of the dangers involved with something, or you have even experienced these dangers; b) *Staff* refers to all the people employed/working in a company; 3. a) Several researchers have reported the distressing conclusions; b) Older youths are convinced by

children to buy them alcohol; 4. a) dropped, fallen; b) suffered; 5. a) had to … survived; b) has been consuming … has never touched

## 2 A British jigsaw

### 1 Wales and the Welsh S. 35

**Caption questions:** 1. Welsh 2. Welcome to Wales

**Comprehension**
1. a) hywl = spirit; b) cawl = a tpye of meat broth; c) Eisteddfod = a competition for artistic activities, e.g. music, poetry, dance
2. a) Only a fifth of the nation speaks Welsh fluently because in the past, the language was banned in school, and the children caught speaking it were severely punished. Also, those who spoke Welsh couldn't succeed in their careers because of peoples' prejudice toward the language and the land.
b) Now it is very popular to speak Welsh. It is required for pupils to learn Welsh until the age of 14, and many adults take evening classes to learn the language.
c) hywl
d) Rugby is important for the Welsh because it is their only chance to beat other countries who are much bigger than they are!
3. a) The Welsh National Assembly was officially opened by the Queen.
b) For the first time in several hundred years, decisions on local matters will be made in Cardiff, not Westminster.
4. –
5. The speaker's intention is to give an idea about Wales and the Welsh to people who know very little or nothing about Wales.

**Language**
accent = ['--] accompaniment = [-'----] atmosphere = ['---] character = ['---] comeback = ['--] curriculum = [-'---] daffodils = ['---] emblem = ['--] generation = [,--'--] hospitality = [,--'---] imaginary = [-'----] laverbread = ['---] pastures = ['--] recipe = ['---] signifiant = [-'---] unpredictable = [,--'---]

### 4 Round Britain crossword S. 39

**Across:**
2. great 3. westerly 4. another way to express *to relax* 4. *to take it easy* is to _____ 9. statistics 13. origin 15. tall 18. Highlands 21. divorced 22. abbreviation for *Master of Arts* 23. voicemail 26. pub 28. What you do with your eyes. 29. spread 32. dense 33. Cars drive on these to get from one place to another. 35. Another way to express *too*. 37. I don't want a copy! I want the _____ ! 38. feeding 39. Abbreviation for *very important person*. 40. Certificate of Secondary Education 41. rural 42. Al 43. rain 45. this 46. Abbreviation for *National Insurance*. 47. Cadbury 49. A famous British dish is steak and kidney _____. 51. That which hasn't changed stays the _____. 52. Abbreviation for *very important person*. 54. The major piece of land of a continent (as opposed to the islands). 56. Abbreviation for *United Kingdom*. 57. climate 60. The numerical results gotten from analysing information. 62. deep 63. Short for *modern*. 65. opposite of *stop* 66. year 68. One of Shakespeare's plays: _____ you like it. 70. 72. capital, east 74. Abbreviation for *as known as*. 75. Opposite of *off*. 77. Synonym for *medicine*. 78. Small brown bird: also the last name of a famous architect who designed St. Paul's Cathedral and many other churches in London. 79. density 82. A short way to indicate that a time is in the morning. 83. Short for *per annum*. 84. Small 86. The abbreviation for *I owe you*. 87. lamp 89. The opposite of *yes*. 91. Abbreviation for *Irish Republican Army*. 93. pier 94. Ashington 96. Nature Conservancy Council 98. born 99. Past tense of *do*. 100. Past tense of *have*. 102. government 105. General word for the cars and trucks on the roads and streets. 107. A scenic region in southwest England.

**Down:**
1. One word meaning *quite a few*. 2. Synonym for *fantastic* 5. Short for *et cetera*. 6. islands 7. Abbreviation for *please turn over*. 8. height 10. subscribed. 11. Do you have a lot of snow and _____ in the winter where you live? 12. Used as a conjunction, this word is a synonym for *because*. 14. non 16. _____ concerts are those where the artists sing in front of the public. 19. Synonym for *thought*. 20. Abbreviation for *as soon as possible*. 23. Having to do with what is seen. 24. When Al cleans the floor he _____ it. 25. learning 27. bed 29. snooker 30. religious 31. Word for a party or social event. 34. delivered 40. cliche 41. Short for *rest in peace*. 42. Articles in English: a, _____, the. 44. Opposite direction of *south*. 48. Birmingham 50. Conditional sentences often begin with the word _____. 51. Shakespeare 53. industry 55. Wales 58. languages 59. Midlands 64. Past tense of *is*. 67. The fee you pay every month to live in an apartment you do not own. 69. steam 71. Famous Shakespeare quote: _____ be or not _____ be, that is the question … 73. urban 76. England 78. Welsh 80. The abbreviation for "Isle of Man". 81. South 82. Synonym for *district*. 85. The _____ of a word can be looked up in a dictionary. 88. pro persona 90. ozone 91. India 95. We're finished with the task. What shall we do _____ ? 97. check 101. body of water 103. open 104. Opposite of *fake*.

### 5 Test: Two towns and two nations S. 40

**Content**
1. Similarities: Both are in England, and both have the same name. Both are also close to the sea.
Differences: One is in the north, one in the south. One is very prosperous, the other is in economic decline.
2. They have agreed to establish a closer connection between the two towns. The object is to try to bridge the gap between the different ways of life, and to understand each other better.
3. A man from the northern Ashington (Bill Gale) happened to see the name of the town when passing on the A24. He contacted a local historian, Daphne Norton, and they began writing to each other.

**Comment**
1. One reason might be the fact that the Industrial Revolution happened mainly in the Midlands and the north, leading to them becoming mainly working-class areas which have now gone into decline. Another might be the advantage the southern Ashington has in being nearer to London.
2. In Germany, one might see a comparison with the East-West divide following the collapse of the communist GDR. Similar is the greater unemployment in the more disadvantaged area, the feeling of having shared hardships, and also the lack of mutual understanding between the two parts. The reasons are historical in both cases, though the details are quite different.
3. –

**Form**
1. The following features are typical of such newspaper articles: the snappy introductory sentence; the frequent short quotations; the short paragraphs.
2. The tone of this article is light and humorous (e.g. " … it was rather hilarious at first." (ll. 39–41) or "It will be interesting to see whether brown ale swilling ex-pitmen …" (ll. 49–50) Sometimes there is a strong contrast between the register of the leaflet (ll. 44–45) and the many spoken remarks quoted. Only the formal register is used in the leaflet (e.g. "explore …"), whereas the speakers sometimes use colloquial phrases (e.g. "We're stuck …" (ll. 5–6) that make their register more informal. Other times, however, the speakers also use a formal register for their comments (e.g. "While we cannot underestimate … (ll. 32–33)).

**Language**
1. a) The two Ashingtons couldn't be more different.
b) Yesterday, they began to try to break down the differences.
c) Mrs Norton has trouble imagining what it is like in the other town.
d) People in the other Ashington know very well that their town is in a prosperous part of the country near London, where many of them work.
2. a) rich; b) poor; c) happened to find; d) drinking (in large quantities).
3. a) has been doing; b/c) called … has learned

# Lösungen zu den Kopiervorlagen

## XtraFile: The British political system

### 1. Government in Britain quiz — S. 42

1. a); 2. b); 3. a), d); 4. a); 5. b); 6. a); 7. a); 8. b); 9. d); 10. d); 11. c); 12. c); 13. a), c)

### 2. The British political system — S. 43

**Parliament**
**The House of Commons:** where the business of government takes place (e.g. new laws are passed) • 659 Members of Parliament (MPs) • one elected from each constituency by universal suffrage • The Speaker is elected by the MPs, and presides over the House but doesn't take part in discussions or votes.
**The House of Lords:** acts mainly in a controlling and advisory capacity but can delay Bills for up to a year • two archbishops and 24 bishops of the Church of England • hereditary peers (over 750 in 1997) • life peers (over 400 in 1997) • In 1999, 92 hereditary peers were elected to retain their seats until the second stage of the reform is completed.
**The Monarch:** official Head of State of the executive and judiciary • officially appoints the Prime Minister • commander-in-chief of the armed forces • "supreme governor" of the Church of England • real powers are very limited and duties are largely ceremonial

**Government**
The winning party is the one that wins the most seats (not necessarily the most votes). • The leader of the winning party becomes Prime Minister (Head of Government). • The Prime Minister forms a Cabinet, a group of ministers, secretaries, etc., who are in charge of important governmental functions. • Important Cabinet ministers = Chancellor of the Exchequer (financial and monetary issues), Home Secretary (internal affairs), Foreign Secretary (foreign affairs)

**Opposition**
The largest minority party in the House of Commons becomes the Opposition. It has its own leader and shadow cabinet.

**The political parties**
**Main political parties:**
Conservative Party (Tories), right of centre • Labour Party, left of centre • Liberal Democrats • Green Party
**National Parties:**
**Wales:** Plaid Cymru (Welsh nationalists) • **Scotland:** Scottish National Party • **Northern Ireland:** Ulster Unionist Party • Social Democratic Party • Labour Party • Democratic Unionist Party • Sinn Fein (political wing of the IRA)

**Current electoral system**
British citizens over 18 may vote. • The Prime Minister decides when elections will be held within a 5-year period. • In General Elections, a simple majority or "first-past-the-post" system is currently employed, where the candidate who gets the most votes in a constituency wins a seat in Parliament. • This system tends to produce strong single party governments. • MPs and their constituencies are closely linked.

**Devolution**
As a result of referendums, Northern Ireland and Wales have their own assemblies, and Scotland has a Scottish Parliament. These governing bodies have varying legislative rights and powers in conjunction with the Westminster Parliament.
**N. Ireland:** On 10th April 1998 (the Good Friday Agreement) a Northern Ireland Assembly was proposed, and the Irish people voted in favour of a New Northern Ireland Assembly on 22nd May 1998.
**Scotland:** A referendum was held on 11 September 1997, and the Scottish people voted overwhelmingly for a Scottish Parliament.
**Wales:** On September 18th 1997 the Welsh people voted by a narrow margin in favour of having a Welsh Assembly.

### 3. British politics game — S. 44

How can the constitution be changed? *By act of Parliament.*
Who is Head of State? *The Monarch.*
Who is Head of Government? *The Prime Minister.*
What is the Monarch's function? *Formally appoints the Prime Minister and many other government officials.*
Where does Parliament meet? *The Palace of Westminster.*
Name the three elements that make up Parliament. *The House of Commons, House of Lords and the Monarch.*
For what functions is the Chancellor of the Exchequer responsible? *Financial and monetary issues.*
Who decides when exactly to hold a General Election, and within which period? *The Prime Minister, within a five-year period.*
How many members are there in the House of Commons? *659*
To which groups do the members of the House of Lords belong? *Bishops and archbishops of the Church of England, hereditary peers (who must now run for office) and life peers.*
What happens in the House of Commons? *New laws are passed and the main business of government is done.*
What is the main business of the House of Lords? *Has a mainly controlling and advisory function, but can delay bills for up to a year.*
Which party forms the government after a General Election? *The party which wins the most seats at a General Election.*
Which party forms the Opposition? *The largest minority party in the House of Commons.*
Which voting system is used at a General Election? *The simple majority or 'first-past-the-post' system.*
What is known as the Good Friday Agreement? *The proposal for a Northern Ireland Assembly which was proposed on April 10, 1998.*
Which parties have played the most decisive role in British politics in the twentieth century? *Two parties: the Conservative Party (Tories) and the Labour Party.*
When was the first election for the Scottish Parliament held? *May 6, 1999.*
Which voting system is used for elections to the Scottish Parliament? *The first-past-the-post-basis for 73 MSPs and a proportional basis from party lists for 56 MSPs.*
Which are the nationalist parties of Scotland and Wales? *The Scottish National Party and the Plaid Cymru (Welsh Nationals).*

### Translation practise (CD-ROM)

*Eine neue Art einzukaufen*
*Dadurch dass immer mehr Geschäfte online gehen, geht man davon aus, dass Verbraucher ihr Kaufverhalten ändern werden. Weil die Konsumenten wissen, dass sie fast alles im Internet finden können, werden sie nicht länger ihre Zeit damit verschwenden, Schlange zu stehen oder in Verkehrsstaus zu stecken. Produkte wie zum Beispiel Software, Bücher, Geschenke und CDs sind problemlos zu bekommen und sollen angeblich billiger sein. Es gibt jedoch einen Nachteil: die Leute verlieren vielleicht die Kontrolle darüber, wieviel sie tatsächlich ausgeben. Dadurch, dass sie alles mit Kreditkarte bezahlen, landen Verbraucher schließlich im Minus.*

### 4. Test: Translation — S. 46

*Australien und die Monarchie*
*Australien war früher eine Kolonie, Teil des Britischen Empires und wurde direkt von Großbritannien aus regiert. Die ersten Siedler wurden vor 211 Jahren als Sträflinge nach Australien geschickt, da die britischen Gefängnisse überfüllt waren. Seit diesem Zeitpunkt steht Australien unter der Herrschaft eines Britschen Königs oder Königin. Ab 1793 fingen die Leute an freiwillig nach Australien auszuwandern, weil sie von dem Reichtum des Landes und dem Vesprechen auf eigenen Grund und Boden angezogen wurden (und auch durch die billige Arbeistkraft der Sträflinge). Diese Siedler kamen von ganz Europa, aber die meisten waren aus Großbritannien und Irland. Bereits Mitte des 19. Jahrhunderts war klar, dass Australien nicht länger ein riesiges Gefängnis war und*

*seine eigene Regierung benötigte. Im Jahr 1901 wurde das Australische Commonwealth gegründet. Aber obwohl Australien heute unabhängig ist, hat es einen britischen Monarchen als Staatsoberhaupt behalten.*

## 3 Making the grade

### 5 Work experience S. 61

**Employer/type and location of company:** menswear company, store in Regent Street, London, first of its type in the country: big, modern, expensive design
**Length of stay:** two weeks
**Feelings before starting work:** very anxious (nerve-wracking night, couldn't sleep, worried about what her colleagues would be like, woke too early)
**First impressions:** shop really nice, people seemed friendly
**Normal duties:** to make the shop look its best, serve customers, stock up, get altered suits from different branches
**Additional duties:** took weekend takings to the bank, helped a German window-dresser
**Good points:** good atmosphere, kind people, enjoyed working as part of team, enjoyed meeting different types of people
**Bad points:** standing up all day (tough on legs), didn't get on with a couple of people (but accepts this as normal)
**Achievements:** earned £2,652 (even though she had no experience of selling), made a good impression on her colleagues, was given an excellent report, she has been asked to go back

**Completing sentences**
1. ... the shop wasn't busy and she had nothing else to do.
2. ... a message was sent straight to the police station.
3. ... panicked and ran to ring the police.
4. ... the police would have come right away.

**Vocabulary**
1. f); 2. g); 3. h); 4. e); 5. d); 6. a); 7. c); 8. b)

**Example sentences** *(CD-ROM)*
1. I know you fear that taking tomorrow's test will be a *nerve-wracking* experience.
2. However, you've revised well, so I'm sure that it *will go smoothly*.
3. Jim had a lot to do yesterday, so we could only talk *briefly*.
5. Trina has lost a lot of weight, so her clothes need to be *altered*.
5. I'm having a *tough* time figuring out what went wrong.
6. Gary woke up *in a state* because his alarm clock hadn't gone off, and he had exactly 30 minutes to get dressed and get to work before an important meeting.
7. She already has one child from her *previous* marriage, and she and her new husband are thinking about having more children.

**Writing a letter**
Siehe 'Skills File', *SB, S. 137.*

### 7 Test: Real life U S. 63

**Content**
1. Elizabeth is not typical because she intends to get a job after leaving school, unlike the roughly 80% of high school seniors who plan to go on to college. Elizabeth has chosen instead to do something she really enjoys.
2. Statistics from the U.S. Department of Education show that although most high school students plan to go on to college, less than half of them (approx. 37% in 1998) actually do so.
3. On one hand Rae Siporin thinks highly of his students' abilities and level of preparation. On the other hand, he thinks they have the wrong attitude to learning. He disapproves of the way they see a degree in strategic terms – just as a means to get a better job. He would prefer them to have a genuine commitment to learning, and to view their degree as a part of a life-long education.

**Comment:** 1./2./3. –

**Form**
1. Techniques used to convince readers: several quotations, both from students and school officials which show how this decision is a good one from several points of view/statistics/directly addressing the reader (ll. 21–23).
2. Techniques to engage audience interest: the article starts with a story and a quote from someone who is average reader age./Colloquial register is used (e.g. "Even if your heart isn't set ..." (ll. 21–23))./Sentences are generally short with simpler structures./To make sure that his point is made, the author writes out the conclusion that readers should already realize from the statistics (ll. 18–20).

**Language**
1. a) where/in which you do; b) who is asking; 2. a) easier; b) hide; c) falling rapidly/plummeting/dropping quickly; d) childish/immature; 3. a) Such a message is inescapable/stated so loudly or clearly that you cannot miss it; b) Enrolment is at record levels; c) The statistics reveal a fact that is very surprising; d) Students are more interested in what a degree will get them than they are in expanding and widening their general knowledge and outlook on life; 4. a) to compete, competitive; b) success, successful; c) to value, value; d) to commit, commitment

## 4 Meet Britain's press

### 1 Using statistics S. 73

**Increase**
**verbs:** to increase, to rise, to grow, to climb, to go up, to improve, to jump, to double, to boom, to explode
**nouns:** increase, rise, growth, climb, improvement, jump, doubling, boom, explosion

**Decrease**
**verbs:** to decrease, to fall, to decline, to drop, to shrink
**nouns:** decrease, fall, decline, drop, shrinkage

**No change**
**verbs:** to stay constant, to stay, to hold, to not change, to not vary
**nouns:** constant

**Adjectives:** slow, slight, gradual, linear, stable, progressive, (un)expected, sudden, surprising, astonishing, significant, rapid, enormous, remarkable, sharp, dramatic, explosive

**Adverbs:** nearly, almost, about, approximately, just under/over, more than, less than, a great deal

**Prepositions:** over, from, to, in, to, Since, In, to, of, at, for

**Prepositions** *(CD-ROM)*
in, by, Since, to, In of, at for, over, from, to

### 4 Working on a regional newspaper S. 77

**Listening for gist**
**Section 1:** Area covered, Readership, News sources
**Section 2:** Who the newspaper is aimed at
**Section 3:** Working day
**Section 4:** Qualifications

**Listening for detail**
**Section 1**
a) The Birmingham Post region is comoposed mainly of the Birmingham area and also the outlying counties.
b) Local, national and international news is covered. There is an emphasis on local news, especially for readers who live outside

## Lösungen zu den Kopiervorlagen

Birmingham but work there and want to know what is going on in the city.
c) The Press Association provides national news, Reuters provides international news, and reporters report on regional and local news.

**Section 2**
The readership of the newspaper has been changing. Traditionally it has been made up mostly of readers who are older and/or male, but lately the newspaper has been attracting other types of readers, such as young people. The paper has done this by having a women's editor and taking on younger writers who write "funkier" articles about topics that interest young people, such as night life and clubs.

**Section 3**
a) Roz uaually works 8 hours per day.
b) She works longer hours when when a story breaks later in the day and she has to finish a feature on it.
c) When she gets to work, she opens her post.
d) She considers most of the press releases she receives to be advertising rubbish and throws them away.
e) Roz writes one feature per day.
f) She covers issues in her features such as stalking, rape, breast cancer, women in the board room, personalities, men who are interesting to women.

**Section 4** –

### 5  Test: Talking in Whispers                                S. 78

**Content**
1. Andres feels excited and hopeful when he sees the American pressman because he hopes that the pressman will let the world know what is happening.
2. The situation is dangerous because the soldiers notice the pressman taking pictures of them being cruel to prisoners. The soldiers don't want him taking pictures, so they try to catch him.
3. *Mögliche Lösung:*
An American pressman in Chile narrowly missed being caught while taking pictures of Pinochet's soldiers abusing their prisoners. The pressman had entered a crowd of people who were looking on as Pinochet's soldiers were hitting their prisoners as they were loaded off of a truck. One of the prisoners, who was already weak and injured, was hit by a soldier with a rifle butt when he did not move fast enough. The American pressman continued taking pictures of these atrocities in order to record them on film until one of the soldiers saw him. The group of soldiers pursued him, but the pressman was able to hand over his camera to an onlooker, presumably a friend, and then escape into the crowd.

**Comment**
1. –
2. When answering this questions, S. should also think about the important "watchdog" function of the press (e.g. Watergate) and not only about the paparazzi aspect.

**Form**
1. The words and sentences are very short, which gives the text a fast tempo and a choppy rhythm. Both make the text seem more urgent and exciting./Sound effects (e.g. click-whirr) are repeated, which helps the reader hear what is going on and feel more a part of the scene./There are many exclamations in the characters' dialogues.
2. Metaphor = "the American cavalry" (l. 2)/Simile = "like wasps to honey" (l. 19–20)/Usage of metaphors and similes help readers to more clearly visualize scenes, and they help readers feel more directly involved emotionally with scenes.

**Language**
1. a) holding; b) pushed; c) seen, taken in
2. a) unfriendly; b) enemy; c) whispered
3. a) Important news must be captured on film by photographers.
b) The guards treated the prisoners terribly.
4. a) A "thrill of hope" means a sudden, strong feeling of expectation, or optimism.

b) "Audible" means a sound which can be heard.
c) "To be captured" in this context means for something to be documented, in this case on film.
d) When you are "paralysed by fear" your are so afraid or terrified that you can't move.

### 5  Welcome to America

#### 1  A conference call                                        S. 88

**Call 1**
Franco's cell phone number: *718 221 8131*
Why Traci is calling: *She needs to speak to Franco urgently.*
What Traci will do now: *She'll try contacting Franco at Alpha.*
What Traci wants Franco to do: *She wants him to call right away.*

**Call 2**
Company where Franco is now: *Alpha Sponsoring*
Franco's surname: *Scicchitano*
Traci's conference number: *245 678 9234*
Time in New York when Traci calls: *7.05 am*
Latest time Franco can call back: *7.30 am*

**Call 3**
Time when Traci calls Sally: *some time after 1 am*
Problem that prompted Traci's call: *The directors of Opus Corporation (clients of International Advertising Inc.) don't like the slogan they were sent. International Advertising will lose the contract if they don't have one ready for broadcast by next week.*
Traci's request: *Sally should start thinking about another slogan so that she, Traci and Franco can discuss this in a conference call.*
How much time Sally has to do this: *20 minutes*
How Sally feels about this: *She says she won't be very creative. (She has a bad headache and is still very sleepy).*

**Call 4**
Why Franco did not respond to Traci's message earlier: *He got the message in the middle of a presentation.*
Why Franco wants the call to be short: *He wants to get back to the party with his business colleagues, as the most important deals are made after the official part is over. He doesn't want to miss anything.*
Time when Traci calls Sally: *around 2 am*
Details of Franco's next meeting in London:
  Name of company: *Robertson's*
  Day of meeting: *Friday*
  Time: *9 am*
  Day of arrival in London: *Thursday*
  How he will get home from the airport: *Dee will pick him up.*
What Franco needs to tell Dee: *his flight details.*

**Further activity:** –

#### 4  Tandem crossword                                     S. 92 & 93

**Across**
1. motels 6. taxes 8. gorgeous 10. near 11. alligator 12. racism 15. retail outlets 18. title 21. hostility 22. sunbelt 27. air-conditioner 28. lot 29. art 31. fast food 33. violence 37. hospitality 38. dream 39. hurricanes 41. swamp 42. coast 43. similar

**Down**
1. minorities 2. tea 3. steamy 4. jet 5. guns 7. segregation 9. rural 13. city 14. state 16. inhabitants 17. trip 19. education 20. suburb 23. gist 24. traditional 25. extra 26. slavery 30. rednecks 32. flat 34. egret 35. crime 36. who 38. deep 39. hot 40. sir

*Diese Lösungen beziehen sich auf die KV im TRB. Abweichungen zur CD-Rom sind möglich.*

## Lösungen zu den Kopiervorlagen

### 5 Test: Notes from a big country — S. 94

**Content**
1. Bill Bryson sees America as big and empty, whereas his fellow Americans think of it as being overcrowded.
2. Visitors may soon be banned from hiking in certain national park areas considered to be overcrowded, even though these areas may actually be very remote./Daniel Boone complained about his neighbours living too close by, even though he could only see smoke rising from where they lived.
3. Visitors consider national park areas to be overcrowded based on the situation in the small area where most of them bring their cars and gather. Of course these limited areas are crowded, but most of the national park grounds are really nearly empty.

**Comment:** 1./2. –

**Form**
1. Bill Bryson uses a humorous, informal and understated tone. He is able to keep this tone informal by using more informal language (e.g. " … as far as I can tell … " (l. 12–13)). He also achieves this by using the first person point of view (e.g. "Yet I may soon find … (l. 21)), and also seemingly addressing his readers at times (e.g. "You can drive for very long periods …") (l. 9)) He entertains his readers by making fun of his fellow Americans, but he does so for the most part in an understated way. (e.g. "Parts of them *are* unquestionably crowded …." (l. 16–19))
2. Bill Bryson compares and contrasts the size and populations of parts of the US with parts of Europe (ll. 1–11). He also contrasts how Americans perceive the density of their population with how this population is actually spread out across the country. In both cases he provides a number of statistics and concrete examples. The effect of this factual and literal comparing and contrasting is that Bryson's makes his point (that Americans have a distorted perception of how crowded their land is) in a very funny and believeable way.

**Language**
1. a) remarkable; b) snug; c) crowded; d) overrun; e) to restrict access; f) to venture; g) foresight
2. a) Parts of parks are undoubtedly/without doubt/clearly/obviously crowded.
b) Yet I may soon be prevented from hiking/be forbidden to hike/not be allowed to hike/be banned from hiking in many areas.
c) Americans have often seen/have frequently been inclined to see things differently.
3. a) consideration; b) curiosity; c) announcement; d) complaint

### XtraFile: The American political system

#### 1 Checks and balances quiz — S. 97
1. d); 2. a); 3. d); 4. a); 5. b); 6. a); 7. d); 8. d); 9. c); 10. b); 11. d); 12. a)

#### 2 Radio address to the nation — S. 98

**Listening**
1. false 2. true 3. true 4. true 5. false 6. false 7. true 8. true 9. true 10. true 11. false 12. true 13. false 14. false

**Joining words and definitions**
1. c; 2. j; 3. a; 4. h; 5. l; 6. g; 7. f; 8. d; 9. k; 10. b; 11. e; 12. i

**Sentences**
*Mögliche politische Themenbereiche:*
– the environment (e.g. an initiative to clean up your community)
– taking better care of young people's needs (e.g. raising money to build a recreation centre where youth can go after school)
– providing more shelter for the homeless
– providing more job training opportunities for young people

### 3 The US political system … — S. 99

*Die Lösungen für die Buch- und die CD-ROM-Version dieser Kopiervorlage befinden sich im SB auf S. 88.*

### Translation practise (CD-ROM)

*Mobiltelefone*
Die Verkaufszahlen von Handys steigen nun schon seit ein paar Jahren. Immer mehr Menschen haben Interesse daran ein Mobiltelefon zu besitzen, nicht nur weil es solch praktische Geräte sind, sondern auch weil niedrigere Kosten sie erschwinglicher gemacht haben. Besonders Schüler wollen unbedingt Handys haben, weil sie für sie immer noch ein Statussymbol sind. Die heutigen Modelle sind viel kleiner und technisch viel besser als die, die noch vor ein paar Jahren verkauft wurden.
Junge Leute wissen sehr wohl, dass Handys hohe Kosten verursachen, es sei denn sie nutzen SMS. Indem sie diese günstigere Art der Kommunikation wählen, können die Benutzer die Kosten begrenzen. Darüberhinaus wird eine neue Sprache geschaffen, da eine Nachricht nicht zu lang sein darf. Sie sollte nach dem KISS Prinzip geschrieben werden: kurz und einfach.

### Test: Translation — S. 100

*Regierung und Politik*
Einem amerikanischen Staatsbürger ist es praktisch unmöglich, den Auswirkungen der Regierung und politischer Vorgänge zu entgehen. Von den verschiedenen Steuern, die bezahlt werden (müssen), über Regulierungen, die die Umwelt und den Verbraucher betreffen, Abstimmungen und Wahlen, bis hin zu Zinsen, die für einen Kredit bezahlt werden müssen, sieht sich der Bürger mit den verschiedenen Auswirkungen politischer Entscheidungen konfrontiert, die von einem gewählten oder ernannten öffentlichen Vertreter auf lokaler, Staats- oder Regierungsebene getroffen werden. Andererseits können die Bürgerinnen und Bürger aber auch ihre politische Welt beeinflussen, indem sie ihre konstitutionelle Freiheit ausüben, die die Verfassung beinhaltet.
Die amerikanische Verfassung geht auf die dramatischen Ereignisse des Kongresses von 1787 in Philadelphia zurück. Die 55 Abgeordneten hatten bestimmte politische Ideale und den Wunsch, eine stärkere Nation zu schaffen. Die Kompromisse, die sie machten, und das Dokument, das sie erstellten, haben sich im Lauf der Jahre klar bewährt.

## 6 Life in the city: Atlanta

### 1 Talking about Atlanta — S. 112

**Order of interview topics**
1. Historic city; 2. Unique neighbourhoods; 3. Urban sprawl; 4. Different cultures and races; 5. Dealing with crime; 6. Successful business centre; 7. Freetime activities; 8. Effects of the Olympics; 9. Southern hospitality; 10. Perspectives for the future

**Topic notes**
**Historic city:** location of Martin Luther King's birthsite and grave and the church where he preached (Ebenezer Baptist Church)/Margaret Mitchell House (where Margaret Mitchell wrote some of Gone With the Wind
**Unique neighbourhoods:** e.g. Buckhead, a fast-paced neighbourhood with very nice homes (mansions), shops, restaurants/Virginia Highlands, a smaller, slower-paced neighbourhood with many different kinds of shops and small restaurants/Little Fivepoints, a funky neighbourhood with biker bars and tattoo parlours/Midtown and downtown, increasingly popular for people to move back to, have lots of art galleries, restaurants, stores, etc.
**Urban sprawl:** The movement out to the suburbs, which in previous years has been massive, is slowing down and people are moving back to the city./People move back because they are tired of traffic, and the quality of life in the city has improved.

! Diese Lösungen beziehen sich auf die KV im TRB. Abweichungen zur CD-Rom sind möglich.

# Lösungen zu den Kopiervorlagen

**Different cultures and races:** People from all over the world live in both spread out and in "ethnic pockets" (e.g. Chinese and Hispanic areas) all over Atlanta.
**Dealing with crime:** Atlanta Ambassador Program: 50–60 unarmed ambassadors who are the extra eyes and ears for the police in the downtown area and fulfill tasks e.g. escorting people to their cars at night (also called the "Friendly Force"). The programme has been successful and is funded by business owners who want to keep their area safer.
**Successful business centre:** Especially financial institutions and technology businesses are attracted to the city./Businesses are attracted by the quality of life, the airport, the generous number of hotel accomodations, the convention center.
**Freetime activities:** sports events, shopping malls, art museums (e.g. High Museum of Art), Fox theatre, more than 8,000 restaurants, CNN and Coca-Cola tours, Centennial Olympic Park, Six Flags Over Georgia (amusement park), the Zoo.
**Effects of the Olympics:** Many more people know about and are interested in Atlanta./This event has attracted new business and tourism./Residents and visitors can enjoy the renovated and new buildings and facilities that were completed in preparation for the Olympics (e.g. Centennial Park, Turner Field).
**Southern hospitality:** This means being friendly, courteous and gracious. In Atlanta people do gracious things like greeting each other in passing, and men still open doors for women.
**Perspectives for the future:** More people and businesses (especially in the technological branch) will continue to come back to the city./As a result there will also be more building of housing, restaurants, etc.

## 5 Test: America's cities …  S. 116

### Content
1. American cities generally show two different faces: the prosperous suburbs with spotless houses and lawns and a majority of well-off white people, and the poor inner cities with decaying buildings and unemployed people (many of whom are African Americans).
2. Urban optimists are positive about America because they point out that indicators of urban decline such as crime, unemployment have been decreasing in bigger cities like New York, Los Angeles and Detroit. They also point out cities like these are gaining confidence and population as a result.
3. After the Second World War, the mostly white middle class started moving out to suburban areas. This didn't turn into a mass movement, however, until the 1960s, when courts enforced school desegregation. After this, the white middle class and their businesses and services left the cities, taxes rose, then the black middle class left. Those who could not afford to go were too poor to keep the situation of the inner cities from steadily getting worse.

### Comment
1./2. –

### Form
1. –
2. Some S may find that this type of opening is good because it is more interesting than standard openings, and therefore makes them more interested in the topic. Others may find this opening distracting and hard to relate to, as some of them may have never been confronted with such a scene before.

### Language
1. a) caricature; b) surface; c) decline; d) deterioration
2. a) contrasting; b) optimistic; c) economic; *(CD-ROM)* 5. nightmarish
3. a) *Contrast* refers to the great difference between outer suburbs and inner cities.
b) Rates for serious crimes have *gone down*.
c) The court decision made the already *large group of white people leaving* turn into a full-scale stampede.
4. a) We have been warned by experts that too many people moving to the suburbs can harm city centres.

b) The mostly white middle classes have deserted the inner cities.
5. a) employed b) pessimist c) risen
6. a/b) Blacks who are unemployed sit on the front steps that are grimy.
7. a/b) If an economic downturn came, cities would probably be more vulnerable …/If an economic downturn were to come …/… cities probably would be more vulnerable …/(standard American English) If an economic downturn would come …

# 7 Glued to the tube

## 1 The Truman Show  S. 127

1./2.
**Truman:**
the main character of a long-running TV soap opera • "Good morning! – Oh, and in case I don't see you …"
**Marlon:**
the main character's best friend • "Went all over. …"
**Lauren:**
the main character's true love (former member of cast) • "We have so little time …"
**Meryl:**
the main character's wife • "Why don't you let me fix you some of this new Mococoa drink? …"
**Christof:**
the producer/director of a long-running TV soap opera • "The world – the place you live in – is the sick place. …"

### Understanding content
1. Some examples: the camera falling from the sky, the radio voice describing the route Truman is driving, his "dead father" appearing again and being dragged away, rain falling only over him, the elevator with no back (Truman sees behind the set), the same cars passing by on the street over and over again, the policeman at the "nuclear accident" who knew his name.
2. Truman wants to go to Fiji because this is where "Lauren's" father said they would be moving to, and Truman wants to find her again.
3. Products are brought to the viewers' attention through clever camera angles and also by "product placement", where the characters point certain items out in an exaggerated way (e.g. Meryl and the Mococoa drink and the "Chef's Pal", the "passers-by" knocking Truman into a billboard with advertisements on it, Marlon holding up the beer he's drinking). Also, during the commentaries about Truman, announcers mention the Truman catalogue (everything on the set can be ordered). There are also advertisements in the form of text running across the screen at some points.
4. "Truman" can be understood ironically as "True – man".

### A Truman trivia quiz
1. Approx. 5,000; 2. 10,909 days 30 years; 3. Pluto; 4,220 countries; 5. Truman's father comes back first as a homeless person and then as Truman's father again.

## 3 Media research  S. 129

*Die Antworten zu der KV finden Sie auf S. 124 im TRB.*

## 4 'The Shock of Recognition' by Art Buchwald  S. 130

### Listening comprehension
1. a) (Mr.) Bufkins, Mrs. Edith Bufkins; b) Henry and Mary; c) Forest Hills High School; d) accountant; e) works in a department store; f) guitar; g) Susie, got married a year ago; h) darned; i) the World Series

### Further activity
a/b) –

### Creative writing: –

140

! Diese Lösungen beziehen sich auf die KV im TRB. Abweichungen zur CD-Rom sind möglich.

## 5 TV board game          S. 131

*Die Seitenzahlen der entsprechenden SB Seiten, auf denen die Lösungen zu den 'Fact'-Fragen zu finden sind, sind auf den Karten vorgegeben. Dies ermöglicht den S die Richtigkeit der gegebenen Antworten zu kontrollieren.*

## 6 Test: TV and me          S. 132

### Content

1. No, he hasn't. Right at the beginning he says "the thing" (i.e. TV) "lost its grip". This implies that it once had a grip on him, that he watched a lot of it as a child. We learn that he only stopped watching when his family moved into an area with bad reception.

2. First of all, TV doesn't set his schedule the way it does for other people, and he is free to do what he wants, when he wants. He is also able to see the world through his own eyes, rather that having it interpreted for him by TV writers and producers.

3. The friendliness of the black woman proved to him that race relations in America were basically OK. At least they were not as tense as the news commentators on TV had been saying in the wake of the OJ Simpson acquittal. (At the time, most whites believed the black football star had got away with the murder of his wife, while most blacks felt he had been framed by the police, and was rightfully found "not guilty" by the jury.)

### Comment

1. *Yes:* There are better things to spend your time on and give your attention to than pop culture, which is mainly trivial and short-lived. The author is right to show contempt for TV series such as *Miami Vice*, which is now mainly remembered for the gaudy fahions of its time!

*No:* Though a lot of pop culture may be trivial and short-lived, total ignorance of it can mean missing a lot of really significant cultural phenomena. It would mean missing out on the music of The Beatles, for example, and knowing nothing of films such as *Casablanca*. Of the three examples he mentions, *Miami Vice* has been largely forgotten, and *Star Wars* can be seen as a modern fairy-tale for children. But the police series *NYPD Blue* dealt with serious social issues, and its hard-edged narrative style has influenced many later TV and film makers. Not to know it means a kind of cultural ignorance that the author should not really be proud of.

2./3. –

### Form

1. In referring to TV, the author uses the terms "the thing" (l. 1) and "the tube" (l. 21). Both express a degree of contempt.

2. This is an example of ironic understatement. The difference in seriousness between his cultural ignorance and the "suffering in Bosnia" is actually so great that we not only believe that the author will "survive", but that he will manage very well indeed.

### Language

1. a) I gradually broke away from the influence of TV and did not relapse/come under its influence again.
b) From… to… , I am totally ignorant of these programmes./I don't know anything about any of these programmes.
c) Programme planners do not set the course of my daily life/What I do during the day is not determined by programme planners.
d) I realized this one night about a month ago.
e) If she hadn't done what she did/If she hadn't helped me, my main financial record would have been lost.

2. a) bad/terrible b) strange/bizarre; c) substitute

3. a)/b) I <u>was watching</u> TV yesterday when suddenly the power <u>went</u> out again!
c) The power <u>had gone</u> off two days before that already!
d) I certainly hope that the power stays on today so that I <u>will be able to</u>/<u>am able to</u> watch my favourite TV show!
e)/f) I <u>have been looking forward to</u> this all week, and I <u>will go</u> crazy if I <u>have to</u> miss this week's episode!

## Worterklärungen zu den Tests

### Children of 8 join alcohol casualty list          S. 23

3 **related** connected with, associated with – 3 **casualty** ['kæʒjʊəltɪ] a hospital department where victims of accidents, violence, etc., are treated – 6 **tenfold** 10 times as many or as much – 10 **unit** *here*: department – 13 **to mature** to become adult, to grow up – 16 **measure** ['meʒə] amount of alcohol in a glass – 17 **illicit** [ɪ'lɪsɪt] illegal – 19 **superficial** [ˌsuːpə'fɪʃl] exterior, external, on the surface – 19 **brawl** [brɔːl] a fight – 26 **alcopop** fizzy alcoholic fruit drink – 29 **off-licence** a shop where alcoholic drinks are sold for consumption elsewhere – 31 **tramp** homeless person

### Two towns and two nations          S. 40

5 **to be stuck** not able to change positions – 6 **solicitor** [sə'lɪsɪtə] *Rechtsanwalt/-anwältin* 7 **parish council** ['pærɪʃ 'kaʊnsl] the elected body of a small rural area in England – 11 **councillor** member of a local council – 12 **leisure** ['leʒə] *Freizeit* – 12 **colliery** ['kɒljərɪ] coal mine and buildings – 15 **pit** *Mine* – 17 **to bridge** to cross – 24 **to stumble across** to find unexpectedly – 27 **eventually** [ɪ'ventʃʊəlɪ] finally – 39 **to twin** to establish a formal relationship between towns and cities – 40 **hilarious** [hɪ'leərɪəs] very funny – 42 **to launch** to start – 49 **to swill** (*inf.*) to drink a lot of s.th.

### Real life U          S. 63

7 **deafening** very loud – 8 **enrolment** *Immatrikulation* – 10 **tougher** more difficult – 15 **startling** surprising – 23 **to put s.th. off** to not do s.th. immediately – 23 **to skip** to leave out or not do s.th. – 24 **to postpone** [-'-] to not do s.th. immediately – 26-27 **undergraduate admissions** the university department responsible for accepting students working towards associate and bachelor's degrees – 27 **UCLA** abbr. for University of California at Los Angeles – 27 **skyrocketing** increasing very quickly – 32/33 **community service** *Sozialdienst* – 36 **to get at s.th.** to do s.th. successfully

### Talking in Whispers          S. 78

13 **to hobble** ['hɒbl] to walk with pain and/or difficulty – 15 **rifle butt** the thick end of a rifle – 21 **to topple** to remove s.o. from a position of power – 22 **villainy** cruel and/or evil behavior – 36 **zip** (*AE = zipper*) *Reißverschluss*

### Notes from a big country          S. 94

11 **hamlet** small village – 14 **moves are constantly afoot** [ə'fʊt] *es wird ständig versucht* – 14 **access** ['--] entry – 15 **on the grounds that** – because – 19 **womb** [wuːm] *Gebärmutter, Schoß* – 24 **to perceive** [pə'siːv] *wahrnehmen, empfinden* – 33 **homesteader** refers to one of the people who became a land owner under the Homestead Act. As a result of this act, which was passed by the US Congress in 1862, settlers who lived and worked on a piece of land for five years could then claim ownership of it. – 33 **dwelling** place where one lives

### America's cities: they can yet be resurrected          S. 116

1 **immaculate** [ɪ'mækjələt] very clean, spotless – 3 **manicured** ['---] cut very neatly – 3 **gleaming** shiny – 5 **surfaced** *gepflastert* – 7 **grimy** ['graɪmɪ] very dirty – 7 **crumbling** falling to pieces – 9 **bleak** very bad – 15 **bankrupt** *Bankrott* – 21 **vulnerable** ['----] *wehrlos* – 24 **disparity** [dɪ'spærətɪ] difference – 27 **vigorous** ['---] *here*: prosperous – 27 **court-mandated** [mæn'deɪtɪd] a legal decision enforced by a court – 32 **huddle** ['hʌdl] a crowd of people – 34 **deteriorating** [dɪ'tɪərɪeɪtɪŋ] becoming increasingly worse

### TV and Me          S. 133

1 **to lose its grip** *here*: to lose its fascination – 4 **Celtics** ['seltɪks] *here*: Boston basketball team – 8 **to be out of it** *here*: to not be up to date – 9 **pop-culture illiterate** [ɪ'lɪtrət] s.o. who doesn't know anything about popular culture – 20 **contrived** [kən'traɪvd] fake – 21 **provincial** [prə'vɪnʃl] simple and unsophisticated – 30 **OJ verdict** the 1995 court ruling where famous ex-football player OJ Simpson was declared not guilty of murdering his wife – 30 **animosity** [ˌ--'---] hostile feeling – 33 **tension** *Spannung* – 36 **to foment** [-'-] to encourage the development of s.th. – 39 **to portray** [-'-] *darstellen* – 40 **host** *here*: a lot – 42 **non-consent** not agreeing to or not going along with s.th.

# Zusätzliche Materialien

## Bücher

| | | |
|---|---|---|
| **Abiturwissen: Landeskunde Great Britain / United States of America** | Klett 929509 | |
| **American Life and Institutions** | Klett 513800 | (Kapitel 5 – 7) |
| **Amerika Wortschatz** | Klett 518910 | |
| **British Life and Institutions** (Neubearbeitung) | Klett 513380 | (Kapitel 2 – 4) |
|     CD | Klett 513382 | |
|     Kassette | Klett 513381 | |
| **Crossroads, USA** | Klett 513472 | (Kapitel 4) |
|     Teacher's Manual | Klett 513473 | |
| **Growing Up: Voices of Youth** | Klett 513950 | (Kapitel 1) |
|     Lehrerheft | Klett 513951 | |
|     Kassette | Klett 513952 | |
| **Grundwissen Landeskunde United Kingdom** | Klett 513460 | (Kapitel 2 – 4) |
| **Literature Live** | Klett 508501 | (Kapitel 1) |
|     Teacher's Book | Klett 508501 | |
|     Kassette | Klett 508502 | |
| **Media and Messages** | Klett 513730 | |
| **The American Dream – Past and Present** | Klett 513610 | (Kapitel 5 & 6) |
| **The American South** | Klett 513620 | (Kapitel 6) |
| **The Truman Show** (Shooting Script) | Klett 577460 | (Kapitel 7) |
| **Urban USA - Life in Three American Cities** | Klett 513760 | (Kapitel 6) |
|     Lehrerbuch | Klett 513761 | |
| **Words in Context, Thematischer Oberstufenwortschatz Englisch** | Klett 519900 | |

## Videos

| | | |
|---|---|---|
| **A Living Society – Britain** | Klett 532330 | (Kapitel 1 – 4) |
|     Lehrerheft | Klett 532332 | |
| **Voices Video** | Klett 533594 | (Kapitel 2) |
|     Activity Book | Klett 533595 | |
|     Teacher's Book | Klett 533596 | |
| **Heartbreak High** | Klett 532364 | (Kapitel 3) |

## CD Roms

| | | |
|---|---|---|
| **Chicago: An American City** | Klett 546399 | (Kapitel 6) |
| **Ireland: The Emerald Isle** | Klett 546903 | (Kapitel 2) |

## Hinweise zur Benutzung der CD-ROM

### Systemvoraussetzung

Windows-PC ab 486er
8 MB RAM
Windows 3.11/95/98/NT/ME
Word für Windows® ab Version 6.0
Grafikkarte VGA/SVGA (256 Farben)

### Inhalt pro Kapitel

**Kopiervorlagen:** eine vereinfachte Version der meisten im TRB erhaltenen Kopiervorlagen inklusive Aufgaben zu den Hörverstehens- und Klausurtests.
**Wortlisten:** A-Z Kapitelwortschatz und A-Z Gesamtwortschatz in dreispaltigem Aufbau: Englisches Wort – Englische Erklärung – Deutsche Übersetzung
**Mind Maps:** je eine *Mind Map* zum Kapitelthema (auch als pdf-Dateien)
**Skills & Grammar files:** eine vereinfachte Version aller *Skills* und *Grammar files* aus dem SB.

### Bedienung

Alle Dateien sind im Word für Windows®-Format (ab Version 6).
Die Dateien können direkt per Mausklick von dem Auswahlmenü der CD-ROM geöffnet werden. Word für Windows® wird automatisch geöffnet.
Um von einer geöffneten Datei zum Auswahlmenü der CD-ROM zurückzukommen, muss das Programm Word für Windows® (per Mausklick auf "X" in der oberen Menüleiste) geschlossen werden.
Die überwiegende Mehrheit der Dateien können nach den eigenen Bedürfnissen der L bzw. S verändert werden, so dass problemlos nach Bedarf und Leistung der Klasse beispielsweise die Aufgaben auf den Kopiervorlagen abgeändert, Wortlisten ergänzt oder gekürzt, die Einträge der *Mind Maps* umgestellt oder die *Skills* und *Grammar files* erweitert werden können. (Die Hilfefunktion von Word für Windows® bietet genaue Informationen und Tipps zur Bedienung des Programms.)
Beim Öffnen der *Mind Maps* von der CD-ROM werden immer zwei Versionen gleichzeitig geöffnet: eine veränderbare Version mit Zeichenelementen und Textfeldern und eine nicht veränderbare Version (pdf-Datei). Die nicht benötigte Version kann einfach geschlossen werden (im Menü 'Datei' 'Schließen' auswählen).

# Acknowledgements

The editors wish to thank all authors, publishers and literary agencies who have given permission to use copyright material. Sources are given next to the texts. The following list acknowledges copyright holders who are not identical with the publishers quoted and also gives specifications requested by copyright holders.

P. 9: Copyright © D.J. Enright, Chatto & Windus, original publishers, Watson, Little Ltd, licensing agents; pp. 10–12: Adapted with permission from *Who Cares What I Think?* © 1994 Close Up Foundation, Alexandria, Virginia, U.S.A.; p. 23: From the article "Children of 8 join alcohol casualty list" by Stephen McGinty, *The Sunday Times*, 24 August 1997; p. 40 Copyright © 1997, *The Guardian*; p. 46: Copyright © 1999, *The Guardian*; p. 63: From the article "Real Life U" by Sean Smith, *Seventeen Magazine*, February 2000, Volume 59, number 2.; p. 78: Approximately 400 words (pp. 39–40) from *Talking in Whispers* by James Watson (Victor Gollancz/Hamish Hamilton, 1983) Copyright © James Watson, 1983. Reproduced by permission of Penguin Books Ltd.; p. 94: © 1998 Bill Bryson. Extracted from *Notes From a Big Country* by Bill Bryson, published by Doubleday, a division of Transword Publishers. All rights reserved.; p. 100: Page 1 from *Introduction to Government* (HarperCollins College Outline Series) by Larry Elowitz, Copyright © 1992 by HarperCollins Publishers Inc., Reprinted by permission of HarperCollins Publishers, Inc.; p. 116 © *The Economist*, London, January 10, 1998.